The Scientific Revolution and the Foundations of Modern Science

The Scientific Revolution and the Foundations of Modern Science

WILBUR APPLEBAUM

Greenwood Guides to Historic Events, 1500–1900
Linda S. Frey and Marsha L. Frey, Series Editors

GREENWOOD PRESS
Westport, Connecticut • London

Library of Congress Cataloging-in-Publication Data

Applebaum, Wilbur.
    The scientific revolution and the foundations of modern science /
    Wilbur Applebaum.
       p. cm—(Greenwood guides to historic events, 1500–1900, ISSN 1538–442X)
    Includes bibliographical references and index.
    ISBN 0–313–32314–3 (alk. paper)
    1. Science—History. 2. Science, Renaissance. I. Title. II. Series
Q125.A54 2005
509.4'09'031—dc22   2004027859

British Library Cataloguing in Publication Data is available.

Copyright © 2005 by Wilbur Applebaum

All rights reserved. No portion of this book may be
reproduced, by any process or technique, without the
express written consent of the publisher.

Library of Congress Catalog Card Number: 2004027859
ISBN: 0–313–32314–3
ISSN: 1538–442X

First published in 2005

Greenwood Press, 88 Post Road West, Westport, CT 06881
An imprint of Greenwood Publishing Group, Inc.
www.greenwood.com

Printed in the United States of America

The paper used in this book complies with the
Permanent Paper Standard issued by the National
Information Standards Organization (Z39.48–1984).

10 9 8 7 6 5 4 3 2 1

To
Ariel, Max, and Benjamin

CONTENTS

ILLUSTRATIONS

SERIES FOREWORD

American statesman Adlai Stevenson stated that "We can chart our future clearly and wisely only when we know the path which has led to the present." This series, Greenwood Guides to Historic Events, 1500–1900, is designed to illuminate that path by focusing on events from 1500 to 1900 that have shaped the world. The years 1500 to 1900 include what historians call the Early Modern Period (1500 to 1789, the onset of the French Revolution) and part of the modern period (1789 to 1900).

In 1500, an acceleration of key trends marked the beginnings of an interdependent world and the posing of seminal questions that changed the nature and terms of intellectual debate. The series closes with 1900, the inauguration of the twentieth century. This period witnessed profound economic, social, political, cultural, religious, and military changes. An industrial and technological revolution transformed the modes of production, marked the transition from a rural to an urban economy, and ultimately raised the standard of living. Social classes and distinctions shifted. The emergence of the territorial and later the national state altered man's relations with and view of political authority. The shattering of the religious unity of the Roman Catholic world in Europe marked the rise of a new pluralism. Military revolutions changed the nature of warfare. The books in this series emphasize the complexity and diversity of the human tapestry and include political, economic, social, intellectual, military, and cultural topics. Some of the authors focus on events in U.S. history such as the Salem Witchcraft Trials, the American Revolution, the abolitionist movement, and the Civil War. Others analyze European topics, such as the Reformation and Counter Reformation and the French Revolution. Still others bridge cultures and continents by examining the voyages of discovery, the Atlantic slave trade, and the Age of Imperialism. Some focus on intellectual questions that have shaped the modern world, such as Darwin's *Origin of Species* or on turning points such as the Age of Romanticism. Others examine defining economic, religious, or legal events or issues such as the building of the railroads, the Second Great Awakening, and abolitionism. Heroes (e.g., Lewis and Clark), scientists (e.g., Darwin), military leaders (e.g., Napoleon), poets (e.g., Byron), stride across its pages. Many of these events were seminal in that they marked profound changes or turning points. The Scientific Revolution, for example, changed the way individuals viewed themselves and their world.

The authors, acknowledged experts in their fields, synthesize key events, set developments within the larger historical context, and, most important, present a well-balanced, well-written account that integrates the most recent scholarship in the field.

The topics were chosen by an advisory board composed of historians, high school history teachers, and school librarians to support the curriculum and meet student research needs. The volumes are designed to serve as resources for student research and to provide clearly written interpretations of topics central to the secondary school and lower-level undergraduate history curriculum. Each author outlines a basic chronology to guide the reader through often confusing events and a historical overview to set those events within a narrative framework. Three to five topical chapters underscore critical aspects of the event. In the final chapter the author examines the impact and consequences of the event. Biographical sketches furnish background on the lives and contributions of the players who strut across this stage. Ten to fifteen primary documents ranging from letters to diary entries, song lyrics, proclamations, and posters, cast light on the event, provide material for student essays, and stimulate a critical engagement with the sources. Introductions identify the authors of the documents and the main issues. In some cases a glossary of selected terms is provided as a guide to the reader. Each work contains an annotated bibliography of recommended books, articles, CD-ROMs, Internet sites, videos, and films that set the materials within the historical debate.

These works will lead to a more sophisticated understanding of the events and debates that have shaped the modern world and will stimulate a more active engagement with the issues that still affect us. It has been a particularly enriching experience to work closely with such dedicated professionals. We have come to know and value even more highly the authors in this series and our editors at Greenwood, particularly Kevin Ohe. In many cases they have become more than colleagues; they have become friends. To them and to future historians we dedicate this series.

Linda S. Frey
University of Montana

Marsha L. Frey
Kansas State University

INTRODUCTION

Research in the history of science has grown substantially in the past fifty years. University courses in various aspects of the subject have multiplied significantly, and dozens of institutions offer Ph.D. programs in history of science. Initially investigated by retired scientists, and then by philosophers and historians, the history of scientific ideas and practices and their cultural influences is now also explored by individuals with interests in sociology and literature. Examining how scientific ideas were born and became part of our knowledge of the natural world can prove useful in mastering scientific concepts and in learning how science advances. New ideas are usually not accepted immediately, and for sound reasons. To understand the new scientific concepts of five centuries ago, as well as those of today, it is necessary to realize that these concepts were frequently in conflict with earlier ones. The relationships between ideas and practices in different branches of science, and the search for themes uniting them, have also been important sources of new and productive developments.

The study of the natural world by scientists from approximately 1500 to 1700 has long been known to have occurred during an era important for the creation of modern science and, indeed, of the modern world. Scientific developments have had significant effects on the ways we live, work, and think. Today's investments in scientific activity and its consequences in time, money, and the number of individuals involved in universities, businesses, and governments far exceed those investments made three to five centuries ago. Yet that earlier period of scientific activity, known as the Scientific Revolution, laid the foundations for modern science and new ways of thinking, not only about the natural world, but about our natures as social beings and as individuals as well.

The term *Scientific Revolution* was coined in the mid-twentieth century and accompanied new modes of thinking about the ways in which scientific ideas emerge, are received, and affect other ideas. Traditionally, scholars of the history of science assumed that scientists in the past thought as today's scientists do, and that therefore there is no point in studying what we now know to have been erroneous views. The assumption was that when a scientific genius overthrew a false traditional view, the "true" view was immediately apparent and accepted. Historians of science today, however, want to know how and why scientists of earlier times thought the way they did. Moreover, today's historians see the history of science not merely as a series of true ideas replacing false ones, but as both affected by and affecting the society and cultures surrounding them.

Just as the nature of scientific thinking has changed, so has thinking about the creation of modern science. One viewpoint is that the foundations of modern science evolved from ideas developed during the late Middle Ages, and that therefore it makes better sense to speak of scientific *evolution* than of a scientific *revolution*. The position taken in this work is that while ideas about the natural world were indeed evolving during the Middle Ages, scholars continued to assume that certain fundamental principles inherited from the ancient world were correct. It was only during the sixteenth and seventeenth centuries that these principles were challenged and overturned in favor of new ones that constitute a basis for many ideas and approaches held today. Although the science of the seventeenth century is not the science of today, it laid the foundations for the study of the cosmos, matter, motion, life processes, and the means of acquiring knowledge of them that are fundamental to modern science.

Concerning a few of the terms used in the text: Some words in common use today did not exist in the sixteenth and seventeenth centuries. No one was known as a "scientist" then, although the designation is occasionally used in the chapters of this book; there were instead "natural philosophers" who were students of "natural philosophy." There was no science known as biology, nor as chemistry. Some words used today had different meanings then. An "atom" was understood quite differently in ancient Greece, in the seventeenth century, and today. Alchemy and astrology were respected sciences and were taught in universities.

I should like to acknowledge that this book has benefited considerably from the criticisms and suggestions of Marsha Frey and Naomi Bernards Polonsky. I am very grateful for their assistance and for the cooperation and forbearance of Michael Hermann of Greenwood Press.

CHRONOLOGY OF EVENTS

1469	Initial Latin translation of an influential number of works on theology and the occult allegedly written in very ancient times by a Hermes Trismegistus.
1527–1541	Paracelsus urges the use of chemical medications and proposes a theory of matter composed of salt, sulfur, and mercury as the prime "elements."
1530–1536	Publication of Otto Brunfels' *Portraits of Living Plants*, the first publication by a botanist of realistic copies from nature rather than fanciful ones from earlier narratives.
1543	Andreas Vesalius publishes the superbly illustrated *On the Structure of the Human Body*, based on his own dissections, and noting several errors in Galen.
	Nicolaus Copernicus' heliocentric theory is published in his *On the Revolutions of the Celestial Orbs*.
1546	Girolamo Fracastoro's *On Contagion* speculates on the spread of plague by "seeds" from an infected person to others.
1553	Michael Servetus describes the pulmonary circulation of the blood.
1572	Observations of a supernova describe something new in the heavens and beyond the sphere of the Moon, challenging an important Aristotelian principle.

1576	Tycho Brahe begins construction of Uraniborg, his observatory, where the most precise collection of astronomical observations made up to that time would be obtained.
1577	Observations of a comet show that its path was beyond the Moon, further challenging Aristotelian conceptions.
1588	Publication of *A Briefe and True Report of the New Found Land of Virginia*, by Thomas Harriot, the first account of the resources and inhabitants of North America.
1596	Founding of Gresham College in London to provide lectures to the public on science and mathematics.
1600	Publication of William Gilbert's *On the Magnet*, based on observation and experiments on magnetism and electricity; it also holds that the Earth is a rotating magnetic body.
1604	Johannes Kepler proposes that light rays are rectilinear, diminish in intensity according to the inverse-square of their distance from a light source, and form an inverse image on the retina of a viewer.
1609	Kepler's *New Astronomy* demonstrates that the planet Mars moves with varying speeds in an elliptical orbit, and he proposes that the Sun provides the force moving it.
1610	In his *Starry Messenger*, Galileo describes what he saw in the heavens with his telescope, noting mountains on the Moon, the satellites of Jupiter, and thousands of stars invisible to the naked eye.
1614	John Napier introduces logarithms as a means of easing calculations.
1619	Kepler proposes that the cubes of the distances of all the planets from the Sun are proportional to the squares of their orbital periods; now known as his Third Law.

1620–1626	Francis Bacon, in a series of books, insists on the importance of fact-gathering and experiments to promote new discoveries, and he describes a model institution for collaborative scientific work.
1625	The first arithmetic calculating machine is designed by Wilhelm Schickard.
1627	Kepler publishes his *Rudolphine Tables*, based on his planetary theories, providing the most accurate and influential means of predicting planetary positions up to that time.
1628	In his *Anatomical Exercises on the Movement of the Heart and Blood,* William Harvey demonstrates how the blood circulates.
1632	Galileo's *Dialogue Concerning the Two Chief World Systems, Ptolemaic and Copernican* presents arguments in favor of the Copernican system by utilizing his discoveries with the telescope and in mechanics.
1633	Galileo is forced by the Inquisition to renounce the Copernican theory and is sentenced to house arrest for the rest of his life.
1637	Publication of René Descartes' *Discourse on Method* and his *Geometry*; the latter provides a foundation for analytic geometry.
1638	Galileo's *Discourses on Two New Sciences* puts forward his novel and influential ideas on moving bodies and the strength of materials.
1644	Descartes' *Principles of Philosophy* explains his ideas on matter and the nature of the universe as analogous to a mechanism.
1647	Blaise Pascal's *New Experiments Concerning the Void* demonstrates that experiments with a tube filled with mercury show that at the top of the tube is a vacuum, contradicting the belief that nature "abhors a vacuum."

1656   Christiaan Huygens invents the pendulum clock, providing significantly greater precision in time measurement.

1662   The Royal Society for the Improvement of Natural Knowledge is established in London to promote the development of science and to spread new scientific ideas. Robert Boyle describes his experiments with a vacuum pump and notes the inverse relation between the pressure and volume of a gas.

1663   Pascal's work on hydrostatics, the weight and pressure of the atmosphere, and the vacuum are published posthumously as *Treatises on the Equilibrium of Liquids and the Weight of the Mass of Air.*

1665   Publication in Paris and London of the first periodicals to feature scientific news.

1666   King Louis XIV of France establishes the Royal Academy of Sciences to promote the experimental sciences and mathematics.

1671   Approximate date of the development of Newton's version of the calculus.

1672   Invention of the first machine generating electricity—a sulfur globe rubbed by a dry hand. Passing sunlight through a prism, Newton shows that white light is composed of a spectrum of colors, and that the light of each is refracted at a different angle. Detailed microscopic examination by Marcello Malpighi reveals the emergence of specific organs in the embryological development of a chick.

1674   John Mayow proposes that certain particles in the air are necessary for combustion, are transmitted to the blood by the lungs, and thereby function to maintain body heat.

1675   Precise astronomical observations by Ole Römer determine that the speed of light is finite.

1677   Microscopic discovery of spermatozoa by Antoni van Leeuwenhoek.

1679	Robert Hooke requests Newton's opinion on the possibility of explaining planetary motion by the principle of inertia and an inverse-square attractive force from the Sun.
1684	Publication of Gottfried Wilhelm Leibniz's account of the calculus, utilizing infinitesimals.
1687	Publication of Isaac Newton's *Mathematical Principles of Natural Philosophy* lays out his laws of motion and universal gravitation, utilizing his key concepts of space, time, mass, and force, and thereby uniting celestial and terrestrial physics.
1690	Christiaan Huygens advances a wave theory of light.
1694	Rudolph Camerarius provides the first detailed explanation of plant sexuality.
1704	Publication of Newton's *Opticks*, based on his experiments, becomes a model for experimentation. The book's appendix also raises important questions about various aspects of nature.
1705	Edmond Halley finds that the comet now bearing his name, and which he observed in 1682, moves in an elongated elliptical orbit over an approximately seventy-year period.
1713	William Derham's *Physico-Theology* and the second edition of Newton's *Mathematical Principles of Natural Philosophy* promote a trend to explain the discoveries of science as evidence for the greatness, wisdom, and beneficence of God.

CHAPTER 1

HISTORICAL OVERVIEW

In the course of the sixteenth and seventeenth centuries, ideas concerning the nature of the universe and explanations of what occurs within it changed profoundly in Western Europe. In 1500 natural philosophers—as scientists were then called—perceived the universe as finite, with the motionless Earth at its center, surrounded by the Moon, Sun, planets, and stars, all of which rested on several homocentric spheres rotating uniformly about the Earth. In 1700 the universe was seen as infinite, and the planets, including Earth, revolving in ellipses about the Sun at varying distances with non-uniform motion. In 1500 the universe was thought to be completely full of matter. In the course of the next two centuries most natural philosophers came to accept the existence of spaces devoid of matter. The behavior of moving bodies, whether falling or thrown, also came to be understood in profoundly different ways.

Knowledge about the world of living things saw similar substantial changes. Anatomical, physiological, and embryological details and processes unknown to the ancients were discovered. The functions of plants and animals were coming to be seen as based on physical and chemical processes, rather than as governed by vegetative or animal "souls." It was learned that sexual reproduction in animals and humans involved the union of sperm and egg, and that processes analogous to sexual reproduction applied in plants as well. Blood came to be seen as circulating rather than ebbing and flowing in the channels of the body.

At the end of the Early Modern period, previously widely accepted beliefs in witchcraft, astrology, magic, and supernatural events brought about by hidden causes began to wane. The inventions of the telescope and microscope enabled further investigation of hitherto unknown worlds. Traditional forms of mathematics were expanded, and new branches of mathematics were developed. Experimentation and the discovery of mathematical laws of nature increasingly became the desired goals of scientific investigation.

These profound changes in the conceptions and practices of natural philosophy constituted significant and decisive breaks with long-held beliefs that originated in Greek antiquity and were modified by scholars in medieval Western Europe and the Islamic world. For several centuries students had learned in the universities of Europe about the achievements of the ancients, such as those of Aristotle (384–322 B.C.E.) in philosophy, on the structure of the universe, on physics, and on the nature of living things; of Claudius Ptolemy (c. 100–c. 170) on astronomy and astrology; and of Galen (130–200) on anatomy, physiology, and medicine. Those achievements came to be seen as standing in the way of a true knowledge of reality. At the beginning of the two centuries under consideration, it was felt that the ancients had gained a true picture of the world. The task of natural philosophy was perceived to be the restoration of truths long lost. In the course of the seventeenth century this was no longer so; the discovery of new things never before seen or understood became the goal. Natural philosophers were now determined, as in Hamlet's instructions to the players, "to hold up as 'twere the mirror to nature," to reflect reality, rather than erroneous conceptions of it.

The pace of change in scientific ideas and practices was now much more rapid than had been the case in previous millennia. This revolution in our beliefs about the natural world and in the ways we try to increase our understanding of it can properly be understood as the achievements of individuals or of groups in the context of the social and intellectual worlds in which they lived and worked.

The European Context

The Scientific Revolution took place in Western Europe rather than in the Islamic world, whose scientists were superior in knowledge and far more innovative during the Middle Ages than those in Europe. In the course of the expansion of Islam, Muslims encountered the works of the ancient Greeks in philosophy, mathematics, astronomy, physics, alchemy, geography, astrology, and medicine, and they were fascinated by what they found. Many of those works were translated into Arabic. Scientists in the Islamic world subsequently built upon and advanced some of the ideas in those Greek sciences. Beginning in the thirteenth century, many books on Greek and Arabic science were translated into Latin and were studied in European universities.

In the course of the later Middle Ages, the Chinese inventions of the compass, of printing, paper, explosives, and the effective rigging of sailing vessels found their way into Western Europe. Yet the Scientific Revolution did not occur in China, whose technical achievements were far superior to those of medieval Europe. Why the study of the natural world by Chinese and Arabic scholars did not result in the revolutionary changes that took place in Western Europe is a topic requiring further historical investigation. Part of such an effort must surely be an examination of some of the unique, important, and relatively rapid changes in European society and culture in the late Middle Ages and the Early Modern period.

Humanism and the Renaissance

Beginning in the cities of northern Italy in the fourteenth and fifteenth centuries, the cultural and intellectual changes known as the Renaissance played a significant role in the changing nature of natural philosophy. Those engaged in learning, literature, and the arts looked to classical Greek and Roman works as models for their growing attention to secular life. With the growth of commerce and changing aspects of civic life, the *vita activa*, or active life, was seen as more important than the medieval ideal of the *vita contemplativa*, the life of contemplation. Classical works in their original Greek and Latin began to be available in Western Europe, along with previously unknown works. Included were works by Plato (c. 427–348 B.C.E.) and other philosophers, works by several mathematicians, and tracts attributed to certain mythological figures, chief among them Hermes Trismegistus, an individual believed to have lived at the same time as, or before, Moses. These and other works had an important effect on thought about the natural world. They emphasized the roles of number and measurement, as well as unity, harmony, and the operations of hidden forces in the universe.

With the invention of the printing press using movable type in the fifteenth century, books began to be published in the various native languages of Europe, as well as in Latin and Greek. Not only works of literature but also treatises on scientific subjects were beginning to be translated, and popular versions of them began to appear. New developments in natural philosophy began to find their way into works of literature, and knowledge of the new scientific ideas became a part of the culture of the upper classes.

The Age of Exploration

In the late fifteenth century Portugal, and then Spain and the United Provinces, sent ships in search of commercial advantages to West Africa and Asia. Subsequent voyages to the Western Hemisphere, carried out as well by France and England, eventually resulted in the creation of colonial empires and the beginning of a world economy. Lands, peoples, flora, and fauna unknown to the ancients and unmentioned in Scripture were discovered. It became evident that there was more in heaven and Earth than had been dreamed of in Aristotle's philosophy.

These transoceanic voyages necessitated the redesign of ocean-going vessels and improvement in the principles of navigation, which in turn necessitated attention to the further development of astronomy, geography, cartography, and instruments useful in promoting those sciences. The study of mathematics and its applications, involving the use of spherical geometry, trigonometry, and algebra, became increasingly important.

Commerce and Economics

Commercial and economic changes in Europe had begun to develop slowly after the eleventh and twelfth centuries. Villages became towns and cities. Businesses were established for trade in various commodities between parts of Europe and Asia. As enterprises grew, they required the creation of institutions and procedures to handle their increasingly complex needs, among which were banking, insurance, and bookkeeping. Here, too, arose incentives for the promotion of mathematical knowledge. The need for effective and profitable insurance policies, as well as interest in the nature of gambling, promoted the

study of probability. Changes in political and social life, class structures, and religion, resulting in the increased transfer of land, placed
increasing emphasis on surveying.

The role of mathematics in everyday life took on increased importance, and the need and desire for greater precision grew. That need
was reflected in the continuing development of architecture, mining,
and the manufacture of clocks and other mechanical devices. Machines
were invented and continually improved for the grinding of lenses for
eyeglasses and for spinning and weaving. Watermills and windmills
were built for the grinding of grain. A knowledge of at least elementary mathematics became a requirement for practitioners in many crafts
to an extent that had not been necessary before.

There began to emerge a new attitude toward and respect for
craftsmanship, for the maker and doer, as well as for the thinker. Natural philosophers and the creators of new systems of thought concerning nature were frequently called architects or craftsmen. Illustrations
showing a divine being using a compass in creating the world was one
symbol of this trend.

Government, Politics, and Warfare

In the sixteenth and seventeenth centuries, the nature of the state
in Western Europe differed in significant ways from the situation in the
Islamic world and in China. Europe was composed of a great number
of independent kingdoms, provinces, principalities, and cities. Chief
among them for their roles in the development of science were the German states, England, France, the Low Countries, and the Duchy of Tuscany and the Republic of Venice in Italy. In the course of those two
centuries the trend within all these states was for greater and continuing consolidation. The number of government departments grew with
time and were divided and subdivided as needed. Government treas-
uries gained increasing attention and became more complex. The re-
quirements of detailed record keeping for tracking population trends,
for purposes of taxation, and for the military services also necessitated
an increase in the use of mathematics.

European governments had to give attention to the changing re-
quirements of commerce, construction, and warfare. A class of skilled
craftspeople called engineers was gradually created to deal with the im-

provement of harbors, efforts in the United Provinces at reclamation of parts of the North Sea, improvements of inland waterways, and the construction of canals. Interest grew in gaining better knowledge of missile trajectories and how to make them more effective, and in the construction of more efficient cannon and fortifications. Problems of logistics and provision of supplies in military campaigns also received increasing attention.

Patronage

Seeking prestige and profit, rulers were led increasingly to act as patrons, not only of artists and poets, but of craftspeople and natural philosophers as well. Undertakings in one kingdom or principality were imitated in others. Patrons would grant their clients money, land, a title, or a combination of them. Rulers sought out well-known astronomers for the improvement of navigation, the casting of horoscopes, or assistance with their own astronomical pursuits. Alchemists were engaged to create new, profitable commodities, and in some instances, novel medical preparations. The earliest societies for the promotion of natural philosophy were, for the most part, supported by patrons. Clients were also sought by the wealthy for managing libraries and collections of botanical and zoological species, and of strange and curious objects. Such positions supplemented and, to some degree, displaced universities as centers of new ideas and practices in natural philosophy.

Scientific Communication

Commerce and the new needs of governments required increased sources of information. Better and more effective means of communication were evidenced in the beginnings of regular coach transportation between some cities; postal services were established in a number of states. Correspondence networks were established among natural philosophers working in various fields, in which ideas and practices were exchanged and debated. Institutions were created to provide lectures to the public on science and technology. The printing press was important in the spread of ideas at a pace more rapid than in previous centuries or than was the case in other parts of the world. In the seventeenth century a number of societies for the promotion of natural philosophy were established, as were journals devoted to the circulation of new discoveries in natural philosophy.

Natural Philosophy and Religion

The Protestant Reformation affected not only the nature of religion in Western Europe, but natural philosophy as well. With the emergence of new denominations of Christianity and challenges to attitudes and practices of the Catholic Church with respect to the role of priests, the sacraments, the Mass, and the organization and governance of the Church, new attitudes arose about the relation of scientific ideas to religious doctrines. Among the important changes in practice for Protestants was the necessity of reading the Bible for oneself to understand more effectively the basis of religious beliefs. An important result was the translation of the Bible from Latin into the native languages of Europe and a subsequent increase of literacy.

Natural philosophy had long been perceived as a handmaiden to theology, which was called the "queen of the sciences." It was now coming to be thought of as independent of theological constraints, with its own methods, functions, and purposes different from those of religion. There were continual debates during the Scientific Revolution over how certain ideas were contradicted by the word of God as given in Scripture. The best-known example is the Copernican theory, which was challenged by a literal interpretation of certain biblical passages. In response, natural philosophers held that passages in the Bible must not be taken literally, that God gave humans the ability to learn more about the ways in which He had created the world, and that we are thereby brought closer to God by examples of His omniscience, omnipotence, and beneficence.

The Watershed

In the course of the sixteenth century there evolved changing attitudes about nature, the development of technology and the crafts, and the importance of observation and mathematics. The most decisive changes in traditional beliefs in natural philosophy in a number of areas took place, however, within the first half of the seventeenth century. The trends noted here seemed to have crystallized at that time. Detailed observation, experimentation, and increasingly precise measurement became important in new ways. A striking cluster of new and significant concepts about the structure and nature of the cosmos, of operations in various physical sciences, in physiology, and about the best methods for gaining new scientific knowledge is evident in those few decades.

Astronomy

The heliocentric theory advanced in 1543 by Nicolaus Copernicus (1473–1543) had very few adherents in the sixteenth and early seventeenth centuries. Among them, however, was Johannes Kepler (1571–1630). He transformed and improved Copernicus' theory by overthrowing what had been axiomatic in astronomy for two millennia, namely, that all celestial bodies must move in circles and with uniform speed. Kepler discovered that planetary orbits were elliptical, and that a planet's speed varied depending on its proximity to the Sun. His discoveries were made possible in part by his utilization of the most precise astronomical observations made up to that time by Tycho Brahe (1546–1601). Kepler's astronomical tables, published in 1627, were significantly more accurate than any then in use. Kepler also insisted that astronomers must also be concerned with causes, and he proposed a hypothesis on the cause of planetary motion based on forces similar to magnetism issuing from the Sun. Galileo Galilei (1564–1642), who was also a Copernican, using a telescope, noted that the Moon, planets, and stars displayed characteristics that were quite different from what Aristotle had taught, thereby weakening certain objections to the Copernican theory. Galileo's discoveries in mechanics also increased support for Copernicus' ideas.

Matter Theory

Traditional beliefs about the nature of matter had also rested for the most part on the theories of Aristotle. One of their most fundamental aspects was a distinction between the heavens and everything beneath the Moon. The Earth was composed of four kinds of matter, consisting of the essences of earth, water, air, and fire; associated with each were various qualities, such as weight, firmness, and liquidity. They were combined in various ways to constitute the substances of our everyday experience. The heavens consisted of a series of nested spheres, perpetually revolving uniformly above the Earth, composed of a fifth element that was perfect and unchanging. The universe was finite, completely full, and devoid of vacuous spaces.

Alternative ideas had been put forward in ancient Greece, both before and after Aristotle. One of them was the theory that the universe was composed of indivisible atoms colliding and moving in an infinite, void space in various combinations that determined the shapes and properties of the substances around us. The most developed theory was that of Epicurus (341–270 B.C.E.) as a part of his philosophy on the means to a good life. Because Epicureanism was seen to conflict with certain aspects of Christianity, Aristotelian theory was supreme during the Middle Ages. In the early seventeenth century the atomic theory and variations of matter as composed of particles were purged of anti-Christian implications and elaborated as a necessary replacement for Aristotle's theory.

Motion

Beliefs about the behavior of moving bodies had also been based on Aristotelian foundations. Aristotelians—also called Peripatetics—distinguished two kinds of motion. All bodies, depending on the matter of which they were composed, tended to move toward their natural places: toward the center of the universe, corresponding to the center of the Earth, or away from the center of the universe. The Peripatetics also held that nothing moved unless it was moved by an internal or external mover, and that bodies fell at speeds proportional to their weights. Medieval Aristotelians held that missiles first moved in the direction they were hurled and then fell directly to Earth.

In the 1630s Galileo Galilei described his experiments, many of which he had made earlier, to determine precisely the trajectories of bodies given an impulse other than vertical and to determine the relationship in directly falling bodies between the increasing distances traveled and successive equal intervals of time. He distinguished between the measurable results of his experiments and assumed ideal results in the absence of friction or resistance. His discoveries were very influential in overturning traditional Peripatetic beliefs and in shaping the subsequent development of mechanics.

René Descartes (1596–1650) held that there was a fixed amount of motion in a universe completely filled with matter. He therefore gave attention to the result of the impact of bodies on one another and concluded that in such instances the total motion is conserved, although the direction of the motions may be changed. Once a body is in motion, Descartes held, it will continue in a straight line until deflected by another body.

With the work of Kepler, Galileo, Descartes, and others, the concepts of force, attraction, inertia, and mathematical laws became central features of efforts to understand and explain the behavior of moving bodies. The culmination of those efforts would come with the work of Isaac Newton (1642–1727) later in the century.

Optics

The nature and behavior of light had, as with astronomy, been one of the mathematized sciences that had come from Antiquity with valid results and methods. Associated with the mathematical results of the behavior of light were theories of vision. It had been known in the ancient world that beams of light were reflected at the same angles at which they struck the reflecting surface, and that a light source at the focus of a parabola would be reflected in a parallel beam. However, the angles of refraction of a light beam passing through various media were unable to be determined precisely until the early seventeenth century, when the mathematical law governing refraction was independently discovered by several scientists. Here, too, precise measurement was a factor in determining a previously unknown result. The sine law was influential in the further development of optics in the seventeenth century. Important discoveries were also made on the nature of color and vision.

Anatomy and Physiology

The discovery by Andreas Vesalius (1514–1564) of a number of errors in Galen's descriptions of human anatomy, and subsequent findings of anatomical features unknown to the ancients, led some to reexamine aspects of human physiology as well. Among the traditional Galenic beliefs about the workings of the body was that the blood ebbed and flowed in the veins and arteries. William Harvey (1578–1657) was determined to find by close observation and experimentation the paths followed by the blood after being pumped from the heart. He carefully observed the functions of the heart and movement of the blood in dying mammals and cold-blooded animals. Measuring the amount of blood pumped by the beating heart, he determined that blood must circulate, returning to the heart, where it is again pumped to the arteries. Here again, then, as had, in effect, been the case with Kepler and clearly with Galileo, motion was slowed so that it could be more precisely measured and its nature and effects determined.

New Methodologies in Natural Philosophy

The early seventeenth century saw increasing attention paid by natural philosophers to determine the best methods for gaining new knowledge about the natural world. The traditional means of explaining natural events proposed by Aristotle was that for every event there were four causes, involving the substance of the object undergoing change, its form, an action initiating the change, and a final cause or purpose. In the early seventeenth century the notion of Aristotle's four causes slowly began to be replaced by the elimination of three of the causes, particularly the final one, and retaining the immediate action as the sole cause. Increasingly, that immediate cause came to be thought of as analogous to mechanical causes, such as those operating in machinery and most notably in clocks. An influential figure in the shift into what came to be known as mechanical philosophy was René Descartes. Descartes insisted that matter moved only when moved by other matter.

Aristotle's theory of knowledge held that newly discovered facts could be explained by seeing how they were related to certain universal principles governing nature. Statements about such facts could be seen as true or not according to whether they logically followed from their relationship to a certain class of absolutely known principles, embodied in logical relationships known as syllogisms. For example: All mammals have breasts; whales have breasts; therefore all whales are mammals.

It was in the early seventeenth century that the logical certainty characteristic of the syllogism was slowly coming to be seen as inadequate for the discovery of new knowledge. Francis Bacon (1561–1626) challenged Aristotelian methodology and insisted on the importance of discovering new facts about nature, collecting as many as possible about the phenomena under investigation. By a process of induction, this would lead to new principles about the natural world. The result would be the growing advancement of knowledge by scientists specializing in the acquisition of such collections of fact. Bacon further proposed a model for a research institution to carry out such studies.

Experiments and more detailed observations were now being undertaken to learn new things about motion and physiology. In 1600 William Gilbert (1544–1603) had published a work on the magnet, in which he detailed a number of experiments illustrating the properties of magnetism. Galileo's precisely measured observations of falling bodies were a pioneering effort at what would increasingly become a goal of scientific investigation. The certainties of mathematics, where applicable, were beginning to be substituted for the certainties of logic. Gradually, it was recognized that relationships in the natural world could be seen as valid, true, probable, or useful, even if not absolutely certain.

In the early seventeenth century, a number of new instruments and means of calculation were invented, thus greatly enhancing the role of measurement and greater precision in the gaining of new knowledge. These inventions included the telescope, the microscope, heat-measuring devices, the air-pump, the barometer, the military compass, logarithms, the slide rule, and calculating machines. Decimal fractions were also beginning to be employed. The telescope and the microscope led immediately to the discovery and exploration of wholly new realms beyond the reach of the unaided senses.

Scientific Communication

The promotion of the new scientific ideas had begun earlier in the century with the creation of societies and organizations to discuss them and with the establishment of lectureships in the sciences. The idea of providing knowledge to a wider audience than students attending universities began with the establishment of an institution in Paris in 1530, later called the *Collège Royal*. In the early seventeenth century associations were formed in Rome, London, Oxford, and Paris to explain new ideas in natural philosophy to a general audience. Practitioners in various branches of natural philosophy established correspondence networks for the exchange of information and to debate the new ideas. All these new discoveries and practices clearly define the first few decades of the seventeenth century as the heart of the transformation of the sciences known as the Scientific Revolution.

It must be noted, however, that in this period the revolutionary changes in thought about the nature of the world were far from readily and universally accepted. Natural philosophy was in flux, and doubts persisted about the profound changes in viewpoint demanded by the new philosophy. As John Donne (1572–1631) wrote in his *Anatomie of the World*:

> The new philosophy calls all in doubt,
> The element of fire is quite put out;
> The sun is lost and the Earth, and no man's wit
> Can well direct him where to look for it.
> And freely men confess that this world's spent,
> When in the planets and the firmament
> They seek so many new; then see that this
> Is crumbled out again to his atomies.

Reception and Development of the New Philosophy

The second half of the seventeenth century built on and extended the achievements and practices of the first half. New ideas began to reach a wider audience. Scientific societies were organized by governments and began to play significant roles in the conduct of experimentation in new areas. Acquaintance with the new scientific ideas became a requirement for the social elites of Europe, and works of popular science appeared in the languages of Europe rather than in the traditional Latin of the learned classes.

The Physical Sciences

Acceptance of the Copernican theory, as modified by Kepler, grew in the second half of the seventeenth century. It was increasingly recognized that planetary orbits were not circular, and that planets did not move equal distances in equal times. New astronomical tables, based on improvements of Kepler's *Rudolphine Tables* of 1627, were published. Planetary position and various astronomical phenomena, such as eclipses, were predicted and observed more accurately with improved telescopes. Important new optical discoveries were made, and new theories were proposed about the nature of light and colors, and on the transmission of light. The finite velocity of light was discovered through astronomical observation, and it was discovered by experimental means that white light is composed of a mixture of colors. The refractive indexes of a number of substances were established more accurately.

In mechanics, studies were undertaken on the behavior of bodies under impact and on laws governing revolving bodies. The concept of a common center of gravity for neighboring masses was proposed. Roles for attraction and inertia were explored as possible explanations for planetary motion. Ideas that had been put forward earlier by Galileo, Kepler, Descartes, Christiaan Huygens (1629–1695), and Robert Hooke (1635–1703) were some of the components of the new and universally applicable laws advanced by Isaac Newton toward the end of the century.

The nature of matter continued to be explored. A variety of particulate theories were proposed to help explain various properties of matter such as density, solidity, and temperature. Belief in the existence of vacuums was strongly reinforced by a series of experiments with pumps drawing air out of sealed chambers. Alchemy remained very much alive and influential. Robert Boyle (1627–1691) and Newton were among its most avid practitioners.

The Life Sciences

The achievement of William Harvey on the circulation of blood was rather quickly adopted and was followed by new discoveries in anatomy and physiology. New taxonomies for animals and plants took into better account the results of detailed examination of fauna and flora and the continuing discoveries of new species in various part of the world. The discoveries of micro-organisms never before known and of minute details of anatomy and physiology in various living things were made possible by the expanding use of the microscope. New theories about the nature of reproduction were debated, and studies in comparative embryology were undertaken. Attempts were made to understand the structure and behavior of animals and plants on analogy with mechanical and chemical processes.

Universities and the World of Learning

The universities of Europe, whose task had been seen as passing on to their students the well-established knowledge attained in earlier ages, were being very slowly transformed from teaching modified Aristotelian ideas, accompanied by new approaches characteristic of the Renaissance, into institutions in which the new natural philosophy was beginning to find a home. There were now a few professors on university faculties who were active participants in developing the new philosophy. The empirical successes of Keplerian Copernicanism resulted in its becoming part of astronomical teaching in some universities, although sometimes with reservations. Galileo's ideas on motion were also beginning to be taught. Medical teaching reflected the discoveries of Vesalius, Harvey, and others.

Scientific societies for the purpose of advancing science were created with sets of rules and restricted memberships. In 1660 an association called the Society for the Promotion of Natural Knowedge was organized in London. In 1662, upon receipt of a royal charter, it became the Royal Society. Shortly afterward the Royal Academy of Sciences was established in France. The purpose of both was to advance science in all its branches. Both issued periodic journals, which were distributed throughout Europe and to which individuals from various parts of Europe contributed. Membership was offered to outstanding scientists from abroad; the Royal Academy did likewise. The rulers of Britain and France established national observatories for the advancement of astronomy.

Religious Responses to the New Philosophy

The idea of a warfare between science and religion was common in the nineteenth century but was completely absent in the Early Modern period. All natural philosophers were religious and sought to reconcile the new natural philosophy and traditional religious beliefs. Apparent contradictions of certain biblical passages, such as the idea of the Earth's motion and hypotheses that the Earth was older than a few thousand years and that it had come into existence through a process of cosmic evolution, were explained by assertions that there are two God-given books—Holy Scripture and the Book of Nature. By learning more about the latter, we could learn more as well about the nature and works of God and be brought closer to Him.

The mechanical philosophy, however, with its goal of developing a self-regulating system of natural laws, was challenged as denying a role for God once He had created the universe. There seemed nothing left for divine Provenance. The Cartesian position that the creation of matter and motion and the laws governing their behavior were sufficient for understanding all natural phenomena was modified by some to include a role for "active principles," spiritual in nature, to account for the motion of bodies. Theological opinions had in a very few cases helped shape new concepts in natural philosophy, but the converse would become increasingly important.

Experimentation

Experiments played an increasingly significant role in the evolving nature of natural philosophy during the seventeenth century. The notion that one must do things, to operate upon nature, to intervene in the physical world, had grown with the increasing influence of magic and alchemy, with the achievements of Galileo, and with the assertions of philosophers such as Bacon that it was necessary not only to observe the world around us but also to wrest knowledge from it.

Novel experiments were conducted in mechanics, particularly on the results of impact. Christiaan Huygens corrected some of Descartes' conclusions and further advanced the laws of collision and the principle of inertia. He also demonstrated that the back and forth motions of a pendulum, whatever their lengths, are truly isochronous only when moving in a cycloidal path. Showing how to make a pendulum move in such a path, Huygens created the first precise clock, increasingly important for the role of precision in the sciences. He examined the nature of a body in uniform circular motion and determined what he termed its centrifugal force.

Experimentation was especially important in the development of pneumatics. Miners had long known that water could not be pumped more than about thirty-two feet, and some began to question why. Beginning about the middle of the seventeenth century, a series of experiments led to the conclusion that the air had weight, and that weight lessened with a rise in altitude. It was further demonstrated that air had pressure, that it would increase as air was compressed, and that its pressure was proportional to its volume. The invention of the air pump led to debates among Aristotelians, Cartesians, and atomists about the existence of a vacuum in chambers evacuated of air.

Experiments were conducted on the nature and propagation of light. Isaac Newton showed by a series of experiments with prisms that white light is composed of a spectrum of colors from red to violet. A hypothesis about the propagation of light in waves was put forward by Christiaan Huygens. Newton determined the minimum sizes of different light waves. Theories of the nature of light, however, as particulate or as waves existed side by side.

New Instruments and Their Discoveries

There were important improvements in telescopes in the second half of the seventeenth century. For the Galilean telescope, with convex lenses at either end, was substituted telescopes based on ideas in Kepler's book on the optics of refraction. A Keplerian telescope, with a convex object lens and a concave eyepiece, was better suited for astronomical observation, since it showed a greater field of view. Moreover, it allowed the insertion in its tube of a micrometer, invented independently in England and in France. This measuring device provided significantly greater precision in the measurement of celestial angles, resulting in the ability to predict astronomical events more accurately.

The microscope became a more effective instrument through the grinding of better lenses, which permitted sharper focus, and the addition of a mirror to provide a sharper image. The most important discoveries, however, were made by Antoni van Leeuwenhoek (1632–1723), the finest grinder of lenses. The microscope revealed that plants were composed of cells. Innumerable new living beings were discovered, as were human spermatozoa and eggs. New discoveries continued to be made in anatomy, physiology, and embryology.

Mathematics

Mathematicians continued to make new discoveries. Analytic geometry was furthered by development of the concept of the analysis of curves by algebraic means, using equations with two unknowns. The concept of infinitesimals led to the most important development in mathematics: the independent development of the calculus by Gottfried Wilhelm Leibniz (1646–1716) and Newton. The use of calculus permitted the subsequent analysis of motion in astronomy and physics in very significant ways.

The Newtonian Universe

The achievements of Isaac Newton in astronomy, mathematics, and optics were the culmination of the discoveries and practices in the physical sciences of the previous century and a half. Newton's three laws of motion and the law of gravitation have played a dominant role in physics ever since he advanced them in 1687. The earlier discoveries in mechanics of Galileo, Descartes, and Huygens and in astronomy of Kepler were brought together in a unified system of universal laws. The Newtonian concepts of space, time, mass, and force embodied in his laws of motion became essential concepts for the subsequent development of mechanics. Newton's laws of motion and the law of gravitation enabled astronomers to plot the positions of celestial bodies with much greater precision. His discoveries in optics and mathematics likewise provided the foundations for further advancements in those areas. The work of Newton marks a fitting close to the era of the Scientific Revolution and the birth of modern science.

CHAPTER 2

ASTRONOMY AND THE COSMOS

For the ancient Greeks, the traditional function of astronomy was to observe the celestial bodies systematically in order to develop geometrical techniques for the creation of tables that could be used to predict the positions of the Sun, Moon, and planets at different times of the year, as well as certain astronomical phenomena such as eclipses. The causes and explanation of celestial motions and appearances was the province of the natural philosopher or physicist, rather than the astronomer. This distinction would be eliminated in the course of the seventeenth century, and astronomers began to deal with both the prediction of the positions of objects in the heavens and larger cosmological issues.

The conception of the nature and structure of the universe as taught by Aristotle was dominant until the sixteenth century, as were the types of geometrical models employed by Claudius Ptolemy some centuries later. The work of Copernicus, however, set a new agenda for astronomers. It was followed by increased questioning of Aristotelian and Ptolemaic conceptions and practices, based on more precise observations than in the past, the revelations of the newly invented telescope, and new theories about the nature and causes of planetary motions.

The Universe of Aristotle and Ptolemy

The Aristotelian universe was finite, spherical, and eternal; medieval Aristotelians, however, both Muslim and Christian, conceived the universe as having been created. The Earth was at its center, and the Moon, Sun, planets, and the sphere of stars all revolved around it. The celestial bodies were each moved about the Earth by a number of uniformly rotating homocentric spheres. Unlike motions on the Earth or below the sphere of the Moon, the heavens were composed of a perfect and unchanging substance—the *aether*, or quintessence, in which all motions were circular and uniform.

Observations of the night sky had been undertaken by the ancient Greeks before Aristotle, and with much greater attention to detail after him. It was clear that the motions of the objects in the sky as observed did not entirely conform to Aristotelian principles. It was obvious, for example, that the notion of uniformly rotating homocentric spheres could not account for the varied lengths of the seasons and the apparent changes in planetary distances from the Earth. Changes at different times in the brightness of the planets and the apparent sizes of the Sun and Moon contradicted the idea that they were equidistant from the Earth at all times. Aristotle's principles, nevertheless, were held to be true. In the practice of astronomy, however, some Aristotelian principles were ignored in order to predict, as effectively as possible, the positions of celestial objects. The greatest achievements in the ancient world in that effort were those of Claudius Ptolemy, who built upon and improved the work of his astronomical predecessors.

Ptolemaic Astronomy

The variation in length of the seasons and the apparent changes in the distances of the planets from the Earth at different times were accounted for geometrically by having the Sun and planets revolve uniformly about points a slight distance from the center of the Earth. Seen from the Earth, the celestial bodies, moving in their *eccentric* circles, therefore appear to move at different speeds at different times of the year. In addition, all the planets are seen periodically to reverse the directions in which they had been moving and then to resume their usual motions. These retrograde motions and the apparent changing distances of the planets and the Moon from the Earth were geometrically described by having them move uniformly on *epicycles*—circles whose centers were carried about on a *deferent*—a uniformly revolving eccentric circle.

To these techniques, Ptolemy, to further improve the accuracy of his geometrical calculating devices, added an *equant*, a point not at the center of an orbit, about which a planet moved uniformly.

These were all described in Ptolemy's chief work on astronomy,

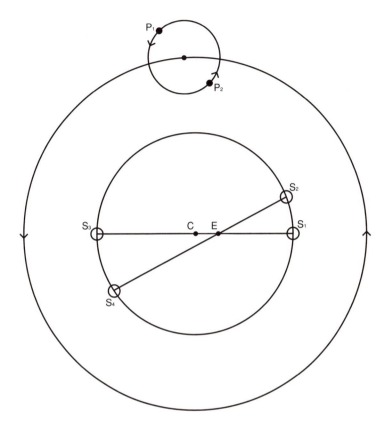

2.1 The Sun revolves uniformly about C, the center of its deferent. As seen from the Earth at E, however, the Sun appears to move more slowly from S_1 to S_2, near the Earth, than from S_3 to S_4, when it is farther from the Earth. A planet, moving uniformly on its epicycle will appear at P_1 to be moving in the same direction as it normally does in the course of its revolution; but at P_2 on its epicycle, it will appear for a short time to be moving in the opposite direction.

which came to be known in the West by its Arabic title, *Almagest*. It remained the chief authority in astronomy for several centuries.

Ptolemaic Astrology

Ptolemy was also the author of the principal text in astrology, *Tetrabiblos* (Four Books). The determination of future events through observation of the orientation of the celestial bodies to one another had

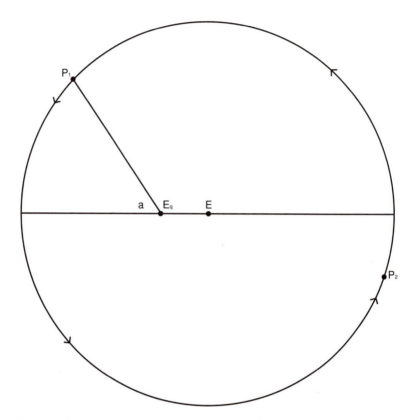

2.2 Angle *a* at the equant, E_q remains uniform throughout the motion of the planet P_1 on its deferent, whose center is at E, the Earth. As the planet approaches P_2, its motion as seen from the Earth would appear more rapid than at P_1.

a lengthy history. Considered a branch of astronomy, astrology required the ability to determine the positions of the planets in the past or to forecast them. Natural astrology was concerned with forecasting the weather, the fates of kingdoms, and catastrophic events. Judicial astrology was concerned with the future of individuals, or their medical prospects, and required the plotting of horoscopes based on the moment of birth of the individual, or of his medical condition. Astrology became part of university curricula in the course of the Renaissance.

Efforts to Improve Ptolemaic Astronomy

In the Middle Ages and the Early Modern period astronomers frequently tinkered with the Ptolemaic devices to improve the accuracy of their predictions. As the states of Western Europe began increasingly to engage in commercial sea voyages, the accuracy of astronomical tables became more important because of their use in navigation. In the thirteenth century King Alfonso X of Castile commissioned the creation of more accurate tables than those in use, and the *Alfonsine Tables*, named for him, were widely used until the later sixteenth century. In the fifteenth century European astronomers began to pay greater attention to the details of Ptolemy's *Almagest*. It became available in its original Greek, and a new translation, along with a manual explaining its use, was published. Astronomical observation, which had seriously lagged in the Middle Ages, was resumed, and useful data collected.

The geometrical procedures employing eccentrics, epicycles, and equants, however useful for the prediction of planetary positions, if taken to represent the real motions of the planets, contradicted the Aristotelian concept of the nature of the universe. The apparent loops in their orbits made by the planets in their retrograde motions and their apparent changing distances from the Earth were inconsistent with the principle of planetary motion from the center of the Earth at all times. Eccentrics and epicycles, however, did maintain the principle of uniform circular motion as characteristic of celestial events. The equant, in contrast, came to be seen as violating the principle of uniform motion because its planet's uniform motion about a point not at the center of an orbit meant that the planet did not move uniformly with respect to the Earth.

The relationship between the useful geometrical calculating devices of the astronomers and the physical principles of the physicists remained a puzzling problem throughout the Renaissance. Although astronomy as an observational and predictive science was based on an assumption of certain physical principles—namely, the Earth at the center of the universe, and uniform circular motion in the heavens— it came to be thought of as a kind of applied mathematics. The real nature of the universe and of celestial events was seen as the province of the natural philosophers. It is not entirely clear, however, that this distinction was universally accepted. This distinction was an issue for some Muslim astronomers, and it would be an important one for Copernicus.

The Reform of Astronomy

Copernican Astronomy

Nicolaus Copernicus learned Aristotelian philosophy as a university student and also made himself a master of Ptolemaic astronomy, but elements of his proposed new astronomy violated some of the principles of both of his ancient predecessors. Among the aims in his goal of reforming astronomy were the elimination of the equant and the creation of a unified system to replace the individual independent calculating devices for each of the planets. In Ptolemaic astronomy a change in the parameters of one planet had no necessary effect on those of the others. Copernicus' system, however, was a unified one where the relations among the planets constituted a whole. Moreover, Copernicus wished to show how certain coincidences resulting from Ptolemy's procedures could be seen as consequences of his own system. He nevertheless continued to employ eccentrics, epicycles, and uniform circular motion in his heliocentric system. Copernicus asserted that he would be satisfied if his system were able to produce results as accurate as Ptolemy's. In his elimination of the equant, Copernicus employed a geometrical device earlier used by a Muslim astronomer; it is unknown how he became acquainted with it. He also continued to have the planets riding on spheres. The earliest version of his ideas was in an anonymous manuscript entitled *Commentariolus* (A Little Commentary), which was circulated among a few individuals.

Copernicus ascribed three motions to the Earth, now conceived as revolving about the motionless Sun. His system was not truly heliocentric, for the planets along with planet Earth revolved about the center of Earth's orbit, which was slightly distant from the Sun. The Earth also rotated; this accounted for day and night and the apparent daily motion of the Sun across the sky. Because the Pole Star retained its position in the northern part of the sky in the course of the annual revolution of the Earth, which rested on the surface of a sphere, it was necessary for the North Pole of the rotating Earth also to rotate in a small circle in the course of a year in order to keep pointing to the Pole Star.

The advantages of Copernican astronomy were several. In Ptolemaic astronomy, the positions of the Sun, Mercury, and Venus relative to the Earth were indeterminate; it was unclear whether the orbit of the Sun was above or below those of the two planets. In the Copernican system their distribution was unambiguous. While the outer planets could be seen in conjunction with the Sun, or at any angle up to 180° from it, Mercury was never seen farther from the Sun than at a maximum of about 28° and Venus at 48°. It was now apparent, with Earth as the third planet revolving about the Sun, why this was so. Further, the retrograde motions of the planets could now be explained as caused by Earth moving more rapidly than the inner planets and overtaking in its annual motion the slower-moving Mars, Jupiter, and Saturn. In Copernicus' system there were six planets, not only the five observable with the naked eye. The nature of the planetary retrograde motions, as well as the sizes and times taken to complete the orbits of the planetary epicycles, could now be seen as reflecting the orbit of the Earth. Epicycles were therefore no longer necessary to fulfill the functions for which they had been invented. Copernicus retained them, however, solely for the purpose of the better prediction of planetary position. Finally, the Copernican system made it possible to determine the relative distances of the planets as proportions of the distance of Earth from the Sun.

Publication and Initial Reception of Copernicus' Work

In 1539 Copernicus was visited by Georg Joachim Rheticus (1514–1574), a young astronomer from the University of Wittenberg who had heard rumors about Copernicus' ideas. He became an early convert and urged Copernicus to publish. Concerned about the response to his radical ideas, Copernicus agreed to have Rheticus publish a preliminary account, which Rheticus did in 1540 in a work titled *Narratio prima* (A First Account). Its reception was favorable enough for Copernicus to agree to publish his full theory. Rheticus oversaw the printing of the first part of the manuscript, but the remainder of the task of supervising its publication was left to Andreas Osiander (1498–1552), a Lutheran minister. In an anonymous foreword to Copernicus' *De revolutionibus orbium caelestium* (On the Revolutions of the Celestial Orbs), Osiander said that its geometrical techniques were an improvement over Ptolemy's, but that the arrangement of the heavenly bodies in the work was not to be taken as reflecting reality. This argument was not the opinion of Copernicus or Rheticus. The book was published in 1543 and reached Copernicus as he lay dying. In 1551 Erasmus Reinhold (1511–1553), using Copernican models, published his *Prutenic Tables*, which were increasingly adopted as an improvement over the Alphonsine Tables.

Very few readers of the *De revolutionibus* during the sixteenth century disagreed with Osiander's opinion. Yet the work was read by most astronomers, and many of them noted their comments on various parts of the text in their copies. It was reprinted in 1566, and it continued to receive detailed analysis throughout the second half of the sixteenth century. Astronomers at the University of Wittenberg, the chief institution of Lutheran higher education, gave it considerable attention. Although Copernicus' heliocentrism was not accepted by those astronomers, his lunar theory, his elimination of the equant, and the tables derived from his work were considered an improvement over Ptolemy.

Problems of the Copernican System

Objections to its heliocentrism were both physical and religious. It clearly conflicted with a literal interpretation of passages in the Bible, but religious objections played no significant part in its reception until the early seventeenth century. Objections on physical grounds, however, were important. If the Earth rotates, why aren't we and objects on its surface thrown off? Why don't objects thrown aloft land to the west of the point from which they were thrown? And if the Earth revolves around the Sun, a star should be seen at slightly different angles when observed six months apart.

Such changes could not be observed, and they would not be until the nineteenth century. If Venus indeed circles the Sun, its brightness should vary considerably between its farthest and closest distances from the Earth; but it does not. Since, according to Aristotle, heavy bodies tend to fall to the center of the universe, which is also the center of the Earth, how do we explain falling bodies on an Earth revolving around the Sun?

To these objections Copernicus answered that objects on the Earth and those thrown aloft participate in the rotating motion of the Earth, giving them the ability to remain on the Earth or to return to the spot from which they had been thrown upward. The

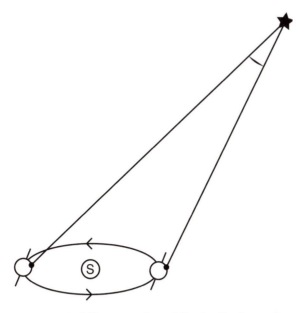

2.3 A star's different angles while the Earth revolves around the Sun.

different angles at which a star is observed at six-month intervals are unobservable because the stars are much farther away than had been thought. The angles are too small to be observed by our instruments. Changes in the brightness of Venus do not show considerable variation because Venus has phases unobservable by us, and these phases are reduced in size as the planet approaches the Earth. Bodies fall to the center of a revolving Earth, according to Copernicus, because of a tendency for bodies separated from a globe to return to that globe when permitted to fall.

Tycho Brahe and Geoheliocentrism

A few individuals thought Copernicus' hypothesis worth considering, but converts were rare. The most important astronomer after Copernicus, Tycho Brahe (1546–1601), was not among them. He devoted his life to the reformation of astronomy and held the most important consideration in that enterprise to be the creation of a series of new and precise observations of celestial bodies. Brahe's observations of a nova that suddenly appeared in 1572 and of a comet in 1577 clearly

2.4 Tycho Brahe seated among his instruments and assistants at Uraniborg. From Brahe's *Astronomiae instauratae mechanica* (1598).

showed that they were beyond the sphere of the Moon. Similar conclusions by other astronomers were important examples of a challenge to the traditional separation in function between the physicist and the astronomer; observations by astronomers had challenged a long-established principle of celestial physics. These observations seemed to contradict Aristotle's ideas that the region beyond the Moon was changeless and that comets were sub-lunar phenomena. They eventually resulted in the abandonment of the concept of celestial spheres.

With the grant of an island just off Copenhagen by Frederick II, the King of Denmark, Brahe built an observatory, Uraniborg (Castle of Astronomy), which he staffed with assistants, a printing press, and instruments capable of the most precise measurements.

In the course of about two decades Brahe made a series of the most detailed and continuous observations of the celestial bodies ever carried out. Among Tycho's astronomical achievements was an improvement in the ability to predict the positions of the Moon. With the accession to the throne of a new Danish king, Brahe was forced to leave Uraniborg; in 1599, and under the patronage of the Holy Roman Emperor, Rudolph II, he moved to a castle near Prague.

Many who rejected the Copernican theory, Tycho Brahe among them, nevertheless recognized that its advantages over Ptolemaic astronomy required a rethinking of the structure of the cosmos. Tycho could not accept the substitution of the Sun for the position of the Earth at the center of the universe, and he proposed a theory, known as geoheliocentrism, in which all the planets revolve around the Sun, which, in turn, revolves around the motionless Earth. This and a few similar geoheliocentric theories were seen for a few decades as a suitable alternative to the Ptolemaic and Copernican theories.

The Early Copernicans

Copernicus' ideas impressed a few contemporaries, including some officials of the Catholic Church, but of those competent in astronomy, Rheticus must be seen as Copernicus' first disciple. In the latter half of the sixteenth century, Thomas Digges (c. 1546–1595), was one of the few individuals open to the Copernican theory. He had carefully observed the nova of 1572 and concluded that it was beyond the sphere of the Moon. His *A Perfit Description of the Caelestiall Orbes* of 1576 included an English translation of parts of Book I of Copernicus' *De revolutionibus*. It also had a diagram showing the stars infinitely extended and at varying distances from the Sun.

It may have been during a visit to England in the mid-1580s that Giordano Bruno (1548–1600), a Dominican monk who had begun to question certain Catholic theological opinions, first encountered the Copernican theory and the idea of an infinite universe. He published several works, the best known of which was *La cena de le ceneri* (The Ash-Wednesday Supper, 1584), giving his theological interpretations of

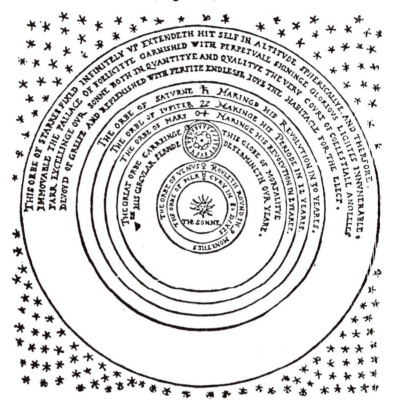

2.5 Thomas Digges' diagram of the stars.

the ideas of Copernicus, of an infinite universe and a plurality of worlds. After being imprisoned for several years and having been sentenced by the Inquisition, Bruno was burned at the stake in 1600 as a heretic, but not, it appears, for his Copernican beliefs.

Simon Stevin (1548–1620), who made important contributions to engineering, mechanics, mathematics, hydrostatics, and many other areas, was the first Copernican in the Low Countries. He published a book, *De hemelloop* (On Astronomy), in 1608, in which he showed the superiority of Copernicus' heliocentric theory over Ptolemy's geocentrism and made some slight improvements in the former. Stevin was but one of a small minority of heliocentrists in the first few decades after the publication of Copernicus' path-breaking work.

Copernicanism Revised and Improved

Johannes Kepler, Planetary Orbits, and Their Causes

Among the few who accepted Copernicanism in the late sixteenth century were Michael Mästlin (1550–1631), professor of mathematics at the University of Tübingen, and his student Johannes Kepler (1571–1630). Kepler went beyond his teacher's Copernicanism in insisting that part of the astronomer's job was to try to account for not only how the planets moved but also why they did so. For Kepler the chief means to account for the motions of the planets lay in the nature of the Sun and in harmonic principles. His first book, *Mysterium cosmographicum* (The Cosmographic Mystery), published in 1596, held that the six planets and their distances from the Sun were related to the five perfect solids, and that the Sun played a role in the movements of the planets. After Tycho Brahe left Uraniborg and moved to Prague, Kepler joined him as an assistant. Upon Tycho's death, Kepler acquired his observations, which proved decisive for his reformation of astronomy.

Kepler made significant changes and modifications in Copernicus' theory. He published *Astronomia nova . . . seu physica coelestis* (A New Astronomy . . . or Celestial Physics) in 1609, based on his analysis of the orbit of Mars. In subsequent works, he applied his discoveries to the rest of the planets. The Sun played a special role in Kepler's astronomy. Kepler discovered that each of the orbital planes of the planets intersected the Sun, and that the Sun lay in one of the foci of each of the elliptical orbits in which all the planets moved. Furthermore, an imaginary line from the Sun to a planet swept out equal areas in equal times. Planetary motion was therefore not uniform, but more rapid when close to the Sun, and slower when distant from it.

The Sun was also the cause of planetary motion. Kepler hypothesized that the Sun rotated and emitted quasi-magnetic forces that swept the planets around, alternately attracting and repelling them, thereby accounting for their elliptical orbits. Kepler also held that the tides are caused by the attraction of the Moon. He later discovered a mathematical law uniting all the planets of the solar system: that the cubes of each of the planetary distances were proportional to the squares of the times taken to complete their orbits. Here again, as in

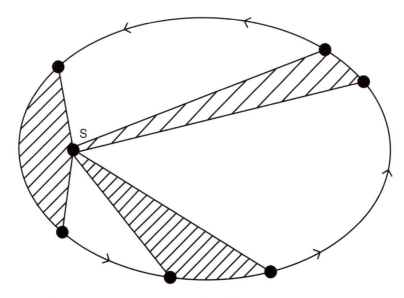

2.6 The Sun in one of the foci of an elliptical orbit. A radius vec-
tor from the Sun to a planet sweeps out equal areas in equal times.

his earliest work, harmonics and harmonic proportions were influential in Kepler's thinking.

Reception of Keplerian Astronomy

As had been the case with Copernican theory, Keplerian astronomy was slow to be accepted. Copernicanism was still rejected by most
astronomers in the early years of the seventeenth century. Kepler's area
rule of planetary motion—that a line from an orbiting planet to the Sun
sweeps out equal areas in equal times—could not easily be applied geometrically; it required the use of approximation, a method thought to
be inappropriate in astronomy. Furthermore, Kepler's speculations on
the cause of planetary motion was also thought be an inappropriate
part of the science of astronomy.

An important consideration in the subsequent acceptance of Kepler's astronomy were the empirical successes of his *Rudolphine Tables*,
named for his patron, derived from his theory, and published in 1627.
The tables predicted planetary positions and celestial events such as
eclipses and the passage of Mercury across the face of the Sun more accurately than any other tables then in use. By the middle of the seven-

2.7 The frontispiece of Kepler's *Rudolphine Tables*
(1627). The pillars of the temple show who Kepler
thought were the most important astronomers before
him. Instruments used in astronomy are also displayed.

teenth century, many astronomers had been won over to planetary ellipses, non-uniform motion, and a role for the Sun in moving the planets. Kepler's elimination of epicycles and the geometrical complexities
employed by earlier astronomers were also noted as praiseworthy.

Galileo, the Telescope, and a New Mechanics

Another early Copernican, Galileo Galilei (1564–1642), however,
was not convinced either of elliptical orbits or of the attractive powers

of the Sun or Moon. His construction and use of a telescope, after his having heard that one had recently been invented, played a very important role in the further weakening of Aristotelian natural philosophy and the promotion of Copernicanism. Turning his telescope to the heavens in 1609, Galileo saw that the planets were more than points of light, that the Moon had mountains rather than a smooth surface, that Jupiter had moons, and that there were innumerably more stars than could be seen with the naked eye, raising the possibility that the stars were much farther than had long been thought. In the next few years it was discovered that Venus had phases, an observation discrediting the astronomy of Ptolemy, but not of Tycho Brahe. These findings were published in 1610 in a short treatise called *Sidereus nuncius* (The Starry Messenger). Galileo and others also discovered spots on the Sun. The observed movements of sunspots across the face of the Sun in the course of about a month, and the movements of the planets in their orbits in the same direction as the sunspots, led Galileo to hint at a role for the Sun in moving the planets; unlike Kepler, however, he refused to speculate further.

Galileo attempted to prove the motion of the Earth by showing that the tides could best be explained by the Earth's daily rotation and annual revolution. He was unsuccessful in this endeavor, but the publication in 1632 in Italian of his *Dialogue on the Two Great World Systems—Ptolemaic and Copernican* indirectly made a strong case for the Copernican theory.

The publication of this work led to Galileo's trial by the Inquisition for heresy; he was accused of having violated an earlier injunction forbidding the teaching of the Copernican theory. Galileo was forced to deny the Copernican theory and was confined for the rest of his life to his home near Florence. His *Dialogue* and Copernicus' and Kepler's works were placed on the Index of Prohibited Books; the Church forbade Catholics to read them without special permission. Galileo wrote nothing more on astronomy and cosmology, but he published his discoveries in the science of mechanics in his *Dialogues on Two New Sciences* (1638). In this work Galileo answered a number of objections to the idea of the Earth's motion and demonstrated how the Earth could rotate without flinging off objects on its surface.

2.8 The title-page of Galileo's *Dialogue*, showing the three individuals—an Aristotelian, a Copernican, and an open-minded individual—whose discussions covered significant issues in debates on the nature of the universe.

New Thoughts about Celestial Motions

On the Causes of Planetary Motion

During Galileo's lifetime a few others promoted the Copernican theory or its Keplerian version with their own work. Ismaël Boulliau (1605–1694) accepted Kepler's elliptical orbits because of the improved accuracy shown by the tables based upon them but rejected his area rule and proposed cause of planetary motion. Jeremiah Horrocks

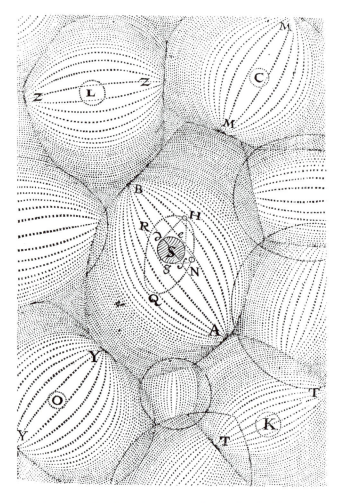

2.9 Descartes' celestial vortices. Note that he has a
planet moving in an elliptical orbit about the Sun.
From Descartes' *Principles of Philosophy.*

(1618–1641), a committed Keplerian, through his corrections to Kepler's tables based on his own observations, was the first to predict and
observe in 1639 the rare astronomical event of a transit of Venus across
the Sun. His theory of the Moon was the most effective of its time, and
he proposed a mechanical explanation instead of Kepler's magnetic hypothesis of the cause of planetary motion. Another figure important in
the transmission of the new astronomy was Giovanni Alfonso Borelli
(1608–1679). Familiar with the work of both Galileo and Kepler,

Borelli proposed that the planets tend to fly off from their orbits, but are attracted by the Sun, and are thus kept in orbital motion.

René Descartes (1596–1650), a Copernican who was familiar with Kepler's and Galileo's ideas, rejected the idea of attraction and forces. He held that the solar system, completely filled with imperceptible matter, was analogous to a whirlpool in which the planets, like something fallen into a whirlpool, are swirled around. Descartes also developed the idea of inertia—that all bodies in motion continue to move uniformly in a straight line unless struck or impeded by another body, a concept that would prove important in later theories of planetary motion.

Astronomers who accepted elliptical orbits had trouble dealing with Kepler's area rule. To carry out the necessary calculations for the production of astronomical tables, a number of them adopted the practice of assuming that a planet moved uniformly about the empty focus of its elliptical orbit; others employed epicycles to generate elliptical orbits. Nonetheless, by the 1670s it was fairly well accepted that astronomers must concern themselves with the means of behind planetary movements as well as the ability to predict them.

Newton, Universal Laws of Motion, and Universal Gravitation

The causes of planetary motion were beginning to receive a good deal of attention by natural philosophers in the 1660s and 1670s. Robert Hooke (1635–1703) proposed that the planets were moved by both the principle of inertia and a centripetal force, a tendency to be attracted to the Sun. A few years later he suggested that the attractive force from the Sun operated according to the inverse-square of its distance. Edmond Halley (c. 1656–1743) showed that a comet becoming visible in 1680, moved in a parabolic orbit, was a periodic phenomenon and would return in about seventy years. His interest in the causes of celestial motions led him in 1684 to suggest to Isaac Newton that he try to prove mathematically how elliptical orbits could be derived from an inverse-square law of attraction and the principle of inertia. Newton undertook the task suggested by Halley, and the results were published in 1687 in his *Philosophiae naturalis principia mathematica* (Mathematical Principles of Natural Philosophy). In it Newton put forward what have become known as his three laws of motion and the law of universal gravitation, that all bodies in the universe attract all others with a force depending on their masses and the inverse-square of the distance between them. Even the Sun was no longer seen as motionless, since it both attracted the planets and was attracted by them. The tendency of bodies revolving about the Sun, when unconstrained, to fly off in straight lines with uniform motion, according to Newton's first law—the principle of inertia—was counteracted by their attraction by the Sun. The work demonstrated that under different conditions, all celestial bodies could be seen as moving in various curvilinear paths, including ellipses and parabolas. Space, time, force, and mass became fundamental components in efforts to explain motions in both the heavens and the Earth.

Summary

The transformation of concepts about the nature and structure of the universe began with increased attention to the relationship between ideas about the causes of the celestial motions and the geometrical calculating techniques used for predicting celestial events. These concerns were supplemented by a significant increase in observational opportunities and precision that challenged long-held beliefs. It took over a century for the heliocentric theory to be accepted by astronomers and several decades for elliptical orbits and the role of the Sun in planetary motion to be accepted. The ancient axioms of uniform circular motion of the Moon and planets and of the unchanging perfection of the heavens were discarded, replaced by ellipses, earthlike mountains on the Moon, planetary satellites, and an uncountable number of stars. By the end of the seventeenth century, a single set of universal mathematical laws was seen to apply throughout an infinite universe. In subsequent generations these laws and continual improvements in the power of telescopes led to increasingly accurate predictions and new discoveries. The decisive event for the further progress of astronomy came with the publication of Newton's *Principia* in 1687.

CHAPTER 3

MATTER, MOTION, AND THE MATHEMATICAL SCIENCES

At the heart of the profoundly changing ideas of the natural world during the Scientific Revolution were radically new conceptions about the nature of matter, motion, light, and magnetism and about the roles of experiment and mathematics in understanding and explaining them. Aristotle's ideas on matter and motion, both celestial and terrestrial, had, in the Middle Ages, captivated natural philosophers, Muslim, Jewish, and Christian, and were modified in various ways to develop them further and to conform with theological opinions. In the Islamic part of the world there were a number of contending ideas about the nature of matter, including versions of atomism. In the medieval Christian West, however, atomism was rejected for its association with what were perceived as some of its immoral and irreligious aspects, and Aristotelian matter-theory remained dominant.

In the development of alchemy Muslims made important contributions to the knowledge and practice of chemical composition and interactions. *Alchemy*, a word of Arabic origin, encompasses not only the nature and reactions of material substances but also theology, hidden forces, and the inner being of its practitioners. The practice of alchemy during the Scientific Revolution was a continuation of the work of medieval Arabic alchemists. The transformation of base metals into gold is the best-known goal of alchemy, but it was not accepted by all alchemists, nor was it the only aim of the art. Among the achievements of Arabic medieval alchemists were the development of new instruments, such as retorts and the still, and such techniques as the processes of distillation, calcination, and filtration. Alchemical ideas and practices were also applied in medicine.

There were efforts during the Middle Ages, both in the Islamic regions and in Western Europe, to develop and improve some of Aristotle's ideas on mechanics. With the invention of the cannon in the West, trajectories and their causes became an important subject of physical study. Muslim natural philosophers gave attention to the balance, weighing, and determination of specific weights. These achievements during the Middle Ages were the starting-points for the creation of revolutionary new principles in the physical sciences during the Scientific Revolution.

Aristotle on Matter and Motion

In Aristotle's thought, all bodies are constituted as a union of matter and form; unformed matter does not exist as an entity with distinct properties or qualities, but is only a potential substance until formed. Some Aristotelian ideas on matter and motion were questioned and slightly modified during the Middle Ages. Theories of matter were proposed that provided unformed matter with aspects of substantiality, such as having a material, corpuscular nature. Such theories were useful in attempts to explain the differences between mixtures and the creation of compounds in which original forms and qualities had been altered. To answer questions about such transformations, some posited the existence of naturally minimal particles of matter.

Matter

Most of Aristotle's fundamental principles, however, were retained. Bodies, their observed qualities and the nature and causes of their motions, were linked in a unified system, which included a distinction between terrestrial matter and the matter of the heavens. Each had unique forms of motion associated with it. Beyond the sphere of the Moon, matter was perfect, unchanging, and rotated as a series of spheres with uniform motion. From the Moon to the center of the Earth, there were four kinds of matter, containing the qualities associated with earth, water, air, and fire. Bodies on the Earth differed from one another according to the ratios of the four elements they possessed. Substances with a preponderance of earth and water tended to move naturally toward the center of the Earth; those substantially made up of air and fire tended to move away from it. Qualities such as density and dryness were associated with the earthy element, plasticity and dampness with the watery one, and so on. The universe was completely filled with matter; empty or vacuous spaces did not exist.

Motion

According to Aristotle, everything that moved was moved by something either external or internal to it. A cart would not move unless pushed or pulled; humans and animals moved as determined by a "soul," or internal principle of movement. Heavy bodies fell at speeds dependent on their weights and proportional to the resistance of the media through which they moved. In unnatural forms of motion, such as in hurled bodies or projectiles, Aristotle had proposed, moving objects continued to move before falling to Earth because as they cleaved the air before them, air rushed to fill the space behind them, thereby providing a means to continue their motion. Later followers of Aristotle explained such motions differently. They proposed that a power, called *impetus*, within a released bowstring, for example, was transmitted to an arrow, which caused it to continue its motion until, its propelling power exhausted, the arrow resumed its natural tendency to fall directly to the Earth.

Ancient and Medieval Alternatives to Aristotle

Matter

There were alternative theories of matter in the ancient world. Chief among them were those known as atomism. Before Aristotle, Democritus (c. 460–370 B.C.E.) had put forward the idea that the world is composed of an infinite number of invisible and indivisible homogeneous particles of matter. They are constantly in motion in an infinite void, and some came together to form our world as well as others. The qualities of various substances are determined by the sizes and configurations of the atoms in groups. Democritus' ideas were further de-

veloped and expounded by Epicurus (341–270 B.C.E.). The Roman poet
Lucretius (c. 95–55 B.C.E.) described the atomic theory in a poem called
On the Nature of Things. Not much attention was paid to the atomic
theory in the Middle Ages.

Another view of matter in the ancient world, developed shortly
after Aristotle, came from the Stoics. Stoicism held that the fundamental substance pervading the entire universe was *pneuma*, a mixture
of air and fire, within which all motions took place. The Stoics therefore rejected Aristotle's elements and his distinction between motions
in the heavens and on Earth. The various qualities of earthly substances
depend on the concentration of pneuma in them. The concentration of
the pneuma in the planets makes them intelligent entities and is the
source of their motion. Stoicism was clearly opposed to Aristotelian
ideas and was known to Renaissance philosophers, but the revival of
atomism limited the appeal of Stoicism.

Motion

In Aristotle's thought, motion had broad connotations and was
equivalent to various changes observed in the world around us. The
nature and causes of motion were of great interest in the universities
of the Middle Ages. Aristotle's theories on the movement of bodies from
one place to another were somewhat modified during the early Middle
Ages and in the universities of the fourteenth century, but without recourse to experimentation. The motion of projectiles, perceived as an
unnatural form of motion, was explained by the projectile's *impetus*, a
cause of its continuing motion, acquired by an arrow, for example,
when it left the bowstring. At the University of Paris different versions
of the impetus theory were applied to theological doctrines, the motions of the planets, and falling bodies. Some philosophers held that
impetus diminished in the course of motion; others, that it even increased in certain motions, such as in accelerated motion. In all instances, however, it was an internal, rather than an external, cause of
motion.

Philosophers at the University of Oxford explored certain aspects
of *kinematics*—the study of motion without attempting to determine
causes. They developed the ideas of velocity and instantaneous velocity and began to explore mathematical relationships governing accel-

erating bodies and uniformly moving ones. They concluded that a uniformly accelerating body during a given time would cover the same distance as it would if it were moving uniformly at the mean speed of the accelerating body. Geometrical representations were developed to demonstrate some of the issues involved, and from them emerged another theorem. It held that in the course of uniform acceleration, the distance covered in the second half of its duration was three times that in its first half. Galileo would later study these ideas, which were influential in the development of his own concepts in mechanics.

Concepts of Matter in the Early Modern Period

The Revival of Atomism

Some of Aristotle's ideas in several areas had begun to be questioned in the early seventeenth century, and interest in non-Aristotelian theories of matter grew as well. Chief among those theories was the idea of matter as composed of particles. Proposals were put forward about the nature of these invisible particles to account for the variety of qualities associated with different substances under diverse conditions. The particles were given characteristics, such as different shapes and sizes, to explain qualities such as specific gravity, fluidity, and temperature. Particulate theories in the seventeenth century may be generally characterized as making this distinction between primary and secondary qualities. Some held that the minute particles themselves possessed various qualities, depending on their sizes, and that they combined into aggregates with the characteristics of certain chemical compounds.

The revival of atomism was given an important impetus by the recovery of an account of Epicurean atomism and the poem of Lucretius. Pierre Gassendi (1592–1655), a French priest, wrote a number of influential works that were a Christianized version of Epicurean atomism. In his view atoms were not eternal, but were the first things created; nor was the universe infinite. Atoms move through the void in all directions, sometimes colliding with one another. They vary in shape, size, and speed, and occasionally they come together to form molecules. The molecules combine with one another to form the objects we perceive. Gassendi's conception of matter discarded Aristotelian characteristics and dispensed with mysterious and occult forces in favor of analogies with mechanical operations.

Alchemy

The practice of alchemy was vigorously pursued during the sixteenth and seventeenth centuries. A good deal had been learned through the transmission of alchemical texts from Muslim sources and translated into Latin beginning in the twelfth century. The chief source of Arabic alchemy was associated with the name, in its Latinized form, of Geber, an eighth-century Persian. An important assumption of Geberian alchemy was that every substance had both perceptible qualities and occult, or hidden, properties that were the opposite of the visible ones. By inverting the hidden qualities, substances could be transmuted into other ones. In the later Middle Ages some Aristotelian components were combined with the alchemical traditions of the Islamic world.

A shortage of gold for currency encouraged some European rulers to engage alchemists to develop alloys for use in coins of standard denominations, the depreciation of which it was hoped would be unknown to the public. Alchemists, however, were chiefly engaged in the creation of a substance variously called an "Elixir" or the "Philosopher's Stone." It had the capability of extending life, curing illnesses, purifying one's soul, and achieving a vast array of desirable ends.

The Church did not look favorably upon these goals, and a number of popes condemned the practice. That condemnation did not keep a number of religious orders from pursuing alchemical goals. In the Early Modern period the role of alchemy and the Philosopher's Stone in the promotion of spirituality became even more important. A substantial literature appeared linking alchemy to biblical passages, including the account of the Creation. Some followers of the new natural philosophy rejected alchemy and its occult forces, but a great many natural philosophers, including Robert Boyle and Isaac Newton, were avid practitioners. A variety of experimental procedures were practiced and widely known. A common belief was that with proper experiments, metals could be made to "vegetate" or grow.

Paracelsianism

Theophrastus Philippus Aureolus Bombastus von Hohenheim, who became known as Paracelsus (c. 1493–1541), was the author of an influential matter theory based on an alchemy with strong spiritual and mystical components. In his bombastic style he chastised Aristotelians and physicians; yet despite powerful attacks from his opponents, his views gained a significant number of adherents in the sixteenth and seventeenth centuries. Paracelsus held that organic phenomena were based on a chemical foundation, the essential components of which were the spirits he called Salt, Sulfur, and Mercury. These spiritual elements were linked to cosmological factors, such as those embodied in astrology. Paracelsus' principal concern was the application of alchemical principles to the cure of illnesses.

Mechanics

Sixteenth Century

An increased interest in the improvement of military technology in the sixteenth century led to some important additional modifications in Aristotelian motion theory. Niccolò Tartaglia (c. 1500–1557), a self-educated mathematician, made notable contributions to the solution of cubic equations and certain geometrical problems. He also published in Italian the first translations in a modern European language of the highly influential *Elements* of Euclid (fl. c. 295 B.C.E.) and works by Archimedes (c. 287–212 B.C.E.). He does not appear to have been familiar with medieval ideas on impetus or on acceleration and claimed that the speed of falling bodies increases as they approach their natural goal.

Tartaglia applied mathematics to the motion of projectiles and was the first to hold, contrary to the opinion of Aristotle and his medieval followers, that natural and violent motion could be mixed. He held that the trajectory of a cannonball was curved throughout its path. He further noted that the maximum range attainable by a missile of any weight, and fired with any explosive charge, occurred when a cannon was elevated 45° from the horizontal. Tartaglia pointed out that specific distances shorter than maximum ranges could be correlated with specific angles of elevation above or below 45°, and relevant tables for the use of artillerymen were created. Here is one of several instances where observation and efforts to provide mathematical solutions to techniques and practices in various crafts and technologies would lead to significant changes in several sciences.

Giovanni Battista Benedetti (1530–1590), a mathematician and successful engineer who had studied briefly with Tartaglia, was also influenced by technological practices, his own and those of others. His approach to the problem of the cause of falling bodies was based on the theory of impetus, which, he held, increased in the course of fall. Benedetti was encouraged by a friend to treat falling bodies mathematically, and he responded by utilizing ideas from the recently published works of Archimedes on specific gravities. Benedetti held, in contradiction to Aristotle, that bodies of the same substance would fall through a given medium at the same speeds, regardless of their weights. The speed of falling bodies would vary, depending on their specific gravities—the proportion of their weights to a given volume. Benedetti implied that his hypothesis would apply precisely only in a vacuum, where all resistance was absent. He also suggested that if two bodies of equal size and joined by a string would fall at a speed equal to that of a body equal in size to the joined pair, it should be clear that the larger body and one-half its size should fall at the same rate. Benedetti's theories became widely known in the latter part of the sixteenth century, and in the 1580s in the Netherlands Simon Stevin (1548–1620) dropped balls of the same size but different weights from a height and found that they fell at the same speed.

Galileo on Mechanics

Galileo was familiar with medieval ideas on motion and the concept of impetus, as well as the objections and alternatives to Aristotelianism proposed during the sixteenth century. He early noted the isochronism of the pendulum, that no matter the length of the pendulum's arc, the times taken in successive oscillations were the same. This movement was analogous to that of the tones of plucked strings, which remained the same for some moments afterward, despite the decline in the volume of sound and the width of a string's vibration. Galileo had very likely aided his father, a noted musical theoretician, in musical experiments of that sort. As a natural philosopher, Galileo was concerned with the properties of naturally oscillating systems and was aware of the growing importance of mathematically oriented craftsmanship in northern Italy.

Initially Galileo rejected the Aristotelian doctrine that bodies fall at speeds proportional to their weights, but he held that they all fall at a uniform speed. He then turned to the idea that bodies fall at speeds proportional to their specific gravities. Testing that notion experimentally by simultaneously dropping objects with greatly differing specific gravities, he found that they landed at the same time. He explained this result by a version of impetus theory in which the degree of impetus gained depended on how high an object had been raised from the surface of the Earth, its impetus draining as it fell. A number of experiments led him to conclude that bodies do not fall with uniform motion.

He then turned to the concept that a falling body accelerates, although it never exceeds a certain limit, nor could its motion ever be reduced to a rule. It was only when Galileo began to experiment with falling bodies that he was able to determine that all falling bodies accelerate uniformly. He did this by rolling balls down the polished channel of an inclined length of wood, and using a water clock, he measured the times taken to reach given distances. The times the balls were released and then ceased rolling to the given distances were determined by releasing water in an elevated container through a tube into a receptacle, then comparing the weights of the water released at different times. He thereby determined that acceleration is a function of the square of the time during which the balls were falling. Or, as he put it, the distance fallen in equal time intervals is as the odd numbers beginning with one. So in the first period of time, the ball fell a given distance; in the second, equal period of time, it fell three times the previous distance; in the third, it fell five time that in the first instance. Therefore, the total distance fallen is proportional to the square of the time during which it fell. These proportions held regardless of the weight of the falling body.

With respect to projectiles, Galileo concluded, as had Tartaglia before him, that their paths were curved, and that the curves in their trajectories while rising were identical to the curves during their fall back to Earth. He also experimented with inclined planes, giving balls a tangential impulse as they rolled downward, and noted that they followed parabolic paths. With respect to bodies dropped from horizontally moving objects, Galileo found that in falling to Earth, they moved in arcs whose shapes depended on their initial velocities. Galileo's concept of compound motion challenged the Aristotelian distinction between natural and forced motions, as did Galileo's thinking on the nature of uniform motions.

When he began his experiments with inclined planes, Galileo believed that it was its impetus that caused a ball to roll downward, and to roll up the plane when given an upward impulse. He reasoned, however, that if after rolling downward to the bottom of the plane it would no longer have impetus, and if there were no impediments or friction impeding its motion, it should continue rolling uniformly about the surface of the Earth. Galileo thereupon abandoned the notion of impetus and also the Aristotelian conception that everything that moves must have a mover.

Cartesian Matter and Motion

The Cartesian Universe

In the middle years of the seventeenth century, René Descartes' ideas were most influential in the promotion of the mechanical philosophy. He attempted to explain all phenomena in mechanical terms, except for the immortal and immaterial nature of the human soul. As with Aristotle, Descartes' concepts of matter and motion were closely linked. Descartes shared some ideas with other natural philosophers on the nature of matter, but differed decisively with atomists on several issues. He thought the extent of the universe was indefinite, and that it was completely filled with matter that was always in motion, as it had been since the Creation. When motion was imparted to the universe, its matter broke up into tiny swirling particles that eventually coalesced into a series of vortices, or whirlpools, one of which is our solar system, carrying planets about their suns.

There are three kinds of matter, according to Descartes, and in the absence of void spaces, the motion of any particle results in the immediate movement of other particles into the space that had been vacated. All the solid and liquid bodies of the planets, and most of the air, are constituted of one type of matter, or element. Another, spherical in form, is interspersed between the particles of the solids, liquids, and air and fills the space between suns and their planets. The third element, which Descartes called the first element, fills the spaces between the microspheres of the second element and constitutes the matter of the stars, including our Sun.

Motion

Descartes believed that God had created laws governing various types of motion, and that it was a function of natural philosophy to discover them. Unlike Galileo, Descartes thought that the search for the causes of motion was important. All moving bodies, he held, had a quantity of "force of motion" and a direction of that force. In collisions between particles, those two factors are altered in conformity with the laws of collision. According to Descartes, a body is moved either when moved by another or, if in motion, continues to move uniformly in a straight line unless encountering something that makes it change its path or speed. He thought of falling bodies as resulting from a force pushing them downward. The concept of attraction and of forces acting over a distance were completely rejected.

Optics

Kepler on Optics

Johannes Kepler's work on optics was undertaken because he saw it, along with mathematics, as an essential component of the practice of astronomy. He wrote extensively on optics and was familiar with the optical ideas of medieval natural philosophers in Islam and the West, among them Witelo, a thirteenth-century scholar. Kepler's first book on optics was published in 1604 and entitled *Ad Vitellionem paralipomena, quibus astronomiae pars optica traditur* (Supplements to Witelo, in Which the Optical Part of Astronomy Is Treated). One of the subjects Kepler dealt with had been a puzzle for his predecessors. Why did sunlight passing through pinholes of any shape—triangles, for example—nevertheless cast circular images? Kepler's answer was that a multiplicity of triangular images passed from the pinhole and were superimposed on the surface receiving the light, resulting in a circular image with a blurred, slightly shadowed circumference. This theory explained why observations of the Moon's diameter during solar eclipses differed from those taken just before or after an eclipse.

Kepler's explanation was quickly accepted, as was his description of the formation of images in the eye. He held that light was refracted through the lens of the eye, and passed, inverted, to the retina, from which it was perceived reinverted. With respect to the nature and transmission of light, Kepler held that it was incorporeal and transmitted rectilinearly in all directions like the surface of a sphere. Light intensity, therefore, diminishes according to the inverse-square of the distance from the light source, a concept derived from a medieval Arabic source.

The Telescope

After Galileo heard of the invention of a telescope, he immediately created his own in 1609. It was very influential not only for astronomy, but also for optics and the craft of lens-grinding. After several improvements, Galileo's telescopes were capable of magnifications of 15–20 diameters. They had concave eyepieces and convex objectives, and they provided a narrow field of view of about one-quarter of a degree of arc. Kepler, from his work on optics, realized that Galileo's telescope could be improved for astronomical purposes. In 1611 he published *Dioptrice*, a term coined by Kepler for investigations of light refracted through lenses. Kepler proposed convex lenses for both eyepiece and objective of a telescope, which yielded an inverted image, but one that was brighter and provided a larger field of view than was seen with a Galilean telescope. Further, it allowed the insertion in the tube of a micrometer, which could precisely determine much smaller celestial angles than could be estimated using a Galilean telescope.

Attempts to create telescopes with successively greater magnifying power ran into problems of image distortion from chromatic and spherical aberrations. Solutions that were tried included the use of lenses with longer focal lengths, leading to the construction of telescopes of successively greater lengths, mounted without the use of tubes. Improvements using this method were minimal. Some small improvements were provided by more effective techniques for lens-grinding and mathematical determinations of the best curves for lenses. Isaac Newton proposed in the 1670s the use of parabolic reflectors as objectives for telescopes to minimize the effects of aberration, and he was the first to construct one, but reflecting telescopes were not to attain effective usefulness for half a century.

The Transmission of Light

A mathematical law governing refraction had been sought for some time, and estimates had long been made of the alteration in the angles of a refracted ray of light. Such a law was independently discovered by several natural philosophers, including Descartes, early in the seventeenth century, but it was only published by him in 1637. From careful measurements of the initial and refracted angles of a light ray passing from one transparent medium through another, it was determined that

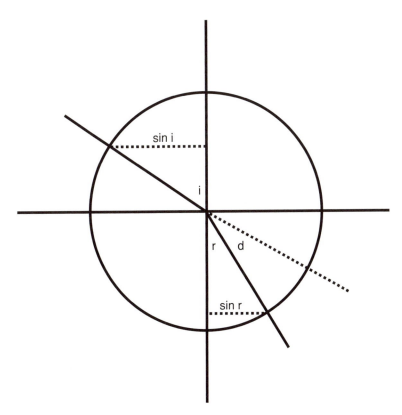

3.1 The sines of the angle of incidence, *i*, is proportional to the sine of the angle of refraction, *r*.

the sine of the angle of incidence divided by the sine of the angle of refraction is equal to a constant unique for the particular media.

Opinions on the nature of light and the means of its transmission
differed. Descartes advanced a mechanistic theory that had some aspects expressed in one work contradicted by those in another. He held
that light is a tendency toward instantaneous motion, transmitted by
the particles of the matter it passed through. Yet in the examples he
cited, the velocity of light depended on the medium through which it
traveled—more rapidly through a denser medium than a rarified one.
The observations of Ole Römer (1644–1701) in 1676 of the eclipse by
Jupiter of one of its moons showed that it was observed some minutes
after it should have been, confirming that the speed of light was finite.

A new aspect of the nature of light was discovered—its *diffraction*,
a term coined by Francesco Maria Grimaldi (1618–1663), after he noticed that light moving past the edges of opaque bodies seemed to split
into bands of light and color on both sides of the edges, leaving a
slightly wider shadow than demanded by a strict linearity. His descriptions were published two years after his death, and in the second
half of the century a significant amount of attention was paid to diffraction and the creation of colors by refraction through prisms and in
thin films of certain liquids. Descartes had advanced the mechanistic
theory that light, when refracted, causes the particles transmitting it to
rotate, resulting in the perception of color. This theory was unsatisfac-
tory for Robert Hooke (1635–1703), since the drops of water in a rain-
bow produce colors although the light passing through them is
rerefracted to its original direction. Hooke produced instead a theory
of colors based on the idea that red and blue are primary colors, and
that white light changes into colored ones as it interacts with pulses
generated in the refracting medium when passing through it.

These ideas were powerfully challenged by the brilliant experiments of Isaac Newton, first published in 1672. In passing a ray of sunlight from a small round aperture into a darkened room through a
prism positioned to maximize refraction, Newton noted that when projected onto a white screen, the light ray formed an elongated spectrum
of colors, instead of a circular one. He designated their sequence as red,
orange, yellow, green, blue, indigo, violet, pointing out that each was
refracted at an angle unique to it. His conclusion was that white light,
rather than being transformed into colored light, is composed of light

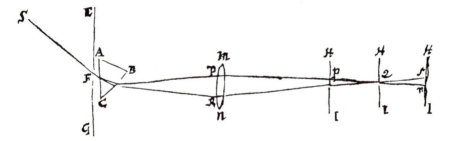

3.2 Newton's experiment on refraction of white sunlight through a prism. From its publication in 1672 in the *Philosophical Transactions of the Royal Society.*

of various colors. It was confirmed by passing the rays of the spectrum through a convex lens, through which they were brought to a focus, resulting in a white ray once again. His conclusion was further supported by his passing individual colored rays through a prism, noting that their colors remained after refraction.

In the 1670s Christiaan Huygens proposed a theory of light in which the particles from a light source, moving through a medium composed of imperceptible particles, produce a series of waves upon impact. Each collision thereupon produces a new wave with a spherical pulse. Huygens called the collective pulses the "principal wave," which we now call a "wave front," thereby producing visible light. The wave theory was not readily accepted; the rectilinearity of light rays in a wave theory would not be satisfactorily explained until a much later date, when it would be shown to be very useful in explaining a variety of physical phenomena.

Magnetism and Electricity

The work of William Gilbert (1544–1603) on magnetism was based on the observations of the compass in voyages during the latter part of the sixteenth century. Gilbert made a series of laboratory experiments with iron magnets, lodestones, and compass needles. His experiments and conclusions were described in *De magnete, magneticisque corporibus, et de magno magnete tellure* (On the Magnet, and Magnetic Bodies, and the Great Magnet the Earth), published in 1600 and accepted by his contemporaries as having established a new science. Gilbert's experiments with spherical lodestones, which he called *terrellae* (little earths), led him to conclude that the Earth was a magnet, and magnetism was an animate, immaterial force responsible for the rotation of the Earth and the cause of the tides. The variation of compass needles from true north and the changes in the inclination of vertically mounted needles in different parts of the world, he explained, were caused by local departures from true sphericity. The association of Gilbert's idea of magnetic terrestrial rotation with Copernicanism made it attractive to Kepler as a cause of planetary motion, but it was erroneous in the eyes of the Catholic Church.

Gilbert used the term *electricitas* to describe the long-known attractive power of amber. He recognized that other substances exhibited similar attractions when rubbed. Unlike magnetic bodies, electrical ones did not have polarity and could not be made to exhibit repulsive effects. For Gilbert, electrical attraction was a local and material phenomenon rather than a cosmic and immaterial one. It was caused by the emission of a certain imperceptible electrical vapor.

Descartes rejected Gilbert's notion of magnetism as an immaterial force. Magnetic effects were explained mechanically by the existence of minuscule channels of two types in magnetic bodies, one with right-handed threads, the other with left-handed ones. Particles were emitted from opposite ends of a magnet, creating vortices around it, and returned to the opposite poles. When they encountered an iron body, they twisted screwlike into its channels, pulling it toward the magnet. For Descartes and other mechanical philosophers magnetism required explanation by material means.

Experiments with the Vacuum

The "Torricelli tube"

Miners had long been familiar with the inability of water to be pumped more than about thirty-two feet high. Galileo, approached about this problem and familiar with the Peripatetic notion that nature abhors a vacuum, but ignoring it, replied that the weight of the water in a tube of such a height was a measure of nature's resistance to the creation of a vacuum. The problem took on a new form with the experiments of Michelangelo Ricci (1619–1682) in the 1640s. He noted that water completely filling a building's downspout that was sealed at the top and bottom, its bottom immersed in a barrel of water, fell to about thirty-two feet when its bottom was opened. Evangelista Torricelli (1608–1647) surmised that the atmosphere has weight, and its weight, pressing on the water on the surface of the barrel, was equal to the weight of the water in the tube. He suggested that mercury, which weighs sixteen times more than water for a given volume, be used in a glass tube sealed at the top with a valve at the bottom, placed in a dish of mercury, would behave in a similar manner. It did, falling to a height of approximately twenty-four inches.

This phenomenon led to a sustained debate over what was in the space between the surface of the mercury and the top of the tube. Aristotelians held that it was filled with matter, Cartesians that it was filled with a "subtle matter," and atomists that it was a vacuum. Blaise Pascal (1623–1662) showed that the level of mercury in the tube remained at the same height under the same circumstances regardless of the shape or height of the tube. He also had the device inserted inside the space above the mercury in a larger tube and noted that lowering the level of mercury in the outer tube lowered it in the inserted one as well. Pascal also had such a mercury-filled tube carried up a mountain, with the height of the mercury measured at different elevations. This appeared to show that the weight of the air, presumably less at higher elevations, did correspond to the weight of the mercury. The tube and its later mechanical versions subsequently became an important instrument in meteorology, the barometer.

Air-pumps were invented in the mid-seventeenth century to evacuate air from sealed vessels, and a number of experiments were performed that demonstrated that air has pressure as well as weight. Otto von Guericke (1602–1686) created the first air pump. In experiments conducted in 1657 and 1663, he demonstrated that two metal hemispheres, evacuated of air and with their circumferences resting against each other, could not be pulled apart by two teams of horses straining to do so in opposite directions.

Air pumps became tools for scientific investigation. Robert Hooke built one for Robert Boyle with a glass chamber to observe experiments conducted in it during and after the evacuation of air. The inverse ratio of volume to pressure at a given temperature was independently dis-

3.3 Otto von Guericke's air pump. From his *Experimenta nova (ut vocantur) Magdeburgica de vacuo spatio* (1672).

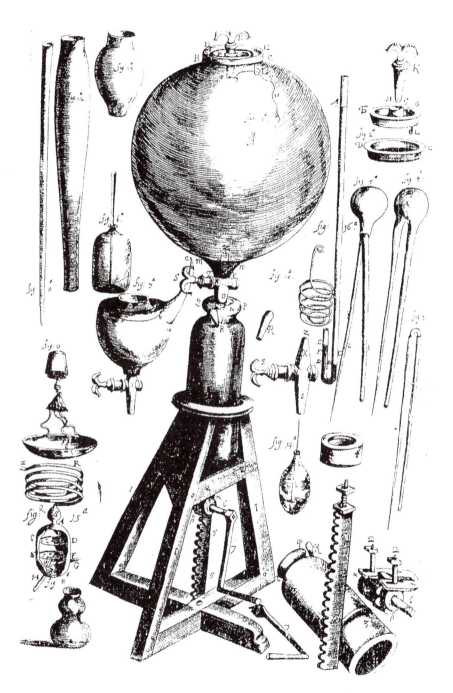

3.4 Robert Boyle's air pump. From his *New Experiments Physico-Mechanical*, 2nd ed. (1662).

covered by Edmé Mariotte (c. 1620–1684) in France and Richard Towneley (1629–1707) in England, but it became known as Boyle's Law. Belief in the existence of vacuums was becoming more acceptable.

Mathematics

By the mid-sixteenth century Western scholars had absorbed the mathematical achievements of the Greeks and Muslims, and Latin translations of their most important works had been published. A process of unification of what had been separate branches of mathematics combined with mechanics continued throughout the Scientific Revolution. Algebra and geometry were reconstituted on new foundations. Problems connected with navigation and insurance stimulated developments in spherical trigonometry and probability. The motions of bodies with varying velocities, moving in straight lines or curvilinearly, led to the creation of the calculus.

Algebra

Algebra is a term of Arabic origin that reflects the development and substantial progress of this branch of mathematics. Our modern symbols for numerals were introduced to the West from the Arabic world, displacing the letters used as numbers by the Greeks and Romans. Equations at first were written with words, not symbols, for their unknown quantities and their powers and were sometimes solved by geometrical means. The use of symbols and numerical solutions for algebraic problems were introduced in the sixteenth century, most effectively by François Viète (1549–1603). The transposition of the terms of quadratic equations so as to equal zero, as well as clarifying the nature of the roots of polynomials, was advanced in the early seventeenth century by Thomas Harriot (c. 1560–1621). The binomial theory was developed independently by both Nicholas Mercator (c. 1619–1687) and Isaac Newton.

Analytic Geometry

René Descartes and Pierre de Fermat (1601–1665) took important steps in the creation of analytic geometry. Fermat saw that plane curves could be correlated with equations with two unknowns. Descartes promoted the use of geometric coordinate systems to solve problems on the relationships within complex curves, notably conic sections. Solutions to algebraic problems by the use of coordinate systems were actively developed in the middle years of the seventeenth century.

Calculus

Problems associated with tangents to curves and finding areas within curved boundaries and volumes within curved spaces were actively studied during the same period. Bonaventura Cavalieri (1598–1657) suggested that lines, areas, and volumes could be thought of as composed of an infinite number of indivisible geometrical components. While condemned by some, the idea was taken up and developed by others. Isaac Newton, in dealing with problems in mechanics, thought that the relation of changing rates of time to distance in motions more complex than in falling bodies could be solved by the use of indivisible time intervals. At about the same time Gottfried Wilhelm Leibniz took a different approach, utilizing sums and differences of geometric infinitesimals. The independent achievements of Newton and Leibniz on problems in the instantaneous rates of change in variables, involving integration and differentiation, gave birth to a new branch of mathematics.

Isaac Newton on Mechanics and Matter

Initial Work on Mechanics

Newton's early work on the motion of bodies under different circumstances resulted in important conclusions. Some became part of his later work; others were modified or radically altered. He began as a Cartesian, but he departed substantially from Descartes in the creation of his own mature system of mechanics. In the 1660s Newton addressed the problem of colliding bodies and concluded that their common center of mass remains at rest, or moves in a straight line with uniform motion. He also studied circular motion and noted the relationship between what he then thought of as centrifugal force and the velocity of the revolving body. Applying that discovery to the motion of the Moon and using Kepler's Third Law, relating the proportion between the times for completion of a planetary orbit to its distance from the Sun, Newton concluded that the Sun's gravitational attraction was nearly equivalent to the inverse-square of its distance from another body.

Newton's Developing Celestial Dynamics

Newton paid little further attention to mechanics until 1679, when, in response to a question from Robert Hooke, he turned his attention again to circular motion and what he now began to think of, as he termed it, centripetal force, a force toward the center of the motion. He now proved mathematically to himself that the tendency of a planet toward the focus of an elliptical orbit exactly varies inversely as the square of the distance between them. Five years later, in response to a reconsideration of the problem urged on him by Edmond Halley (c. 1656–1743), Newton, in two and a half years of intensive work, undertook a reformulation of celestial dynamics. The result was the creation of his laws of motion and gravitation, demonstrated in one of the most influential work ever published in the history of science.

The *Principia*

Newton's *Philosophiae naturalis principia mathematica* (Mathematical Principles of Natural Philosophy) was published in 1687. It immediately resulted in the recognition of Newton as the leading scientist of his age. Although the principle of universal gravitation was rejected by strict proponents of the mechanical philososphy of Descartes, its power to solve various problems in celestial and terrestrial mechanics was rapidly seen. The achievements of Kepler and Galileo were able to be derived from Newton's three laws of motion and universal gravitation. The *Principia*, slightly revised, was republished twice in Newton's lifetime.

Newton subdivided his work into three Books. Book I dealt with the motions of bodies, principally in the heavens, on the assumption of an absence of resistance. Since all bodies attract all others, Newton dealt with the complexities involved in the mutual attractions of two and three bodies, such as those affecting the motion of the Moon and the tides. Book II applied mechanical principles for the first time to the solution of problems of motion in resisting media and definitively demonstrated that the Cartesian vortices assumed to be moving the planets could not account for Kepler's laws. Book III addressed detailed problems in the motions of celestial bodies. It proved that those motions result from a tendency for them to fly off from each point of their orbital paths with an inertial motion, counteracted by an inverse-square attraction proportional to the distance from the central body, resulting in closed orbits. Book III also provided mathematical demonstrations of the nature of the tides, comets, and other phenomena observed in the heavens.

Hypotheses on Matter

Newton hypothesized in one work that all bodies are pervaded by a medium more subtle than air, composed of particles with a tendency to expand. They fill the the universe, are mutually repulsive, and are the medium, an "aether," through which light and heat are transmitted. He also suggested that this medium is less dense in heavenly bodies, and that pressure from the space around those bodies may be the cause of gravitation. Magnetic and electric phenomena might occur through the emission of subtle effluvia composed of particles. Newton admitted that he did not know much about these hypothetical particles. In a revision of the work in which these hypotheses had been expressed, he voiced his favorable opinion on atoms and vacuums, rather than in the existence of fluid media.

Newton spent more time on alchemy than on mechanics, read very widely on the subject, and conducted a great many experiments in his own laboratory. He does not seem to have been interested in the transformation of other substances into gold, and it is not clear what he sought in his pursuit of alchemy. He was in the company of many natural philosophers in seeking to learn how various substances can be converted into other ones. Above all, they sought the existence of the Philosopher's Stone and its role in their spiritual purification and that of the world. Newton seemed to be seeking a component of his universe not found in a strictly mechanical concept of nature.

Summary

Aristotelian concepts of matter and explanations of physical phenomena in the mathematical sciences, such as mechanics and optics, were decisively transformed during the Scientific Revolution. Matter was assigned properties distinct from those exhibited in its various forms. There was sound experimental evidence for the existence of vacuums. New aspects of the behavior of light were discovered, as well as formerly unknown mathematical relationships in the science of optics. The distinction between natural and unnatural motion was no longer relevant, nor was the presence of a mover necessary for motion with the development of the concept of inertia. Bodies were shown to fall with uniform acceleration according to a mathematical law. Newton's laws of motion and universal gravitation were the culmination of the continuing and growing efforts to learn about physical phenomena through the use of mathematics and experimentation.

CHAPTER 4

THE NATURE OF LIVING THINGS

The study of the various life forms and the processes taking place within them had been part of natural philosophy in Antiquity. As with other aspects in the study of the natural world, Aristotelian concepts and approaches were dominant. New components, however, were added from things learned in the practice of medicine in the ancient world and in the Early Modern period, from the discovery of new plants and animals in the sixteenth and seventeenth centuries and, above all, by the application of detailed observation and experimentation characteristic of the new approaches to the study of nature during the Scientific Revolution.

Traditional Concepts

Forms of Life and Their Modes of Operation

The division of living things into three kingdoms—vegetable, animal, and human—began in the ancient world. Each was governed by a "soul" unique to its type. Plant forms had what Aristotle had called a vegetative soul, a source of a plant's ability to absorb nourishment, to grow and to reproduce itself. Animal souls had vegetative functions, but had in addition functions associated with mobility. Humans had both vegetative and mobility functions, but they also possessed the ability to think.

The taxonomy, or classification, of plants and animals had a hierarchical form. In descending order, botanical species began with distinctions between trees, shrubs, and grasses. Animal species were divided into two large categories, those with blood and the bloodless. Each was further subdivided. The blooded group included quadrupeds that gave birth to live offspring, egg-laying quadrupeds, birds, and fish. These also were subdivided according to skeletal structure or other distinguishing features or characteristics of behavior.

There were variations of this system in the medieval West, but the hierarchical character of taxonomy persisted, associated with increased perfection and moral value as one moved up the scale. In the medieval Christian world there was a conception that all living entities, and spiritual ones as well, such as angels and archangels, were part of a *scala naturae*, or ladder of nature, ascending from the lowest worms up to the right hand of God.

Human Organs and Their Functions

Greek and Roman Antiquity saw a considerable growth of knowledge about human anatomy and physiology. The leading authority in the ancient world on these subjects was Galen. He published voluminously, and his descriptions of the human organs and their functions were adopted in medieval Islam with slight modifications, then transmitted to Western Europe. Galen's works, along with Arabic commentaries on them, were translated into Latin, and their ideas became part of the curriculum in the medical schools of European universities.

The dissection of human cadavers for the study of anatomy had been practiced several centuries before Galen. Dissection may have been frowned upon in Galen's time, for it appears he never dissected a human corpse. He did, however, dissect animals and even experimented on living ones. Human dissection was subsequently forbidden by the monotheistic religions. In Western Europe in the later Middle Ages, however, dissection began to be carried out in the case of homicides where the cause of death was not apparent. By the fourteenth century, dissection had become a standard part of medical education as a means of demonstrating features of Galenic anatomy.

The Galenic system emphasized three significant organ systems associated with the heart, liver, and brain. Each functioned in a particular way to help carry out the vegetative, mobile, and reasoning operations of the body. Among the bodily functions performed by these organs and others were the maintenance of bodily heat, movement, gestation, development and growth, sensation, and volition. The heart is the source of innate heat, which it distributes together with "vital spirits" to all parts of the body. The movement of the blood in the heart, veins, and arteries is as follows: the contraction of the heart—systole— carries blood to the lungs, where the blood is cooled for the proper maintenance of the body's heat. The blood flows and ebbs in the arteries and veins, each of which have different functions. The *chyle*, the nutritive material in what has been eaten or imbibed, is brought from the stomach and intestines by the veins to the liver, where it is transformed into blood. The brain converts the "vital spirits" brought to it by the blood into a means for carrying out mental faculties, sensation, and movement through the nerves.

Medicine during the Renaissance

Medical Education

From Antiquity until modern times in Western Europe most illnesses and medical problems were treated, not by doctors, but by family members, friends, neighbors, or local healers familiar with traditional treatments that had been passed from generation to generation. Physicians had been trained in schools in the ancient world and in medieval Islam, but not in the West until the establishment of universities in the twelfth and thirteenth centuries. By the thirteenth century medicine had become a distinct profession, with regulations governing the qualifications of its members and admission to it. In medical schools in the universities of Western Europe, ancient traditional and modified Islamic practices were the dominant forms of instruction. By the fifteenth century the attainment of a Bachelor of Arts degree was required for admission to medical school. Three or four years studying medicine awarded a student a Bachelor of Medicine degree and enabled him to become a practicing physician. The degree Doctor of Medicine required additional work at a medical school.

The teaching of anatomy was done by the professor, seated high above a cadaver, reading from Galen or another authority while the dissection was carried out, usually by a barber, to illustrate the Galenic descriptions. Those performing the dissections were usually trained by having been apprenticed to one experienced in dissection. An assistant

4.1 Medical students observing a professor carrying out a dissection. From
Barthélemy Cabrol, *Ontleeding des menscelycken lichaems* (1663).

to the professor pointed to the parts of the body being described. A student was fortunate to have seen one such demonstration in the course of his stay in medical school. This would change with the appointment of Andreas Vesalius (1514–1564) as a professor of surgery at the University of Padua in 1537. He came down from the professorial chair to perform his own dissections and showed the parts of the cadaver to the students. Vesalius' practice was then followed in other medical schools.

Another important innovation in medical teaching took place in the sixteenth century. Upon attaining a medical degree, the former student was required to go through a period of clinical training at a hospital or to serve as an assistant to a physician. An important advance in this practice took place with the adoption of clinical teaching at a patient's bedside, where a case history was taken by a student, symptoms noted, and notes provided to the professor, who then commented on the case.

The appropriate use of medicines also became part of the medical curriculum during the Renaissance. Padua also led in the establishment of courses in what was called *materia medica*, drugs to be used for the cure of illnesses or amelioration of their symptoms. Most such medications were of plant origin, with a few derived from animals and minerals. Some had been passed down from ancient times; others began to be used during the Middle Ages. Students gathered their own specimens from areas near their university. Beginning in the 1540s, universities created their own gardens for growing medicinal plants and the instruction of students in recognizing them and learning their uses.

The Reform of Anatomy and Its Practice

About the beginning of the sixteenth century a few medical professors began to do their own dissections and, although followers of Galen, trusted their own findings when they differed from Galen. They also saw their work as necessary for the promotion of surgery, long neglected by physicians, as a part of medical practice. The most notable achievement in these efforts was made by Vesalius with the publication in 1543 of his *De humani corporis fabrica* (On the Structure of the Human Body).

Vesalius had dissected many cadavers and noted a considerable number of errors in Galen's anatomical work. Among them was Galen's description of the human jawbone as consisting of two parts; Vesalius had always found the jawbone to be a single bone. He also questioned Galen's account of the septum, separating the right and left parts of the heart, as having invisible pores through which blood passed from the right ventricle to the left. Vesalius said that he had found no such pores. He also found no evidence of the existence of a "miraculous network" that Galen held to be below the brain. These and other discoveries called into question some of Galen's physiological explanations, but it would be some time before Galenic physiology was effectively challenged.

Vesalius' findings were incorporated in his *de fabrica*, a 650-page work, which was beautifully illustrated and superbly detailed to a degree never before attained by any other anatomical work. The illustrations, closely supervised by Vesalius, were made by artists from the studio of the noted artist Titian. Each illustration was accompanied by detailed anatomical accounts. *De fabrica* was enormously popular from the time of its publication, but its expense encouraged Vesalius immediately to prepare a shortened version, an *Epitome* of his *de fabrica* for the use of medical students and novices.

Vesalius' *de fabrica* resulted not only in the revision of anatomical textbooks, but in changes in the practice of dissection as well. Dissections for the instruction of medical students had been performed for two centuries by beginning with the inside and proceeding outward. First, the abdominal and thoracic cavities were opened and their organs displayed. The dissection then proceeded to the head and limbs. Vesalius' approach began with the structure of the body, its skeleton, and then moved on to the muscles. Successive plates showed the outer muscles peeled back to reveal the muscles beneath them. Next came depictions of the blood vessels, and after them, the details of the various internal organs. Vesalius emphasized that the progress of anatomy depended on further and continuing research that might even contradict his own findings, as proved to be the case. A second edition of Vesalius' *de fabrica*, in 1555, contained many corrections and revisions of the first edition. Because individuals differed with respect to the size, shape, and to some degree in the positioning of their anatomical parts, Vesalius cautioned that many bodies must be examined before anatomists could generalize about human structures.

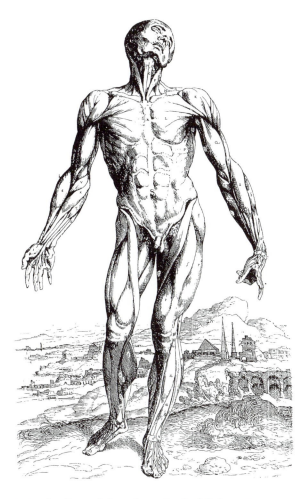

4.2 The first of the plates in *de fabrica* on human muscles.

Further Anatomical Discoveries

The new attitude in anatomy about seeing for oneself led to additional discoveries by Vesalius' successors at the University of Padua. The fallopian tubes, through which ova pass from the ovaries to the uterus in the female reproductive system, were discovered by Gabriele Falloppio (1523–1562). Bartolomeo Eustachio (c. 1510–1574) improved Vesalian anatomy and discovered the pasage from ear to throat that bears his name. Girolamo Fabrici (c. 1533–1619) discovered that the veins have valves. During the sixteenth century detailed investigations in comparative anatomy were undertaken, and much was learned about similarities and differences in the anatomical structures of humans and a variety of animals. Studies of human and animal embryos and the stages of their development were also pursued.

The Nature of Medical Practice

The principal theory of the nature and causes of diseases was based on the humoral theory. It arose about 400 B.C.E. in ancient Greece and was derived from the notion that everything on the Earth is composed of four elements, earth, water, fire, and air. Each has particular qualities associated with it: earth, cold; water, moisture; air, dryness; and fire, heat. The balance among the four humors—blood, yellow bile, black bile, and phlegm—in our bodies determined the status of our health; an imbalance was the cause of illness.

This long-held concept was incorporated by Galen, in the second century, into a comprehensive medical theory. He held that food and drink are converted in the body into the humors. Each humor is associated with two qualities: blood is hot and wet, yellow bile hot and dry, black bile cold and dry, and phlegm cold and wet. Their proportions in the body are determined by a number of things, including one's occupation, the astrological sign of one's birth, the season of the year, among other factors. An individual's personality was also associated with the dominance of a certain humor: blood was dominant in confident people, black bile in melancholy ones. Diagnosis yielded the necessary remedies, which might include a better diet, blood-letting using leeches, and drugs of various sorts, including one to cause vomiting.

These remedies were of little help in combating new diseases that appeared during the Renaissance. The contact of Europeans with the New World brought new venereal diseases and fatal epidemics to Europe. Sexually transmitted life-threatening diseases had been unknown in Europe before this. Infection, contagion, and epidemics were thought to be caused by "corruption" of the air, resulting in a corruption of the body. A theory of how diseases were spread was put forward in 1546 by Girolamo Fracastoro (c. 1478–1553), which held that diseased persons emitted invisible particles that then passed to others or to their clothing or utensils. The rise of particulate matter theories in the seventeenth century lent support to this view, and observations with the microscope brought forward the notion that invisible insects might also be a cause of contagion.

Pharmacology

Medical practice was also changed by a new theory of disease and the use of new medications. Paracelsus and his followers were instrumental in challenging, and eventually overthrowing, the humoral theory. Paracelsus completely denied the existence of the humors and that there were four elements, insisting that there were three: *salt, sulphur,* and *mercury.* Illness was caused by chemical imbalances and could be treated and cured by drugs, including some composed with heavy doses of minerals. The association of chemistry with medicine was reflected in the introduction of courses in chemistry in medical schools and the growing recognition of the importance of experimentation in the creation of new medications.

Professional pharmacists first began to dispense drugs in the thirteenth century. By the sixteenth century they were licensed by many municipalities, and pharmacy underwent some important changes. New medications, including those proposed by Paracelsians, came into use. Plants discovered in the New World and in Asia began to be used for new medications. Pharmacopoeias, books listing standard pharmaceutical recipes and the ways to make them, began to be published.

Surgery

Surgery was another medical practice that changed during the Early Modern period. It had been carried on in most of Europe during the Middle Ages and the Renaissance by craftspeople, most of whom were illiterate. In some parts of Europe, notably Italy, some physicians also practiced surgery, and medical schools offered courses in it. The best anatomists of the sixteenth century, from Vesalius onward, all practiced surgery. Some of them wrote manuals on the subject, incorporating their own discoveries and improvements. Surgeons dealt with the body's surface, setting fractures; treating burns, diseases of the skin, and gunshot wounds; and performing amputations. One of the most skillful and important surgeons of the sixteenth century was Ambroise

Paré (c. 1510–1590). He had not gone to medical school, but had learned the craft through his apprenticeship to a barber-surgeon and spent most of his career as a military surgeon. He replaced certain traditional methods, challenging some practices taught in medical schools for the treatment of wounds. His new methods tended to improve the chances of recovery. He also improved the design of surgical instruments. Paré, who wrote treatises describing his surgical procedures, had considerable influence in both the sixteenth and seventeenth centuries.

Botany and Zoology

The term *botany* was created during the Scientific Revolution to encompass the study of all aspects of the nature and lives of plants, rather than to deal with them primarily for their use in medicine. Several events triggered these new interests. The reprinting and translations of classical Greek botanical texts provided a preliminary stimulus. The discovery of many plants unknown to ancient authorities in the course of European expansion around the world led to a rethinking about the nature and classification of plants and to investigations into the ways in which they functioned. The same was true of animals. The invention of the microscope in the seventeenth century brought knowledge of entirely new organisms and details in the structure and function of all living things.

New Flora and Fauna

Books describing and illustrating plants, known as herbals, were common in the Middle Ages. They were far from accurate, however, and the plants described were linked to legends and what were thought of as their religious, magical, and medical properties. This was also true of traditional bestiaries, books describing animals, living as well as imagined. The discoveries of new species, however, coupled with a growing emphasis in art on the depiction of reality, led to the creation of new herbals and bestiaries depicting and describing them with much greater accuracy. The multivolumed *Portraits of Living Plants* by Otto Brunfels (c. 1489–1534), published 1530–1536, was the first step in this development. It was quickly followed in 1542 by the publication

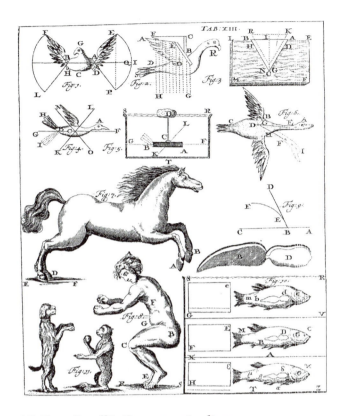

4.3 From Borelli's *De motu animalium.*

of *Notable Commentaries on the History of Plants* by Leonhart Fuchs (1501–1566).

The role of patronage in the depiction of portraits of the patrons of artists stimulated a more realistic depiction of plants and animals. Patrons were also important in the development of zoos, botanical gardens and museums originating from their private collections and cabinets of curiosities. Municipalities became active in the sixteenth century in establishing public gardens, and were eager to include varieties from other parts of the world. Europe had begun to import maize, potatoes, tomatoes, tea, and coffee from other parts of the world, but plants with exotic flowers were also eagerly sought. In the latter part of the seventeenth century, plants were being depicted in their entirety, including their roots, and in the stages of their growth.

Similar changes were taking place with respect to animals. The leading figure in the unusual studies being made about the animal world was Conrad Gessner (1516–1565). Naturalists sent him descriptions of physical appearances, behaviors, and specimens from all parts of the world. Gessner wrote and edited dozens of works, and his *Historiae animalium* (Histories of Animals) was published from 1551 to 1587. Detailed anatomical studies were undertaken by others, as were studies in animal embryology. The influence of the mechanical philosophy on the study of animal physiology may be seen in Giovanni Alfonso Borelli's (1608–1679) posthumous *De motu animalium* (On the Motion of Animals), 1680–1681. Borelli relied on mechanical explanations to account for movements such as walking, flying, and swimming, as well as the functioning of muscles and internal organs. He also used physical concepts such as centers of gravity and the lever, and in his explanations he referred to chemical processes.

New Taxonomies

Several new taxonomies were created in the sixteenth and seventeenth centuries. Most were based on Aristotle's system, but they were modified to account for European species unknown to Aristotle and for those from other parts of the world. Ulisse Aldrovandi (1522–1605) wrote many treatises on animal taxonomy, most of which were published well after his death. His system, and those of others, made alterations in the Aristotelian schema, employing certain anatomical and behavioral criteria. New plant taxonomies employed leaf shapes, flower or seed characteristics, or habitat as a basis for classification.

The New Physiology

Modifications of Galenic Physiology

Differences with the nature of physiological functions in Aristotelian and Galenic interpretations also arose in the sixteenth century. They chiefly concerned the absence of spiritual factors involved in those functions. Paracelsus, however, insisted on the existence of an *archaeus*, an internal alchemist, producing chemical changes through spiritual means and thereby governing physiological processes. The discovery that the blood circulates, rather than, as Galen had it, ebbs and flows in various ways in the arteries and veins, had the most important consequences for the development of physiology. A preliminary step in that development was Vesalius' discovery, contrary to Galen's description, that blood does not pass directly from the right to the left side of the heart through the septum, the thick wall separating both sides of the heart.

Shortly afterward, Michael Servetus (1511–1553) published in 1553 a description of the movement of the blood from the right side of the heart to the lungs and back to the heart's left side. Servetus, a physician, was considered heretical by both the Catholic Church and Protestants because he questioned the existence of the Trinity. In a work on theology, in which Servetus held that the divine spirit is in the blood, he described in a few pages the pulmonary circulation, unaware, as were all anatomists in Europe, that it had been discovered in the thirteenth century by an Egyptian physician. Servetus, from anatomical observation, saw that blood passed from the right side of the heart to the left, after passing through the lungs, where it was mixed with air. His discovery never reached the medical world because, fleeing the Inquisition, he went to Geneva, where he was burned at the stake by Calvinists, along with almost all copies of his book.

Just a few years later pulmonary circulation was rediscovered by Realdo Colombo (c. 1510–1559) at the University of Padua, who published a work on anatomy in 1559. From autopsies and animal vivisection, Colombo noted that the pulmonary vein, from the right side of the heart to the lungs, always contained blood, not air, as had been thought. Passing from the lungs to the left side of the heart, having absorbed air or something in it, the blood was brighter and more reddish than blood coming to the heart from the veins of the rest of the body. Colombo also described the systole of the heart, its contracted phase, associated with the heartbeat, as the active stage in the motions of the heart. This theory contradicted the traditional Galenic view of the role of the heart's diastole—its expanded and relaxed stage—in drawing blood into the heart, rather than pumping it out.

Another professor at the University of Padua, Girolamo Fabrici (c. 1533–1619), a highly respected surgeon and anatomist, also made important discoveries in anatomy and physiology. In the 1570s he discovered the valves in the veins. In keeping with his essentially Galenic and Aristotelian outlook, he interpreted their function as the slowing down of the flow of the blood to the body's extremities in order to keep the blood from excessive concentrations in certain parts of the body. The valves also served, in his view, to strengthen the veins and to keep them from stretching. By tying a band firmly about an arm in order to make a vein and a valve in it appear in the arm's surface, he demonstrated that the veins all opened toward the heart. Then, stroking the vein with his finger toward both sides of the valve, he showed that the blood could pass the valve easily only in the direction leading to the heart.

The Circulation of the Blood

William Harvey (1578–1657), who had been a student at the University of Padua, had attended Fabrici's lectures on anatomy. He was therefore familiar with Fabrici's discoveries about the valves in the veins and his insistence on the study of the anatomy and physiology of animals to broaden our knowledge of human anatomy. Harvey considered the blood as the living and most fundamental part of the body because it was the first thing to be distinguished in the development of an embryo. Blood also clearly functions, he thought, to help maintain and sustain the powers of the body's organs, a view somewhat different from that held by the Galenists. For them, the heart and arterial blood functioned primarily in the distribution of heat and substances in the air throughout the body.

Determined to discover the true motion of the blood, Harvey traced the sequences involving the motion of the blood in the movements of the heart, its valves, and its flow patterns by observing them, moving slowly, through his vivisection of cold-blooded animals and dying mammals. He determined that the heart's contraction is its only active motion, one by which blood is expelled from the heart's auricles, its upper chambers, through valves leading to the ventricles below them. From there the right ventricle pumps blood to the lungs, from which it returns to the heart's left auricle, whose valve opens to allow the blood to pass into the ventricle below. The blood then moves to the aorta, from which it is distributed by successively smaller arteries to all parts of the body. Blood in the body's extremities is carried by increasingly larger veins to the right auricle of the heart. Successive heartbeats continue the process just described. Harvey also concluded that the pulse in the arteries results from the contraction of the heart, and that the valves in the veins function to keep the blood from flowing away from the heart.

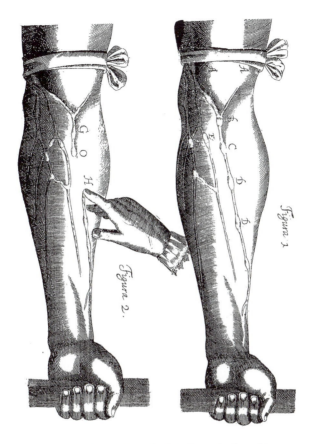

4.4 Harvey showed, as had Fabrici before him, that by pushing the blood through distended veins, it could only flow toward the heart. From Harvey's *De motu cordis*.

Despite these findings, he did not immediately come to the conclusion of the circulation of the blood. It was only after a few years of additional work, and a shift of his attention to the continuous succession of heartbeats from what occurs during a single heartbeat, that Harvey came to the conviction that the blood circulates. The amount of blood in the body could not possibly be the result of a process by which the blood was being continually created, and despite the repeated pumping of the heart, it never runs out of blood. Harvey could only surmise that blood passes from the smallest arteries to the smallest veins through invisible passages. He published his results in 1628 in his *Exercitatio anatomica de motu cordis et sanguinis in animalibus* (Anatomical Exercises on the Movement of the Heart and Blood in Animals). Despite some initial resistance, his theory was fairly rapidly accepted.

The Oxford Physiologists

Inspired by Harvey's achievement, a number of physicians centered around Oxford University began to learn more about the role of blood in the body. They saw that the passage of blood to the lungs and back to the heart changed its color from dark to bright red. Richard Lower (1631–1691) and others questioned the idea that the function of the heart lay in its ability to impart heat and "vital spirits" to the blood. They assumed that the air in the lungs, or something in the air, an *aerial nitre*, as it was called, added a significant and nourishing component to the blood and, therefore, to the proper functioning of the body. The lungs functioned to remove the waste products accumulated by the blood in the course of its circulation. Lower also calculated, assuming complete elimination of blood from the ventricles with each contraction, the rate at which the blood circulates, concluding that it does so thirteen times in an hour. This was much more rapid than had been suspected. He and his colleagues also experimented with animals, injecting air directly into the blood, to note its effects, and also performed the first blood transfusion, at first on animals and eventually on a human.

Microscopy

The invention of the microscope shortly after, and very likely inspired by, the invention of the telescope in the first decade of the seventeenth century brought discoveries of new organisms and novel details of anatomy and physiology in all living things. Magnifying glasses had been known from ancient times, but the microscope was the first magnifying instrument with compound lenses. The growing ability to grind lenses to curvatures other than spherical led to improvements in the magnifying and resolving powers of microscopes and of single lenses as well. Spherical and chromatic aberrations, as well as decreased illumination, beyond limited magnifications, however, resulted in poor resolution. The design of an improved microscope, de-

4.5 Robert Hooke's microscope. From his *Micrographia* (1665).

scribed and illustrated by Robert Hooke in his *Micrographia: or Some Physiological Descriptions of Minute Bodies Made by Magnifying Glasses* of 1665, made it a popular instrument. It was capable of being tilted for the user's convenience, and the specimens under examination could be viewed under a reflected light. Later improvements during the next few decades included substage illumination, changeable lenses for different magnifications, and the use of slides for the mounting of specimens. Techniques such as freezing, drying, injecting with wax, and dyeing for the preparation of specimens were also developed. The extent of magnification with single lenses had been significantly developed, and the best ones exceeded the magnifying powers of microscopes with compound lenses.

The Microscope and the Invisible World

The earliest microscopic investigations were of insects. A microscopic study of the anatomy of the bee was published in 1625. Micro-

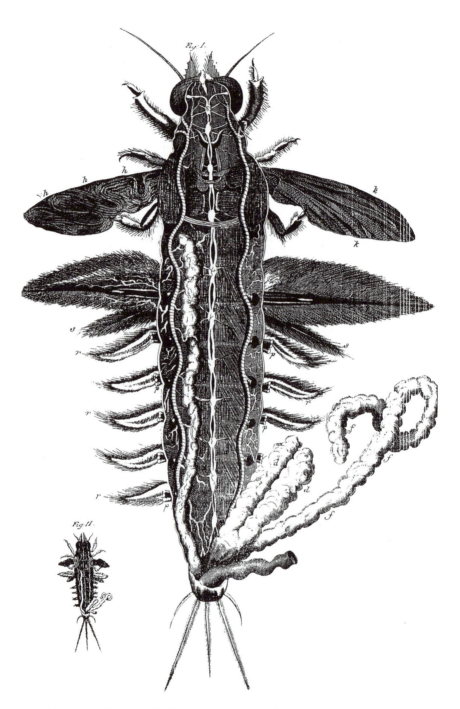

4.6 Anatomy of a may-fly through Swammerdam's microscope.

scopic details of the eye of the fly were described and illustrated a few years later. The appearances of seeds, glands, and human tissues under the microscope were published in books devoted to the newly detailed life forms. Robert Hooke's very popular *Micrographia* had several dozen beautifully engraved illustrations of insects, molds, seeds, and slices of cork. He discovered that cork is composed of cells; that discovery eventually led to the generalization of the cellular nature of living things. The anatomy of a may-fly was detailed with the aid of a microscope by Jan Swammerdam (1637–1680) in his posthumously published *The Book of Nature* (1737–1738).

Antoni van Leeuwenhoek, a clothing merchant and land surveyor, was the best lens-grinder of his day. Using a single lens with a magnifying power of over 250 diameters, he examined hundreds of objects and communicated most of his observations to the Royal Society of London, which published many of them. Leeuwenhoek became an international celebrity for his work in microscopy. His interests centered on the minute structures of organisms and the means governing reproduction and growth. He examined objects living and dead, among them the cells of various woods, salt crystals, dental bacteria, and muscles. His most important discoveries included the red blood cells, several microorganisms, and the spermatozoa of humans and a number of different animals.

Among the most important microscopical discoveries in the seventeenth century were those made by Marcello Malpighi (1628–1694), who discovered in 1661 the capillaries joining arteries and veins, thus confirming the circulation of the blood in the manner surmised by Harvey.

Generation

The use of the microscope brought new thinking about the nature of *generation*, the term given to what we now call reproduction. Aristotle had written on the subject, proposing that some living things come into existence by epigenesis, the creation by spontaneous generation, or alteration, of the forms of substances. He held that lower forms of life such as grubs or larvae emerged from mud or decaying organic matter. Others posited the generation of insects, plants, and vermin from non-living substances. Aristotle also explored the idea that

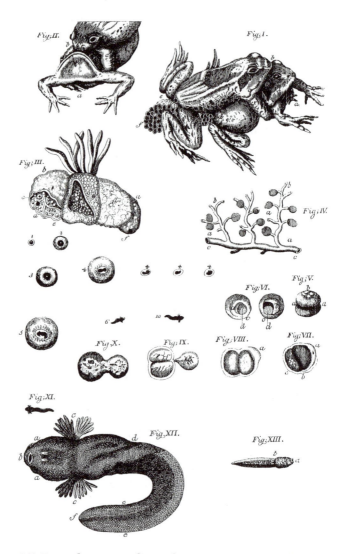

4.7 Reproduction in frogs, from mating, to the development of tadpoles. From Jan Swammerdam, *The Book of Nature* (1737–1738).

the developed forms of living organisms arose from similarly formed early stages in the process of generation.

Details of embryonic processes in animals had been observed in the ancient world and the Middle Ages with differing results. The collection of such data increased in the sixteenth century, notably through observation of incubated chicken eggs at various stages after having been laid. William Harvey made many such observations and concluded that all living things came from eggs in which the forms of organs evolved from shapeless matter in the course of embryological development. The microscope provided details of generation and growth unavailable earlier.

Around the mid-seventeenth century the use of the microscope and experiments testing the idea of the creation of life forms from nonliving matter led to challenges to the theory of epigenesis and its replacement by the idea of preformation. The microscopical studies of insects showed that they had sexual organs and reproduced sexually. Marcello Malpighi and other microscopists described in minute detail the first appearance of cells and their organization into the first stages in the development of organs. The function of the ovaries in producing ova was soon discovered, and the description of spermatozoa by Leeuwenhoek led to the new notion of reproduction through fertilization. Spontaneous generation was discarded, at least for some time, by the demonstration by Francesco Redi (1626–1697) that when rotting organic matter is kept in tightly sealed jars, no organisms can emerge from it. All existing organisms, it was concluded, can only be the offspring of parents. The preformationists were of two camps. One group held that all organisms existed in the invisible primary structure of their species in ova; the other as fully formed minuscule individuals in spermatozoa. Preformationism remained the dominant approach until the nineteenth century.

Summary

The discovery of many new plants and animals unknown to the ancients led to detailed studies of their forms and the processes governing their activities, and it engendered efforts to create new, more appropriate taxonomies. The increasing use of observation and experimentation during the Renaissance to discover the details of human anatomy brought about important challenges to traditional conceptions. The work of Andreas Vesalius transformed the investigation and teaching of anatomy and encouraged the search for new anatomical discoveries. During the Scientific Revolution new ideas from physics and chemistry began to be applied to a limited extent to the study of living things. The new anatomy resulted in the questioning of traditional ideas on physiology and in important discoveries that marked a turning-point in the departure from Aristotelian and Galenic principles. Although William Harvey did not entirely abandon those principles, his discovery of the circulation of the blood was such a turning-point. The use of the microscope, beginning early in the seventeenth century, brought additional changes to the study of anatomy and physiology and led to new discoveries about the nature of living things and their reproduction.

CHAPTER 5

New Methods for the Advancement of Knowledge

Close observation, experimentation, mathematics, and measurement were all significant in the creation of the Scientific Revolution. Mathematics and measurement had long been important in certain traditional branches of science, but during the Scientific Revolution they were employed in new ways and, together with detailed observations and experiments, they advanced knowledge attainable in no other way. New theories about how to understand nature better stressed the importance of some or all of these practices. Considerations about the best methods for the advancement of knowledge also included new ideas about causes and the nature of explanation, which did not fully replace Aristotelian approaches until about the mid-seventeenth century.

Aristotelian Methodology

A Hierarchy of the Sciences

Aristotle, following a general characteristic of ancient Greek thought on the importance of classifying by rank in all sorts of areas, held to a hierarchy of the sciences. The highest form of thinking was in the realm of metaphysics, concerned with the nature of existence, of causes and of substances in the most abstract sense. Then came physics, the study of nature, or the science of changes and movements that we see all about us. Mathematics is abstracted from nature and is therefore not a fundamental characteristic of the study of nature as Aristotle defined it. Aristotle recognized, however, that some of the physical sciences—astronomy, optics, mechanics, and harmonics—were mathematical in nature. These came to be called "mixed sciences" by later Aristotelians and were to prove important in the development of the Scientific Revolution. Still lower down in Aristotle's taxonomy of the branches of learning were branches of technology and the crafts, as well as what we now call the social sciences, such as economics and psychology.

Rules of Reasoning

Aristotle and later philosophers gave a good deal of attention to proper methods of reasoning and the avoidance of errors in thinking. The rules of correct thinking were essential for the effective mastery of all sorts of knowledge. The basic form of logic was that of the *syllogism*, which deduced a characteristic of a subject by determining its membership in a class whose members shared that characteristic. One example of the variety syllogistic forms is "Socrates is a man; all men are mortal; Socrates is therefore mortal." Useful as it is, this came to be seen during the Scientific Revolution as not being very helpful in gaining new knowledge about natural phenomena. For Aristotle, in the study of natural philosophy, it was necessary to determine the essential nature of the objects of concern. The world is composed of a variety of objects—substances—both material and immaterial, each with its attributes. The essential natures of objects and events observed in the world must be determined in order to establish the causes of change through logical analysis.

Aristotle's Causes

In the matter of explanation, Aristotle proposed that everything that happens has four causes. The primary cause is the tendency for things or processes to attain, or respond to, an inherent goal or aim. Second was the material cause, the substance of which the object under consideration consisted. Third was the formal cause, depending on the shape of the object. Everything in the world exists as formed matter. The fourth cause was the immediate cause, an event precipitating or maintaining a change of any sort. These four causes operated in the heavens as well as on the Earth. The celestial causes included a Prime Mover, the purpose behind the circular motions of all celestial objects, which were moved by spheres composed of the element *aether*, and thereby moved the planets attached to them. On the Earth: A bed exists because of a plan to construct one; the bed is made of wood, with its parts attached to provide a given form, and the work of the carpenter who made it.

A New Epistemology

Epistemology, the philosophical inquiry into the nature of knowledge, the means of its acquisition, its suppositions, and validity, changed substantially in the course of the Scientific Revolution. The value of logic was not denied, but the complexities of life and the urge to gain new knowledge of a world found to be more complex than conceived by the ancients gave rise to new theories about the most effective ways of learning about the natural world. Greater emphasis would be placed on doing coupled with thinking as the best way of gaining such knowledge. Reasoning by deduction from new and well-established premises to sound conclusions and by induction from new observations and experiments to useful hypotheses and theories were characteristic features of the Scientific Revolution.

Magic and the Occult Sciences

Aspects of the practice of magic were influential in shaping new approaches to gaining knowledge of the natural world. Magic and conceptions about the supernatural had existed in Antiquity. In Western Europe magic had been divided into two types: white, or natural, magic and black magic, or magical events occurring with the assistance of demons or evil spirits. The medieval Church had frowned on magic, but in the course of the Renaissance, magic and the operation of occult, or hidden, forces in nature became an important component in thinking about the nature of the world. In part this change resulted from the arrival in Europe of a series of manuscripts believed to have been written by Hermes Trismegistus, "the thrice-great Hermes," a statesman, philosopher, and religious thinker who lived in Egypt well before the development of Greek culture. The Hermetic writings were later found to have been written by several authors in the Hellenistic period. Also arriving in the West was the Kabbalah, Hebrew texts on the relation of words to numbers, the knowledge of which, like the Hermetic corpus, could enable one to achieve things otherwise impossible by the methods of traditional natural philosophy. Belief in witches was also common, as were beliefs in astrology and the alchemical transformation of some metals into others or to make them grow through proper alchemical practices.

There were several ways by which results in the occult sciences were achieved. Since spiritual causes had long been seen in all religions to affect and explain changes in individuals and in the larger world, the extension of the concept of unseen forces as causing natural events seemed reasonable. One such commonly accepted cause was the concept of correspondences, chiefly in the form of *macrocosm/microcosm* relationships. It was widely believed that aspects of cosmic or large-scale structures are reflected in smaller, analogous ones. The twelve traditional signs of the zodiac are each analogous to specific organs of the human body. The four types of matter—earth, water, air, and fire—correspond to the four seasons and the humors of the body. These analogous relationships may also possess causal aspects, as in the alignments of the planets and the weather or the prospects for one's recovery from illness. The causes may yield positive or negative results, commonly referred to, respectively, as *sympathy* and *antipathy*. An example of a sympathetic effect is the theory that a wound might be healed by the application of a remedy to the instrument that caused the wound.

A proper understanding of the Scientific Revolution requires analysis of the relationship between the new and more effective methodologies that emerged in the Early Modern period and the growing interest in magic and the occult sciences during the Renaissance. A good case can be made for the idea that belief in the occult sciences, but more particularly in their practices, was an important factor in the development of the Scientific Revolution. Whereas witchcraft, correspondences, microcosm-macrocosm relationships, and the character of a sorcerer or magician were not particularly helpful, the rites associated with white magic represented an important aspect of the growing belief that it was possible to achieve desired results by intervening in nature. The use of spells, rites, and the invocation of assistance from spirits was an aspect of the idea that one must not only observe nature but also intervene in it to achieve desired results. More important was the experimentation conducted by practitioners of the occult sciences to achieve their hoped-for results. The increased perception of the importance of mathematics, associated by many during the Renaissance with magic, in understanding the world, as advocated in the recently available works of Plato, was also significant in the new approaches to the acquisition of knowledge.

Francis Bacon and the New *Organon*

Francis Bacon (1561–1626), eager to promote a useful method for the growth of knowledge, proposed a new *organon*, a new tool, describing the most effective practices for achieving that goal. He strongly emphasized the importance of empiricism, the acquisition of facts learned from observation, either directly or through experimentation. It is necessary to collect and correlate as many facts as possible in order to then be able to create generalizations from which those facts, as well as others, would flow—thus leading to new knowledge. It was important, however, to seek counterinstances to test the validity of the rules induced from the observations. Experiments are important in extending the range of our observations by forcing nature to reveal aspects of it hidden to us by our ordinary experiences. Bacon also laid out four erroneous ways of thinking that retarded the advancement of knowledge. In his *Novum organum* (A New Instrument) of 1620, he described the existence of "idols," as he called them, that hinder correct and effective thinking. The Idols of the Tribe, the Cave, the Market Place, and the Theater are restrictions imposed on us by our sensory abilities, individual aberrations, society and language, and erroneous philosophies.

The *Novum organum* was only one part of a vast undertaking by Bacon to create a firm foundation for the growth of knowledge. He projected a six-volume series of books, collectively entitled *Instauratio magna* (The Great Instauration), a grand renewal of our knowledge of the natural world. The project was never completed: among its published segments was *De augmentis scientiarum* (On the Growth of Knowledge, 1623). It is concerned with establishing that knowledge must grow, and not merely be collected and passed on as traditional wisdom. Bacon emphasized the importance of the history of natural phenomena and the collection of data from observations, experiments, and technology. In a forceful way, Bacon presented the notion and goal of progress. Technology was the engine of progress: printing, the compass, and gunpowder had changed society more substantially than the cogitations of the greatest philosophers. Bacon held that knowledge is power, not only in the political sense but also in its ability to yield useful results for the benefit of humankind. These ideas were linked to religious concepts: Bacon saw the advancement of knowledge as a return to the ideal state in the Garden of Eden. In his *New Atlantis* (1626), a utopian account of the discovery by some voyagers of a scientific research institution, Bacon suggested that the development of science was a collaborative enterprise and proposed the organization and activities of scientists in ways that would further their investigations. That work became a model for those who, later in the century, created the scientific society named the Royal Society of London.

The Mechanical Philosophy

The new ideas concerning the proper pursuit of natural philosophy were given various names. The term *mechanical philosophy* seems most appropriate because the model to explain change was seen as analogous to the operation of machines. The mechanical philosophy received an important impetus from the increasing reliance on and importance of machines in economic and everyday life. Leonardo da Vinci (1452–1519), the political philosopher Thomas Hobbes (1588–1679), and René Descartes compared learning how nature works with learning how a watch works by taking it apart. Things happened because objects were pushed or pulled. The motions, collisions, and speeds of material objects were seen as important means of explaining natural events. Mathematical relationships and experimentation were significant aspects of this new approach to causes. In the course of the Scientific Revolution all but the immediate cause of the traditional Aristotelian four causes were rejected. The material and formal causes became irrelevant. The traditional first causes, goals, or purposes were to be rejected in explanations of natural events.

Cartesian Methodology

The ideas of René Descartes were the most decisive influence in the development of the mechanical philosophy. He, like Bacon, sought a sound basis for a philosophy of nature that would allow for the progress of knowledge. Although a skilled experimenter, Descartes paid less attention to the importance of experimentation than did Bacon. Descartes attacked formal logic as useless and primarily a tool for expressing what was already known. One must begin by doubting received opinion. In his *Discourse on Method* (1637), Descartes emphasized the importance of arriving at certainty by proper thinking about the principles governing natural phenomena. He began with a dualistic conception of the nature of existence, holding that the universe consists of two distinct entities, the material and the spiritual. God created the universe, which contained both components. Everything in the created world, except the human soul, immortal and capable of thinking, consists of particles of matter in constant interaction. For Descartes, the universe was completely full, there were no vacuums, and the concept of attraction was anathema. The motions of individual particles, or clusters of them, can account for all natural phenomena, including the motions of the planets, magnetism, the transmission of light, and the behavior of animals. The bodily functions of all living things, including humans, could be explained by mechanical means. Descartes tried, not very effectively, to explain mechanically William Harvey's description of the circulation of the blood. Descartes, did, however, successfully account for muscular reflex actions by mechanical means. Descartes was an excellent mathematician and played an important role in the development of geometric algebra. In his view the certainty of mathematics and universal agreement about the results of mathematics provided an additional model for the way science ought to develop.

Mathematics and Natural Philosophy

During the Scientific Revolution there were several reasons for the increased use of mathematics in the study of nature. Classical mathematical works became available and were mastered during the Renaissance. The mathematical achievements of the ancient Greeks were built upon and applied to problems in navigation, engineering, architecture, and various crafts to a greater extent than had been seen in previous ages. In art as well, mathematical techniques were employed to make artistic representations more effective. The discovery of perspective, using geometrical ratios to provide accurate renditions of how things are seen both near and far and to give the appearance of three-dimensionality, had a tremendous impact on the development of art. Albrecht Dürer (1471–1528) employed a device to assure accurate proportions between parts of a scene he was trying to reproduce. The increased emphasis on realism in art and in the study of nature was coupled with the certainty provided by mathematics.

Those sciences, relying on mathematical components inherited from Antiquity, such as astronomy, optics, and music, made significant progress in the early years of the seventeenth century through novel applications of mathematical analysis. The achievements of Tycho Brahe and Johannes Kepler greatly improved accuracy in the prediction of astronomical events. Kepler pointed out that the intensity of light diminishes in an inverse-square ratio with distance from the light source. Angles of incidence and refraction in different media had long been measured, but the sine law of refraction was independently discovered by Thomas Harriot (c. 1560–1621), Willibrord Snel (1580–1626), and René Descartes early in the seventeenth century. Newton would later measure the angles at which light of various colors was refracted.

Music had been seen from ancient times as a branch of applied mathematics and was taught that way in the universities. Mathematical relationships between different tones was well known. Galileo conducted experiments to determine mathematical ratios between strings emitting different tones and their lengths and the distances covered by the center of a vibrating string.

New Applications of Mathematical Analysis

Mathematical analysis in areas where it had not been applied before, and in conjunction with experimentation, marked an important development of the Scientific Revolution. In mechanics Galileo, seeking to find the relationship between the distance fallen by an object and the time during its fall, carefully measured segments of the distance and time to determine their ratios. The result was a striking revision of long-held ideas about the nature of motion. After Galileo several experimenters measured the results of the impact of bodies of different or similar weights upon each other. The ratios of the speed of whirling bodies to distances from their centers was determined by Christiaan Huygens. Newton's formulation of his second law of motion involved mathematical determinations in moving bodies of changing relationships between velocity and/or direction of motion. His principle of universal gravitation involved quantitative determinations of dis-

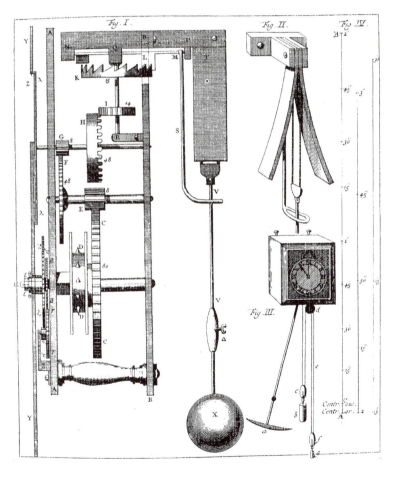

5.1 Christiaan Huygens' diagram of his pendulum clock. From his *Horologium oscillatorium* (1658).

tance and mass. The discovery of laws of nature expressed in mathematical form had become the ideal in natural philosophy.

The importance of measurement in the emerging new natural philosophy was becoming apparent in the life sciences as well. William Harvey and his successors thought it important to measure the amount of blood leaving the heart during systole. Giovanni Borelli applied mechanical principles to certain aspects of animal and human activities. Interest in measurement and the pursuit of greater precision often required the slowing of motion to ascertain more effectively the resulting effects. This may be seen in Harvey's slowing of the motions of the heart and in Galileo's use of inclined planes to slow the motion of falling bodies. The search for greater precision and detail brought the inventions of the microscope, the thermoscope, the barometer, the telescopic micrometer, the pendulum clock, and the odometer. The pursuit of greater effectiveness and rapidity in managing the increasing complexities of calculation led to the use of decimal fractions, the publication of trigonometric tables for smaller and smaller angles, the development of calculating machines, and the creation of logarithms. All these applications and mathematical developments were essential components of the mechanical philosophy.

Experimentation

Experimentation had not been entirely absent in Antiquity or the Middle Ages, but it was insignificant in a natural philosophy dominated by an emphasis on thinking rather than doing. This view slowly began to change in the sixteenth century, but a pronounced change occurred very early in the seventeenth century.

Experimental Design

Galileo's efforts to determine the true paths of projectiles and of falling bodies, involving the use of experiment and measurement, required the design of experimental apparatus that would approximate as closely as possible the ideal conditions implied by the mathematical relationships being sought. Galileo used inclined lengths of wood, with highly polished grooves, down which he rolled steel balls to minimize friction. Harvey, too, had to design his experiments and observations on blood flow to allow effective and detailed observation by slowing the movement of the blood.

Conclusions determined from experimental results were sometimes subjected to further tests by varying the original experiments or by conducting new experiments. Blaise Pascal's trials with mercury-filled tubes were made under different conditions, utilizing a variety of shapes and sizes, and at different elevations. Robert Boyle's air pump had a glass chamber, so that different objects could be inserted, activated, and observed under conditions of partial or total evacuation of air. Under the latter condition, a simultaneously dropped feather and coin landed at the same time, an experiment duplicated in the twentieth century on the airless Moon. Newton subjected the initial results of his experiments with light refracted through a prism to further tests of the apparent constitution of white light by rays of different colors. Refractions of each color in the original spectrum resulted in no change in color; and bringing the spectrum to a focus, blending its colors back into white light, appeared to validate his theory that white light is composed of a mixture of light of separate colors. An important aspect of all these experiments is that they were repeated more than once and were described in such a way as to be able to be reproduced by anyone who followed the same procedures.

Invisible Causes and Mathematical Descriptions

Galileo, who had been initially concerned with the causes of falling bodies, abandoned attempts to find them upon discovering the mathematical relationships that expressed how they fell. There seemed to be no way to discover those causes with a similar mathematical certainty. The proponents of the mechanical philosophy, in contrast, continued to seek the immediate causes of various phenomena by postulating motions of invisible particles as the causes of certain phenomena. By the end of the seventeenth century, a purpose or goal could not be assigned as a cause of phenomena; but for effects not easily explained by perceptible mechanical means, the assignment of a property or tendency would suffice. Magnets tended to attract iron. The relationship of air pressure to the height of mercury in a barometric tube could be explained by assigning a property to air—its elasticity, its tendency to expand. Because mechanical philosophers were generally dissatisfied with occult forces such as Newton's universal gravitation that could not be explained mechanically, many simply referred to it as a natural property of all bodies. Despite vigorous objections to the concept of universal attraction upon its publication, its great success in explaining in incontrovertible mathematical terms, motions in the heavens and on the Earth successfully silenced those objections.

The New Philosophy and the Wider Culture

Thus far have been noted how social and cultural changes in Europe during the Early Modern period affected ideas on the nature of natural philosophy. The new approaches and achievements in the study of nature in turn began to affect the culture at large in this period, though to a limited degree. Those effects, greatly enhanced by further scientific developments, would profoundly affect life and culture throughout the world in later centuries. During the Scientific Revolution, however, effects of the new philosophy could be seen in popular culture, the arts, and the universities and in the creation of new institutions.

Popularization

There were increasing efforts during the Scientific Revolution to provide those who were literate, even if they were of the lower classes, with the new scientific ideas of the natural philosophers, written in the various European languages. Among the most popular works were almanacs, issued annually, providing not only astronomical and astrological information but also weather predictions and the best times for planting. They cost little and, with the Bible, were frequently the only printed works in a household where at least one member was literate. In the early seventeenth century, some almanacs explained the Copernican theory and, by mid-century, some of Kepler's ideas and even his tables that were used for the calculation of the positions of celestial bodies in the course of the year. Kepler's ideas had even spread across the ocean. In 1662 an almanac published in New England explained that the planets dance "illiptical Sallyes, Ebbs and flowes," responding to "Magneticall Charmes" issuing from the Sun.

In the sixteenth century there began to appear translations of clas-

sical ancient works in mathematics and natural history into the vernaculars of Europe. In the seventeenth century, books on modern science, such as those written by Galileo and Kepler, originally written in
Latin, were being translated. Latin was slowly beginning to be replaced
as the language of learning, and the educated elites and members of
the middle classes were targeted by some natural philosophers as an
additional audience for treatises on new scientific ideas written in the
vernacular. Galileo wrote his *Dialogue Concerning the Two Chief World
Systems—Ptolemaic and Copernican* in Italian. Although after Galileo's
trial by the Inquisition the book was placed on the Index of Prohibited
Books, in 1633, that did not keep it from being disseminated and read.
Three years later it was translated into Latin so that it could be read
by those who knew Latin, but not Italian. Descartes wrote his *Discourse
on Method* (1637) in Latin but in 1644 translated it into French. Robert Hooke's *Micrographia* was written in English. Newton described his
optical experiments in English in his *Opticks* of 1704. It was translated
into Latin two years later.

In addition to translations of works describing the new scientific
concepts, books were written to explain those concepts to the common
reader in a more easily understandable form. One of the greatest popularizers of science was John Wilkins (1614–1672), who wrote books
on astronomy and mechanics. One of these, *A Discourse Concerning a
New World & Another Planet* (1640), reprinted six times by the end of
the century, explained and defended the Copernican system as improved by Kepler and Galileo. It appeared at a time when arguments
from Scripture and common sense carried more weight among laypersons than scientific arguments. Wilkins further published *Mathematical
Magick* (1648), a text on elementary mechanics, which also reached a
large audience. The most popular work of all, explaining the Cartesian
version of the Copernican theory, was by Bernard le Bovier de
Fontenelle (1657–1757). His engagingly written *Entretiens sur la pluralité des mondes* (Conversations on the Plurality of Worlds) of 1686
was an immediate success, often reprinted and translated into several
languages.

The ideas of Copernicus, Kepler, and Galileo also appeared in a
number of poems that showed how widely understood those ideas
were. John Donne (1573–1631) read Kepler's book, *De stella nova* (On
the New Star), published in 1606, on the appearance of a new star that

had recently been observed in the heavens. In several works Donne referred to novas as challenging the Aristotelian concept of the perfect
nature of space. In his *Biathanatos* of 1608, he cited Kepler's book as
his source for a critique of

> Aristotle's followers, . . . who defending the Heavens to be inalter-
> able, because in so many ages nothing had been observed to have
> been altered, his Schollars stubbornly maintain his proposition
> still, though by many experiences of new Stars, the reason which
> moved *Aristotle* seems now to be utterly defeated.

Poets also seemed interested in meeting the authors of the new scientific ideas. Donne met Kepler on a trip to the Continent in 1619; and
John Milton (1608–1674), on his trip to the Continent in 1638–1639,
paid a call on Galileo. Milton, referring to Kepler's theory of the cause
of planetary motions, in Book VIII of his *Paradise Lost* has the angel
Gabriel ask Adam

> What if the Sun
> Be centre to the World, and other Stars,
> By his attractive virtue and their own
> Incited, dance about him various rounds?

The Universities

In the course of the Renaissance there was growing impatience
with logic and the transmission of Aristotelian ideas as the foundation
of university curricula. The discovery of ancient alternatives and of new
goals and styles of life brought with them a questioning of the traditional modes of learning. The practitioners and proponents of the New
Philosophy argued that university teaching needed to be reformed.
Mathematics and experimentation, so fundamental to the new natural
philosophy, had little place in the fundamentally Scholastic orientation
of the universities, where traditional texts reigned supreme.

This situation began to change, more readily in some universities,
but not at all in others, in the course of the seventeenth century. Most
of the innovative natural philosophers had attended universities, and
a substantial number of them were members of university faculties.

Certain of Copernicus' ideas received a favorable hearing at the University of Wittenberg in the second half of the sixteenth century. Rheticus, Copernicus' first disciple, and Reinhold who although not a convert constructed the first Copernican astronomical tables, had taught there. Johannes Kepler learned his Copernicanism from his professor of astronomy at the University of Tübingen. Galileo taught at the universities of Pisa and Padua; Newton taught at the University of Cambridge. The medical schools were more receptive to the new ideas. Their professors, notably at the University of Padua, took important initiatives to advance knowledge in anatomy, physiology, and embryology. The task of a professor was no longer to transmit and analyze the works of Galen, but to discover new things unknown to the ancients and to teach them to their students. Medical professors were also eager to learn more about botany, zoology, and chemistry to increase the effectiveness of medicines.

By the second half of the seventeenth century the impact of the New Philosophy was beginning to be felt in a number of universities. Cartesianism began to enter the curricula of several of them. Mathematics—in many institutions, very elementary mathematics—had long been part of the undergraduate curriculum, but mathematics began to receive greater emphasis, first in Protestant universities and Jesuit institutions, which were less bound by tradition than older universities. The gradual absorption of the new learning by the leading universities contributed to its acceptance, as did the easing of concerns about challenges to Scripture. Universities alone, however, were not seen as providing sufficient resources and opportunities for the advancement of knowledge. Faculty members and others joined together to create societies to conduct experiments and to promote and transmit new knowledge.

An Expanding Audience

Among the goals of Renaissance humanism was to transmit the knowledge of a changing world to a public audience, including those who had not attended a university. King Francis I established an institution in Paris in 1530 to provide lectures in mathematics and medicine, as well as ancient languages and philosophy. Initially called the

Institution of Royal Lecturers, it was renamed the *Collège Royal* in 1610. Although distinct from the University of Paris, both institutions occasionally shared speakers. An institution with a somewhat similar function was created in London. The will of Thomas Gresham, a businessman and diplomat, bequeathed his home and an endowment for the establishment of Gresham College. It was founded in 1596 to provide lectures in both Latin and English in seven subjects, among which were astronomy, mathematics, and medicine. Its lecturers had attended Oxford and Cambridge universities and frequently returned to them as professors when openings bcame available. By the 1640s Gresham College became a gathering-place for natural philosophers to meet for discussions after the lectures.

By the early seventeenth century the transmission and exchange of scientific ideas had became an important means to develop and spread the ideas of natural philosophy, chiefly through letters that could be received in days or in a few weeks from one part of Europe to another. Many scientists sent and received hundreds of letters in the course of their careers. A few individuals, known as "intelligencers," undertook to serve as intermediaries for the transmission of scientific intelligence, or information. One of the most important was Nicolas-Claude Fabri de Peiresc (1580–1637). He corresponded with hundreds of individuals from his home in France and wrote and received thousands of letters, many of which he had an assistant copy and forward to another recipient. Marin Mersenne (1588–1648) was another such "clearing-house." From his monastery in Paris, Mersenne corresponded with Galileo and Descartes, among many others. In London, Samuel Hartlib (c. 1600–1662) carried out similar functions.

Scientific Societies

The creation of formal organizations to promote scientific research and to transmit new ideas and experimental results to a wider scientific audience was a new and important development. In 1603 Federico Cesi (1585–1630), descended from wealthy members of the nobility, founded the *Accademia dei Lincei*, the Academy of Lynxes, in Rome. It was named after the keen-eyed felines and was organized to promote the advancement of natural philosophy. Its most distinguished

5.2 The frontispiece of *History of the Royal Society* by Thomas Sprat (1667) shows a bust of King Charles II as founder and patron of the society, flanked on its right by the society's president and on its left by Francis Bacon, whose goals were an inspiration for the society.

member was Galileo. It did not long survive, but other societies continued to be formed and to flourish. Among the new groups for the discussion and promotion of new scientific ideas in the seventeenth century were the Montmor Academy in Paris, which flourished for a decade, beginning about 1653. In the 1640s a similar group, the Oxford Philosophical Society, was created. Under the patronage of the Duke of Tuscany, the *Accademia del Cimento* (Academy of Experiment) was created in Florence in 1657 to carry out experiments in the new natural philosophy.

In 1660 some natural philosophers who had been at Oxford, including John Wilkins, Robert Boyle, and Robert Hooke, came to London and, merging with a group that had met regularly at Gresham College to discuss natural philosophy, created a scientific society. Two years later the society received a royal warrant and became the Royal Society for the Promotion of Natural Knowledge. Its members saw themselves as followers of Francis Bacon. It was a dues-paying, self-governing organization that elected its officers, a council, and new members. It had a paid demonstrator of experiments, Robert Hooke, and heard lectures about scientific work both in Britain and elsewhere. Its secretary, Henry Oldenburg (c. 1619–1677) kept minutes of the society's meetings and was a very active intelligencer, carrying on an international correspondence in Latin, English, French, Italian, and Dutch. In 1665 he founded the *Philosophical Transactions of the Royal Society*, which shortly became the Royal Society's official publication. The Royal Society and its journal became a model for other scientific organizations.

In 1666 a similar organization, the *Académie Royale des Sciences* (Royal Academy of Sciences) was established in Paris by King Louis XIV, but with significant differences in organization. Its members were chosen, from both France and abroad, by a minister of the king, were paid handsome salaries, and were expected to evaluate requests for patents. Established at the same time were an observatory and a journal providing reports on the activities of its members, as well as reports of scientific work done elsewhere. King Charles II of England created a Royal Observatory at Greenwich, then a suburb of London, with a paid astronomer as its director. The creation and support of scientific institutions by governments would grow substantially in the following centuries.

Summary

Aristotle's concepts of method and of explanation in natural philosophy were superseded in the course of the Scientific Revolution. Greater emphasis was placed on the collection of facts and intervening in nature by experimentation to gain new facts and to test hypotheses. The determination of mathematical relationships and "laws" that explained observed phenomena, and from which new ones could be deduced, became an ideal. The Mechanical Philosophy rejected the role of purpose and hidden forces in causal explanations in favor of analogies with mechanical processes. Scientific activity became much more of a collaborative enterprise through correspondence between natural philosophers, the organization of scientific societies, and the publication of journals.

CHAPTER 6

RELIGION AND NATURAL PHILOSOPHY

A fundamental part of the cultures of all peoples is their attempts to understand the origin of the world and its inhabitants, the causes of the natural phenomena affecting their lives, and how best to deal with one's mortality. These universal endeavors are reflected in their religions. Until relatively recent times, conceptions about the natural world and the growth of knowledge about it were almost always entwined with religious beliefs. Aristotle equated his highly abstract god with the prime mover, the fundamental cause of the motions of the heavenly spheres. For Aristotle the deity and the universe were both eternal, and there was no role for divine providence in the workings of the world. The theologies that developed in Judaism, Christianity, and Islam differed in fundamental ways from Aristotle's view. The very high regard in which Aristotle's philosophy was held required serious attention to those theological differences.

With the development of the Catholic Church and its institutions in Western Europe, and as the state religion in all its governments, natural philosophical ideas were subject to theological analysis and control for the prevention of heresy and threats to the social order. Europe in the Early Modern period was the scene of powerful religious differences and contention. The Reformation not only broke what had been the Universal Church into several pieces but also was a source for varying approaches to new scientific ideas. Because religious beliefs were universally held, there were some instances where they may have played a role in the shaping of those new ideas. The effects of science on religious beliefs during the Scientific Revolution were minimal, but would become significantly greater in later centuries.

Aristotle and Christianity

The translations in the twelfth and thirteenth centuries of Aristotle's works from Arabic, into which they had earlier been translated, into Latin, along with commentaries on them by Muslim philosophers, had a profound effect on the universities of Western Europe. Aristotelian concepts became the foundation of the undergraduate curriculum and advanced studies for degrees in theology, medicine, and law. Medieval and Early Modern Aristotelianism consisted of a general agreement on Aristotle's principles and conclusions, although there were considerable variations in their interpretations. While the earliest Christians, in their efforts to establish the importance of divine revelation, reacted against the intellectual methods, achievements, and what they saw as the arrogance of the philosophers, their medieval descendants became eager to absorb those methods and achievements.

Theological Modifications of Aristotle

Problems arose, however, over some of Aristotle's ideas that contradicted established Christian beliefs. Aristotle held that the universe was eternal and uncreated, that there is no divine intervention in the natural order, and that the soul dies with the body. Intense debates about the relationship of Aristotle's thought to the established beliefs of Christianity and about what were perceived as efforts to supplant the primacy of theology and faith by natural philosophy and reason initially led to efforts to forbid the study of Aristotle. Those efforts were of no avail. The desire to reconcile Aristotle's thought with the fundamentals of Christian belief were eventually achieved at the University of Paris through the work of Thomas Aquinas (1225–1274). The Church adopted Aristotle's philosophy as its own, but suitably modified. In the second half of the thirteenth century some professors at the university of Paris were so committed to Aristotle's philosophy that they insisted on teaching it exactly as Aristotle taught it, without theological modifications. In 1277 the bishop of Paris condemned as heretical over 200 propositions derived from Aristotle's thought, including a few propositions of Thomas Aquinas'. In addition, the doctrine of "two truths," that something might be true in philosophy but false in theology, was severely condemned. Nevertheless, the highly respected work of Thomas Aquinas was officially adopted shortly afterward, and he was canonized as a saint in the fourteenth century.

The Reformation

The challenge to Catholicism initiated in 1517 by Martin Luther (1483–1546) in nailing his ninety-five theses to the door of a church in Wittenberg affected not only theology and religious beliefs and practices but also the relations between science and religion. Luther was followed by others opposed to Catholicism, but who differed in various ways from Luther's positions. These efforts at a reformation of religion were shortly followed by the Catholic Church's Counter-Reformation, aiming to restore Protestants to the Catholic faith, eliminate heretical beliefs, and reform certain practices that had weakened the late medieval Church, and led to the Reformation. A number of wars ensued, particularly in the German-speaking part of Europe, and Europe was divided into Catholic and, chiefly in Northern Europe, a variety of Protestant countries and regions. Since at that time each state had an official religion, individuals holding a different one, or what were considered heretical doctrines, tended to be persecuted and even tortured or killed. For his heretical views, Giordano Bruno was burned at the stake in Rome, Realdo Colombo was killed in Geneva, Johannes Kepler, a Lutheran, thought it best to leave Catholic territory for Protestant areas, and Galileo was forced to renounce his Copernican views by the Inquisition. Yet, in the world of learning, continuing relationships between those of different faiths continued to serve the advancement of natural philosophy. After leaving Denmark, Tycho Brahe, a Lutheran, had as his new patron the Catholic Holy Roman Emperor, as did Kepler after him. Rheticus, a Lutheran, traveled from Wittenberg to Catholic West Prussia to live with Copernicus and study his astronomy. William Harvey, a member of the Anglican Church, studied at the University of Padua in the Catholic republic of Venice.

Luther, Calvin, and the Jesuits

Martin Luther characterized Copernicus as a fool who wished to turn astronomy upside down, but that position was modified by the work of his principal theologian, Philip Melanchthon (1497–1560), whose influence at the University of Wittenberg was important in keeping Copernican ideas alive and helping to advance them. The University of Wittenberg was one of several universities in the German states established to promote Lutheran theological principles and practices. Melanchthon stressed the importance of teaching new scientific knowledge, and his university reflected that aim. Rheticus, Copernicus' disciple, and Reinhold, who calculated the first Copernican tables, had taught at Wittenberg. Johannes Kepler learned his Copernicanism at the University of Tübingen, another Lutheran institution.

The religious beliefs of John Calvin (1509–1564) were very influential in the Swiss lands, in parts of the German territories, in the Spanish Netherlands, and in England. Calvin never directly addressed the new ideas in natural philosophy; he did, however, interpret some biblical passages that referred to natural phenomena as a means by God to explain his divine creation in a manner intelligible to humans. Learning the true shape of the heavens came through the work of astronomers, and not by a literal interpretation of biblical passages. The literal interpretation of biblical passages would become an important issue in debates on the relations of science and religion, as it still is today.

The Society of Jesus, founded by Ignatius Loyola (1491–1556) in the course of the Counter-Reformation, became heavily involved in the promotion of the Catholic faith in various ways. A significant aspect of those efforts was their founding of schools and universities, and teaching in them as well as in others. The Collegio Romano, founded by Loyola in Rome, early emphasized the teaching of natural philosophy and became a model for universities later established by the Catholic Church. Jesuits actively pursued aspects of the new natural philosophy and constituted a core of the most knowledgeable members of the Catholic Church who were familiar with and contributed to the new science.

Religion, Literacy, and Science

An important effect of the Reformation was an increase in literacy in the various languages of Europe. Protestants of various sects thought it important for believers to be able to read the Bible themselves. That had not been possible for the great majority of the population who had never learned Latin, the official language of the Bible during the Middle Ages. Luther translated the Bible into German. There had been English versions before King James, who in the early seventeenth century commissioned a group of scholars to translate the Bible from its original languages. That version, named for him, remained the standard English version for many years. While the language of learning and of the great majority of books on natural philosophy remained Latin, in the course of the seventeenth century books on science began to be written in the various European languages. The knowledge of natural philosophy was thereby spreading to a wider audience and was no longer the province of those with a university education, where a knowledge of Latin was still an important requirement.

Religious Responses to the New Natural Philosophy

With acceptance of the need for study of the new scientific ideas by Catholic and Protestant leaders came a fear of those ideas as potential challenges to the divine inspiration of Holy Writ. In response, the new natural philosophy was linked by its advocates to religious doctrines, and thereby justified, particularly where it seemed to contradict traditional beliefs. The belief that the pursuit of science promotes sectarian or even atheistic views was expressed from time to time. People should be concerned less with the functions of the natural world than with the state of their souls. In response, some pointed out that God had given humans the ability to discover hitherto unknown details about the workings of the world. The pursuit of natural philosophy was therefore a means of bringing one closer to God. Francis Bacon linked the new philosophy to the coming of the Millennium, a belief common in his day, through his project for the advancement of science, and thus to usher in an anticipated return to the ideal state symbolized by the Garden of Eden.

Heliocentrism and Biblical Interpretation

The heliocentric theory of Copernicus and his followers proved to be one of the most significant issues among perceived threats to fundamental religious beliefs. There are several passages in the Bible referring to a motionless Earth and a moving Sun. In the seventeenth century the contradiction between heliocentrism and a literal interpretation of biblical passages would become a significant source of debate on the relationship between natural philosophy and theology. For several decades after the publication of Copernicus' work, however, it was not a significant issue. Copernicus was a devout Catholic and a member of the governing body of his cathedral. His radical ideas on the structure of the universe raised no objections from his Church, and in 1536 he was even urged by a cardinal aware of those ideas to publish his results. There were some negative comments by a Church official immediately after the publication of Copernicus' masterpiece, but the Church took no official position. Osiander's preface, denying the physical truth of the Copernican system, may have played some role in its failure to be seen as a challenge to biblical passages.

All natural philosophers during the Scientific Revolution saw their efforts as exhibiting formerly hidden details of God's creation. Johannes Kepler's first book, his *Mysterium cosmographicum* (The Cosmographic Mystery) of 1596 opens with his assertion that his aim is to reveal the hidden pattern in God's creation of the universe. Inspired in part by Plato's vision of the creation of the universe by the deity in accord with mathematical relationships, Kepler proposed that the reason the solar system has only six planets, including Earth, is that God's model was the five perfect solids, each of which was made up of equal faces and equal angles. Each, in a certain sequence, defines the distances separating the six planetary orbits. Kepler also saw the division of the system into its center, circumference, and the intervening space, as reflecting the Trinity. God the Father is represented by the Sun, which, while immobile, is the source of the motions of the planets.

The weakening of certain Aristotelian cosmological ideas by astronomical observations, such as those of nova, and particularly through the use of the telescope, removed some objections to the Copernican theory. Galileo felt more confident about the theory after additional observations, such as the phases of Venus, which indicated that the planet revolved about the Sun. The observation of sunspots led Galileo into a vigorous debate in 1612 with a Jesuit astronomer, Christoph Scheiner (1573–1650), through correspondence with a third party, over the nature of sunspots. Galileo's ideas were published in 1613 and made clear his acceptance of the Copernican theory. This may have resulted in increasing attention within the Catholic Church to theological implications of Galileo's Copernicanism. Galileo fell out of favor among the Jesuits and, though defended by some members of the clergy, he was accused by others of heretical opinions and was attacked from pulpits.

Galileo and the Church

Galileo was denounced to the Inquisition in 1615 and, to defend himself, wrote out his opinions on the relationship between natural philosophy and theology in a series of letters to supporters and to the mother of his patron, Christina, Grand Duchess of Tuscany. The letters were not published during Galileo's lifetime, but were circulated among his friends and acquaintances. In the letter to the Grand Duchess, Galileo pointed out that there are passages in the Bible that clearly cannot be taken literally, as in references to God having feet and hands, forgetting past events, and feeling repentance. He went on to say that we were given the abilities to perceive and to reason, and we were thereby better able to understand God through increased knowledge of His creation. Galileo reported that he once heard a cardinal say that the purpose of the Bible is to teach us how to go to heaven, and not how heaven goes. The workings of nature can be determined only on the basis of sense experience and demonstrated conclusions. Galileo, with prescience, warned that once heliocentrism was decisively and indisputably proven, its condemnation by the Church would reflect badly on it. Theologians, ignorant of the science of astronomy, should stick to what they know. Galileo's letter concluded with an interpretation of the miracle of Joshua at the battle of Jericho that attempted to show that the halting of the Sun's apparent motion did not contradict the Copernican theory.

In the same year as Galileo's letter to the Grand Duchess, Paolo Antonio Foscarini, a friar and theologian, published a work showing some of the implications of Galileo's discoveries, and he asserted that the Copernican system was not contradicted by the Bible. Foscarini sent a copy of his book to the leading theologian of the Church, Robert Cardinal Bellarmine (1542–1621), who responded that it was acceptable to speak of the Copernican system hypothetically, but that Scripture and the opinions of theologians should not be contradicted. Bellarmine went on to say that if there were indisputable proof of the motion of the Earth, traditional opinions would have to be reconsidered, but he had seen no such proof and strongly doubted that there was any. The Holy Office, the body directing the Inquisition, determined that a heliocentric system was both scientifically false and heretical.

The pope directed Cardinal Bellarmine to instruct Galileo not to expound the Copernican system, and Bellarmine did so in 1616; Galileo accepted the prohibition. The Church then condemned Foscarini's book as heretical and placed Copernicus' book, *On the Revolutions of the Celestial Orbs*, on the Index of Prohibited Books, forbidden to be read by Catholics without special permission, until it should be corrected. A book written by a Spanish priest in the later sixteenth century, asserting that the Copernican theory was not contradicted by Scripture, and Kepler's *New Astronomy* were also placed on the Index. These prohibitions had very little effect on the growing acceptance of the Copernican theory, even in solidly Catholic countries. The restrictions did, however, result in Catholic natural philosophers, notably the Jesuits, opting in their publications for the Tychonic system with its immobile Earth and revolving Sun.

Galileo received the election of Maffeo Cardinal Barberini (1568–1644) as Pope Urban VIII in 1623 with great pleasure. Cardinal Barberini had been very friendly to Galileo, who dedicated his new book on scientific method, *Il saggiatore* (The Assayer), published in 1623, to the pope, who praised the book highly. They met several times the following year, and Galileo felt encouraged to believe that the Church might ease its condemnation of the Copernican system. The pope, however, cautioned that discussions of the merits of the heliocentric system must remain within the bounds of the decree of 1616. Galileo then began to write his *Dialogo sopra i due massimi sistemi del mondo Tolemaico e Copernicano* (Dialogue Concerning the Two Chief World Systems—Ptolemaic and Copernican). An official license to publish the work was received in 1631, and it was published the following year.

Galileo's work was written as a discussion and debate among three individuals—a natural philosopher presenting the new ideas in astronomy and mechanics, an Aristotelian, and an open-minded individual weighing the ideas being advanced. The book was an immediate success and quickly sold out. Galileo felt he had kept within the limits imposed by the Church. The pope, however, became very angry; it is not entirely clear why. Perhaps he felt that the simple-minded Aristotelian in the *Dialogue* was meant to represent the Church's official position and thus mocked it, and that it was a thinly disguised pro-Copernican work. Galileo was thereupon brought before the Inquisition on suspicion of heresy. He was forced to deny the truth of the Copernican theory on threats of torture and excommunication, and aged, ill, and becoming blind, he was sentenced to house arrest for the rest of his life. His *Dialogue* was placed on the Index of Prohibited Books.

The trial of Galileo did not stem the growing interest in and acceptance of Copernicanism and its Keplerian version. A notable exception was René Descartes' withholding from publication his book on the Copernican system of the world. His heliocentric system, however, was described in another, later work. Other Catholic Copernicans disguised their convictions in various ways. Some substituted the revolutions of the satellites of Jupiter to explain the causes of celestial motion in order to mask their belief in the heliocentric theory. Others advanced the geoheliocentric theory of Tycho Brahe, in which the planets circled the Sun, which revolved about the motionless Earth at the center of the system. It was nevertheless clear that the Aristotelo-Ptolemaic system was no longer accepted.

A New Relationship

Traditional conceptions of natural philosophy as a handmaid to religion were transformed in the course of the seventeenth century. Some challenged the new scientific outlooks for promoting deism, or even atheism, by denying the truth of Scripture. The new natural philosophers answered by denying the validity of literal interpretations of certain passages in the Bible, which were written to appeal to the common understanding of ordinary people. Furthermore, the pursuit of natural philosophy with our God-given intellectual abilities helps us better understand the creation of what was called the "Book of Nature" and brings us closer to God. Centuries earlier St. Augustine had said that the function of the Bible was not to teach us about nature. Galileo, Kepler, and others held that the Book of Nature was not designed to prepare us for salvation. They urged that natural philosophy and theology should be seen as distinct areas with their own methods and criteria, and that their practitioners should not intervene in one another's provinces. Descartes' distinction between the two kinds of entities created by God, the material and the spiritual, appeared to serve the same purpose. Religious issues were to be avoided in the discussions and publications of the scientific societies.

Responses to the Mechanical Philosophy

In the late Middle Ages there were two delicately balanced strands of thought in theology concerning the nature of God. It was thought that God would use rational means to achieve His purposes and, at the same time, had the ability to exercise His will in any manner He chose. Some natural philosophers during the Scientific Revolution emphasized God's voluntaristic nature, explaining miracles as a manifestation of it. What we learn through observation and other empirical means are not so by necessity and can be undone at God's will. Others, like Descartes, saw the laws of nature as sufficient and adequate explanations for all events in the universe. Aspects of the the atomic theory, of Descartes' mechanical philosophy, and of the chemical philosophy associated with Paracelsus were disturbing to Catholic and Calvinist theologians alike. Their theories of matter seemed to leave no active role for God in the operations of nature. Moreover, Descartes' description of the creation of the universe differed from that in the Bible and, in omitting the account of the origin of original sin, challenged an important component of true religious belief. In addition, his assertion that the universe was governed by fixed laws of nature ordained by God, raised the question of God's role in the universe since the Creation. If everything in the universe worked on the principles of mechanics, where was there room for the role of spiritual factors? Could all miracles be explained on rational, mechanical grounds? It would appear that after the Creation, God had nothing to do—an obviously dangerous idea.

A number of natural philosophers, concerned about the dangers of a thoroughgoing materialism, proposed that the mechanical philosophy include an active participation by God in the operations of His natural laws. Henry More (1614–1687), a member of the faculty at Cambridge University, proposed that the universe is filled not only with matter but also with a "Spirit of Nature," an incorporeal entity as the means by which God's design for the operations of nature is carried out. Isaac Newton was similarly concerned about a role for providence in the operations of a lawlike universe. He proposed that there were non-material "active principles" carrying out the will of God, who was present throughout the universe, as seen in alchemical operations, optical phenomena, and the cohesion and attraction of bodies.

In 1715 a debate began between Gottfried Wilhelm Leibniz and Samuel Clarke (1675–1729), a spokesman for Isaac Newton, over the nature of God and His relation to the laws of nature. In a series of five letters to Caroline, Princess of Wales, Leibniz argued that Newton's position that God is present everywhere in the universe and is actively involved in managing it assumes that God's work was imperfect and required His constant intervention to correct it. Clarke's response was that Leibniz was imposing restrictions on God's will and abilities.

The Creation and Age of the Earth

Biblical Chronology

There was a great deal of interest in the sixteenth century in reforming the Julian calendar to have it coincide with the actual length of the year and to bring the religious events of the year in better conformity with the proper times of the year. Astronomical observations were important for that purpose and were utilized in the reform of the calendar bearing his name by Pope Gregory VIII in 1582. There was also interest in dating events cited in the Bible and in determining the precise age of the Earth. Investigations into biblical chronology were undertaken by several, who estimated the ages of individuals and generations, as well as utilizing astronomical phenomena mentioned in the Bible. Joseph Scaliger (1540–1609), in a work published in 1583, using data from Copernican astronomical tables and events mentioned in the Bible, and in pagan accounts, arrived at a date for the Creation of a little more than 5,500 years before his time.

Slight variations in the exact date of Creation were advanced in the seventeenth century. Johannes Kepler, preoccupied with biblical chronology for several years, concluded in his *Rudolphine Tables* of 1627 that the proper date was 3983 B.C.E. Another biblical chronologist, who published his work the same year as Kepler, Denis Petau

(1583–1652) came up with the same year for the Creation as Kepler had but, with greater precision, gave the time as October 27, forty-two seconds after 9:05 AM. Isaac Newton would later amend Petau's date by adding five years. Kepler and others were also interested in verifying the actual year of the birth of Jesus by analyzing astronomical references in the Bible. Kepler came to the conclusion that Jesus was born four or five years earlier than had been thought, a conclusion generally accepted today, unlike the dates given for the origin of the world.

After more than four decades of investigation, James Ussher (1581–1656), Archbishop of Armagh in Ireland, utilizing the regnal dates of rulers mentioned in the Hebrew Bible and links to non-scriptural sources, arrived at a date for the creation of the world a few years earlier than those of his predecessors. In his results, published in 1650 and 1654, he asserted that the Creation took place on Sunday, October 23, 4004 B.C.E., after God had created the initial unformed matter at about 6:00 PM on the previous day. When the Church of England accepted that date as authoritative, it was included in the King James version of the Bible in the eighteenth century.

Geological Analyses and Biblical References

In the seventeenth century there was growing interest in the structure of the Earth and its history since the Creation. Descartes provided an early example of efforts to apply the mechanical philosophy to the subject. He suggested how the Earth had come to be formed from the swirling vortex about the Sun, and that the Earth had layers, which were formed in certain ways by the particles composing it. Subsequent efforts at explaining features of the Earth and its history in terms of the mechanical philosophy were expressed in a manner consistent with references in the Bible. Several theories of the Earth paid a good deal of attention to the biblical Deluge. One held that the layers of the Earth's crust were laid down after the Flood, in a sequence reflecting the specific gravities of the matter composing the layers. The Flood was also responsible for the fossils found in the Earth's crust. Thomas Burnet (c. 1635–1715), in his *Telluris theoria sacra* (Sacred Theory of the Earth), published in several parts from 1681 to 1702, was influential in promoting the idea that the Earth had a physical history. He proposed six stages in the history of the Earth that included references to the Garden of Eden, Noah's flood, the future destruction of the Earth by a great conflagration, and a return to Paradise with the second coming of Christ. Before the Flood, the surface of the Earth was smooth and without mountains or oceans. Afterward there were changes reflecting the terrestrial features with which we are familiar. At the end of the final stage the Earth will become a bright star. Burnet was vigorously attacked both for violating Scripture and for neglecting to provide explanations based on mechanical philosophy.

One of Burnet's defenders was William Whiston (1667–1752), whose own theory, published in his *New Theory of the Earth* (1696), on the creation of the Flood by the passing of a comet near the Earth, found favor with Newton. The very great influence of Newton, after the publication of his *Principia*, led some, including Whiston, to propose theories of the creation of the Earth utilizing principles of Newtonian cosmology. Whiston's theory was that the opening verse of *Genesis* describes two distinct divine actions: the creation of the chaos that would become the heavens, and a subsequent decision to create the Earth. The latter was done by having a comet moving about the Sun in an eccentric orbit become the Earth, and the chaos vanished. Earth moved in a circular orbit about the Sun and was without poles, seasons, or rotation. Another comet struck the Earth, making it revolve at an angle to the plane of its orbit and bringing water up from the interior of the Earth. Whiston was attacked and defended, as Burnet had been, but his works were widely read and reprinted many times.

During this period there were also efforts to gain knowledge about the history and future of the Earth by close observations of changes on its surface. Edmond Halley (1656–1743) proposed that the age of the Earth might be determined by investigations and measurements carried out over many years involving silt movement in rivers and streams and the degree to which saltiness grew in the seas and saline lakes. He estimated the age of the Earth as somewhat more than the few thousand years estimated by Archbishop Ussher and others, but he contended that the Earth was certainly not eternal. Here too were developments where discoveries or hypotheses about the natural world were seen by some clerics to contradict passages in Scripture. Halley was denied appointment to a university position in 1691 because of rumors that he believed in the eternity of the world.

Physico-theology

In the latter part of the seventeenth century there were efforts, particularly in England, to demonstrate the wisdom and beneficence of God by the results achieved through the experimental philosophy. Many works were written to show how the new discoveries of natural philosophy were evidence of intelligent design on the part of the Creator. Such works continued to appear after every new scientific discovery until well into the nineteenth century and continue today, although to a lesser degree.

Unorthodox Religious Opinions

Accusations of heresy were not limited to the Catholic part of Europe. It is doubtful that any of the natural philosophers associated with the Scientific Revolution were atheists, although accusations of atheism were not uncommon. The philosopher Thomas Hobbes (1588–1679) was frequently accused of being an atheist. Influenced to some degree by Descartes, Hobbes differed from him, and from almost everyone else, by having God as a material entity, but in a unique manner appropriate to His divinity. He was not persecuted for his opinion, because of the favor of King Charles II of England. Persecution for unorthodox religious belief took different forms. Johannes Kepler, a devout Christian, was refused Communion by the pastor of his Lutheran church, for Kepler's disagreement with what was at the time an aspect of Lutheran belief, the presence of Christ everywhere in the world. Kepler was forced to go to a neighboring town for its service. Edmond Halley, in addition to being passed over for an academic appointment, had his ode to Newton in the first edition of Newton's *Principia* significantly modified by others in its second and third editions to eliminate phrases that might be construed as representing unorthodox opinions. William Whiston, who had been appointed by Newton as an assistant, and succeeded Newton in his professorship of mathematics, was removed from his post after writing several tracts raising questions about the Trinity. Newton did not come to Whiston's help at all, even though Newton clearly denied the Trinity, a fact he kept secret his entire life.

Boyle and the Bentley Lectures

Robert Boyle had strongly supported a number of religious activities throughout his life, such as paying for translations of the Bible, encouraging missionary work, and writing theological treatises. He left a sum of money in his will to provide a series of annual lectures demonstrating that the achievements of natural philosophy tended to prove the existence of God by showing how the nature of the natural world in its intricacy and apparent design could only be explained by the existence of an omniscient and omnipotent Creator. The first to give a series of Boyle lectures was Richard Bentley (1662–1742), who exchanged four letters with Newton to become familiar enough with his ideas to enable him to deal with them effectively in his lectures. Bentley's lectures, entitled *A Confutation of Atheism from the Origin and Frame of the World*, were given in 1692 and published the following year. They drew heavily on Newton's concepts of matter, his laws of motion, and his theory of universal gravitation. Bentley's lectures became a model for arguments from design as proofs for the existence of God in subsequent centuries.

Summary

The idea originating in the Enlightenment of a warfare between science and religion throughout history can receive no support from the attitudes toward religion held by natural philosophers during the Scientific Revolution. Throughout the Early Modern period religious beliefs were intertwined with new concepts about how the world worked. Despite the Protestant Reformation and the Catholic Counter-Reformation, and the wars and persecutions they gave rise to, communication and collaboration between natural philosophers of different religious persuasions continued to take place. Fears that the new ideas threatened the truths of Revelation, chiefly by the Copernican theory, led the Catholic Church to ban them as heretical and to forbid the teaching of those ideas. Nevertheless, by the end of the seventeenth century most Catholic intellectuals accepted them. Despite his condemnation, Galileo remained an international scientific star throughout Europe. The mechanical philosophy, replacing traditional ideas about how to gain knowledge, was adapted to provide a role for God in a lawlike universe. New scientific discoveries came to be presented as evidence for the existence of a wise, omnipotent, and beneficent God.

CHAPTER 7

INFLUENCE OF THE SCIENTIFIC REVOLUTION

The modern world has been shaped by many factors, including the growth of science. In the wake of the Scientific Revolution, the development of science over the past few centuries has had significant effects on economic, political, and cultural life. Scientific ideas and practices are known to a much wider audience than was the case before the Scientific Revolution. The sciences are now learned, practiced, and supported quite differently than they were in the seventeenth century. Today's scientific institutions are both similar to and different from those that evolved during that century. Yet there can be little doubt that the results of the employment of experimentation, mathematics, precise measurement, and new instruments had powerful effects on the subsequent development of science and on the ways we work, live, and think.

The Enlightenment

In the eighteenth century the movement known as the Enlightenment had at its core a belief that knowledge of the natural world had progressed and would continue to do so. This progress was made possible, it was thought, through the investigation by rational means of various aspects of the world around us. Events not easily explained should not be attributed to miracles, divine intervention, or magic, but should be investigated by the use of reason and, where possible, by close and comparative observations and experiments. Many of the *philosophes*, the intellectuals of France and other countries in the second half of the eighteenth century, saw themselves as living in an enlightened age, an Age of Reason, sharply distinguished from what they called the "dark ages" preceding the Renaissance and the scientific achievements of natural philosophers from Copernicus to Newton. Some intellectuals sharply questioned traditional religious opinions. Belief in deism, in the existence of a God who does not, nor ever did, intervene in the world was common among the *philosophes*. Unitarianians, who denied the Trinity, created their own churches. A few philosophers were agnostics, and a very daring few, atheists. While the Enlightenment emerged in England, and was later centered in Paris, its views were taken up and promoted by thinkers in other parts of Europe.

The Age of Newton

Isaac Newton was considered a man of the Enlightenment. His achievements were so well recognized and acknowledged by the time of his death in 1727 that he was given a state funeral, and was laid to rest in Westminster Abbey, the traditional burial place of Britain's royalty. Alexander Pope wrote,

> Nature and Nature's Laws lay hid in night;
> God said, Let Newton be!—And all was light.

Newton's brilliant achievements in physics, his invention of the calculus, and his experiments and discoveries in optics were seen as models for the investigation of nature and the further development of the sciences. His achievements had been built upon those of his predecessors in the Scientific Revolution, but it was the genius of Newton that laid a foundation for the much more rapid developments and the discovery of new laws in the sciences of mechanics, astronomy, electricity, heat, and chemistry.

The Physical Sciences

Mathematical analysis of all sorts of theoretical problems in mechanics rapidly advanced, but it was in astronomy that notable advances were made in precision and the ability to predict actual planetary and stellar positions. Entirely new discoveries in physical astronomy were made that went beyond the study of the celestial bodies carried out in the seventeenth century. William Herschel (1738–1822), using improved telescopes, with the assistance of his sister Caroline Herschel (1750–1848), discovered a planet, Uranus, the existence of which had been totally unknown before then. He also discovered that the brightness of stars, which had been thought to depend on their distances from us, varied at similar distances, after finding stars of different brightnesses that revolved about one another. The nature of astronomical investigation was further enlarged by Herschel in his efforts to learn the shape of the universe by mapping the distribution of stars in our galaxy.

Electricity became the leading experimental science with the invention of the Leyden jar in 1746, enabling the creation of very large electrical charges. The discoveries of electrical attraction and repulsion, that electricity could be conducted over significant distances by various means, and that lightning was an electrical discharge stimulated a great many further experiments and resulted in a substantial growth of knowledge. By the end of the century, aspects of electrical phenomena had begun to be quantified. The most notable example was the determination by Charles Augustin Coulomb (1736–1806) in 1785 and 1787 that the force of attraction between opposite electrical charges and of repulsion between similar charges varies as the inverse-square of the distance between them.

Chemistry became a wholly new science in the eighteenth century through a series of experiments that added to the knowledge of chemical processes gained by alchemists and physicians in earlier centuries. The discovery that various chemicals, in an analogy with the physical states of water as solid, liquid, and gaseous, could also have different states depending on the application of heat, was an important stage in the process. Experiments also revealed that gases of various kinds, which we now designate as carbon dioxide, nitrogen, hydrogen, and oxygen, were present in the atmosphere, each with unique properties. The final step in the creation of the new science of chemistry was the discovery through experiment and measurement by Antoine-Laurent Lavoisier (1743–1794) of the role of oxygen in combustion, its combination with certain metals, and its capability of being removed from metals under proper conditions. Water was shown to be a compound of hydrogen and oxygen, and elements and compounds were distinguished in a wholly new and rational manner, providing a foundation for the further development of chemistry.

The Life Sciences

Aspects of the mechanical philosophy applied to the world of living things was coming to be seen as inadequate in the study of natural history and physiology during the eighteenth century. Natural history included the descriptive sciences such as anatomy and botany, as well as the classification of life forms; physiology dealt with how animate beings functioned. Carl Linnaeus (1707–1778) created a classification system for plants based on the recently discovered sexuality of plants and the details of their structures. He developed the binomial system of classification with the use of two Latin names, the genus and species of the organism. In the study of living things, the increased knowledge of chemistry was vital. Botanists learned that the leaves of plants absorb carbon dioxide and emit oxygen through sunlight falling on them, and that the nutrition of plants can be absorbed from air and soil. New observations on the generation, growth, and regeneration of bodily parts in plants and animals led to questioning the adequacy of approaches characteristic of the mechanical philosophy in such investigations. The discovery of laws and mathematical relationships in those and similar areas would have to wait for a later time.

Creation of the Social Sciences

The successes of the physical sciences encouraged the *philosophes* to believe that laws governing the behavior of individuals and social groups could also be found, to the benefit of humankind. Economics, with its mathematical basis, was a likely candidate, and efforts were undertaken to determine means for the improvement of the economic conditions of nations. The outstanding effort was Adam Smith's *Wealth of Nations* (1776). The creation of a science of political life was pursued by several *philosophes*, including Voltaire and Montesquieu, whose *Spirit of the Laws* (1748) was very influential. Investigations were conducted into the social evolution of human beings, such as by Jean-Jacques Rousseau in his *Discourse on the Origin of Inequality among Men* (1750), although it challenged the belief that the progress of science had improved the moral condition of humankind. It may, however, be seen as the beginning of anthropological inquiry through the issues it raised. Efforts at the creation of a science of human nature and psychology were also pursued. The criterion of reason that was applied to the social world had profound political consequences. The nature of the social order and of the class structure of society began to be questioned. Social and political crises and ideas about a need for new and rationally constructed governments would lead to revolutions replacing monarchical governments and to the creation of republics and democracies.

Popularization of Science

Knowledge of the new scientific ideas was perceived as a necessary part of the culture of the upper and middle classes. Some entrepreneurs earned a livelihood by giving public scientific lectures and demonstrations. Books were published in a number of European languages explaining the new scientific discoveries in terms intelligible to a lay audience. The goal of explaining all scientific knowledge, showing the interrelationship of its branches, as well as discussing issues in philosophy and social theory, was carried out in the *Encyclopédie* under the editorship of Denis Diderot (1713–1784) and Jean le Rond d'Alembert (1717–1783). It was published in twenty-eight large and beautifully illustrated volumes from 1752 to 1772. The encyclopedia was based on a proposal by Francis Bacon more than a century earlier and included articles on the most advanced technologies in manufacturing, the crafts, and trades. It reflected the scientific and social aims of the *philosophes* and was seen as a foundation for the future growth of knowledge.

The Organization and Structure of Science

Science as a Profession

A small number of natural philosophers in the seventeenth century were employed by universities and the academies of sciences in Europe or were paid salaries by patrons. Most natural philosophers practiced their sciences as hobbies or activities incidental to their primary occupations, chiefly as physicians or members of the clergy. By the nineteenth century, scientists began to constitute a distinct profession, whose members came from various segments of society. Becoming a scientist required specialized training at a university, judgment by one's peers, and a full-time commitment to one's scientific work. The term *natural philosophy* was replaced by *science* and by new names for traditional sciences, now grown larger in scope, as well as for new sciences. Philosophy became a separate and distinct discipline from science; it continued to pursue its traditional inquiries, other than the ways in which the natural world works. The new sciences began to find a place in university curricula. Universities came to be thought of as institutions, not only for passing on the learning of the past, but where new discoveries were to be made and scientists trained.

The Fission and Fusion of Scientific Disciplines

With the growth in tempo of the progress of scientific knowledge, traditional sciences began to split into separate and distinct sciences or sub-sciences. Astronomy added the study of the stars, their composition and distribution, to the study of the solar system. Physics added to mechanics the specialties of electricity, magnetism, and thermodynamics. Chemistry, divorced from alchemy, divided into inorganic and organic branches. The study of the Earth's surface branched into geology, oceanography, and the study of fossils. Investigation of the forms and nature of living things, christened "biology" in the early nineteenth century, came to include taxonomy, anatomy, physiology, evolution, genetics, and a host of specialties involving the variety of different life forms and their processes. At the same time branches of what had been distinct sciences merged to become new ones, among them electrochemistry, thermodynamics, electrodynamics, and biochemistry. They soon developed their own subdivisions, as did wholly new areas of investigation, undreamed of during the Scientific Revolution, such as evolution. As the sciences grew, a similar branching and merging of disciplines took place among the societies for the exchange and advancement of scientific ideas. The Royal Society of London and the Royal Academy of Paris were models for the establishment of similar societies in Prussia, Russia, the United States, and a number of nations in

Europe and around the world. By the nineteenth century there were sometimes several such organizations in a single country.

Scientific Education

The continued growth of science and its increasing role as an important component of business and government led to the incorporation of science as an essential part of school curricula from elementary grades through the university. As institutions for the training of engineers were created, beginning at the end of the eighteenth century, and as universities subsequently added engineering departments, courses in mathematics and various sciences became a fundamental part of such training. The degree of Doctor of Philosophy, created during the Middle Ages, now had branches specialized in the sciences and was a requirement for employment as a scientist.

Scientific ideas were presented to a wider public in works in all the European languages. Popular lectures on scientific subjects appealed to members of the nobility and the middle classes, who attended in large numbers. By the late eighteenth century Britain's institutions to provide evening classes for working people to improve their job skills and opportunities included courses in mathematics and the sciences. Museums, planetariums, zoos, aquariums, botanical gardens, and libraries were founded, sometimes originating from private collections, and were made available to the public. Scientific ideas and references to science also began to find their way into literature during the Scientific Revolution. The process expanded considerably in later years, with scientific concepts expressed in poetry, novels, plays, and science fiction.

The Support of Science

Shortly after the Scientific Revolution scientists were employed by governments to a limited degree to assist with the granting of patents and the improvement of navigation, exploration, and the mapping of territories. In the course of World War I governments came to realize that scientists and engineers were important for the realization of their military objectives. Agencies were established and maintained after that war, and scientific research was supported to a limited degree. World

War II made a profound difference in governmental support for scientific research. Government laboratories and research facilities were established and agencies created to fund research and the education of students intending to become scientists.

Two other principal locations for the conduct of scientific research were industry and the universities. The first industrial scientific laboratory was created about the middle of the nineteenth century, when it became clear to chemical companies in Germany that chemists could create new and marketable compounds. It was soon followed by the establishment of scientific laboratories in a number of industries to improve existing products and to create new ones. Scientists on the faculties of universities were expected to advance scientific knowledge in their fields of expertise. Support for those activities frequently came from industry and government.

The Ways We Live and Think

Science, Technology, and the Economy

The appearance of *homo sapiens* many millennia ago was accompanied by the ability to craft improvements in shelter, protection from the elements, and the acquisition of food, as well as to continue to build upon those achievements in succeeding generations. For most of history this ability bore little relationship to what became known in ancient Greece as natural philosophy. That situation was profoundly altered after the Scientific Revolution. Although the Industrial Revolution in the eighteenth and early nineteenth centuries did not owe its beginnings and early years to the growth of science, it nevertheless received substantial impetus in the nineteenth and twentieth centuries from developments in electricity, chemistry, and thermodynamics, the foundations of which were laid in the development of scientific methodology during the Scientific Revolution. The further development of those and other sciences led to significant improvements in technology. The steam engine was replaced by electric and gasoline engines, ice and fans by refrigerators and air conditioners. The generation and transmission of electricity also brought the telegraph, the telephone, and the various means of wireless communication so much a part of life today. Developments in chemistry led to the creation of a host of new materials, increased food supplies, improved health, and increased longevity. The ways we live, work, travel, communicate, and entertain ourselves have been profoundly shaped by the application of science to technology.

Government and Politics

The new and more effective weapons, along with scientific-technical improvements in vessels and navigation, made possible the creation of the colonial empires of the nineteenth century. Today the former colonies aim to improve their societies by adopting the scientific and science-based techniques of their former rulers. Improvements in means of transportation and in explosives through science-based technology have changed the character of war and made facilities for the manufacture of weapons prime targets. The substantial expenditures by governments on scientific research have become a political issue, resulting in debates and decisions about the amounts and distribution of funds among competing research entities. International scientific cooperation, along with competition, common during the Scientific Revolution, continues today.

Challenges to Ranking and Worthiness in Various Categories

Ancient and medieval thinkers tended to attach varying degrees of value and rank to the components of different classification systems: people, living things, metals, the sciences. In philosophy, metaphysics was superior to physics, which in turn was superior to mathematics. Gold ranked higher than silver, ants were better than worms. With the growth of the mechanical philosophy, these rankings tended to become irrelevant. Matter was matter, no part of which was more noble than another. This elimination of the relative values of objects did not apply at first to humans. Despite the persistence of racial, ethnic, national, and religious biases to this day, beginning in the late eighteenth century scientists began to question the existence of traditional physical and intellectual distinctions determining the relative worth and abilities of different groups of human beings.

Science and Religious Modifications

Beginning in the late seventeenth century, a medieval concept intended to demonstrate the existence of God, the argument from design, began to be applied to scientific discoveries. As one complexity after another in the structure and organization of the world was discovered, each was seen by some as evidence of creation by an omniscient and omnipotent intelligence. The initial resistance by some in the early nineteenth century to geological evidence of the great age of the Earth faded as evidence accumulated. In the second half of that century, Darwinian evolution, based on the extended age of the Earth, was sharply resisted, since one of its central features was the role of chance. Such objections were eventually overcome through figurative and metaphorical readings of certain biblical passages and through interpretations of the evolutionary process as having been directed toward the creation of human beings. In the course of time, as science advanced, religious ideas could no longer be said to shape science. Scientific developments appeared, instead, to bring with them some modifications to religious beliefs.

Summary

The nature of science in the Early Modern period was revolutionary because it broke decisively with traditional ideas and ways of doing science that had changed only slightly since ancient times. Moreover, its revolutionary nature was characterized by its ability to increase the tempo in the growth of knowledge and the creation of new sciences in later times. The new principles of scientific investigation established during the Scientific Revolution brought substantial advances in the way we live through the application of science to existing technologies and through the creation of new ones. The broadening of scientific knowledge to the population at large has had important effects on the way the operations of nature are seen, as well as on religious beliefs.

BIOGRAPHIES

Francis Bacon (1561–1626)

A philosopher, essayist, statesman, and lawyer, Francis Bacon attained the rank of Lord Chancellor, the highest legal official of the English government, but he was removed from office in 1621 for taking bribes.

Much of his writing was concerned with the uses of knowledge both for the promotion of national interests and for the advancement of our knowledge of nature. Among his goals was the reform of natural philosophy by exposing the errors in thinking that held back that advancement and promoting practices and ideas leading to new knowledge. His ideas were put forward in their most advanced form in his uncompleted and extensive collection of works, written in Latin, titled *Instauratia magna* (The Great Instauration), 1620–1626.

Bacon attached a significant amount of weight to history in general, to the collection of facts in natural history and technology, and to experimentation. He saw the development of technology as shaping historical change, citing the importance of the invention of printing, gunpowder, and the compass (all of which had been invented in China) in the development of civilization. As a firm believer in progress Bacon heaped scorn on traditional natural philosophy. Progress in the advancement of knowledge and in improvement in the conditions of life could best be attained by the use of rational practices and modes of organization in the pursuit of knowledge.

In his best-known and important work, *Novum organum* (A New Instrument), Bacon wrote a critique of contemporaneous philosophical systems and laid out the sources of four kinds of illusions or faulty ways of thinking. He went on to provide an example of his insistence on the importance of collecting as many facts as possible in an analysis of heat, concluding, contrary to common belief, that it was a substance, that heat arose from motion. The work also described experiments of different kinds and how to perform experiments in the

Courtesy **Whipple Museum of the History of Science,**
Wh.3594, University of Cambridge.

best possible fashion; it also distinguished some experiments as more
important than others.

In subsequent works he provided other examples of his "natural
histories," collections of as many facts as possible about various phenomena as foundations upon which natural philosophers could build
principles characteristic of those phenomena. One of these concerned
the weather. Another was a collection, written in English, of a thousand experiments and observations, both ancient and modern, which
became his most popular work during the seventeenth century. His
New Atlantis was a work of fiction in which he described an organiza-

tion that employed Baconian methods to learn new things about the operations of nature. It was a collaborative enterprise that greatly enlarged knowledge, thereby increasing the powers of humanity as a whole. In later years English natural philosophers saw Bacon's vision as essential to their work and attempted to model the Royal Society for the Advancement of Knowledge upon it.

Bacon was familiar with the ideas not only of the ancients but also of the moderns. He put forward a speculative system containing elements from a number of other students of nature. For Bacon the universe was finite, geocentric, and completely filled with matter, and therefore his view differed from those of Copernicus, Gilbert, Galileo, and the atomists. His opinion on the various types of matter composing the heavens and the Earth was derived from the ideas of Paracelsus.

Bacon was widely read in the seventeenth century, and those of his works written in English were translated into Latin, the language of learning. His ideas were adopted by a wide variety of individuals from various countries, of differing religious persuasions, and used to support a variety of causes. In general terms his works may be seen as promoting the ideas that natural philosophy must be based on the acquisition of as many facts as possible through observation and experiment, that anyone was capable of contributing to the sciences, and that research must be organized and conducted in a planned and systematic manner. Bacon's ideas were eagerly adopted in the seventeenth century as essential components in the creation of a new natural philosophy.

Robert Boyle (1627–1691)

A son of one of the most wealthy and influential men in Britain, Boyle was educated both in England and on the Continent, where he experienced a religious conversion that shaped the rest of his life. In 1655 he joined a group of natural philosophers meeting at the University of Oxford and hired Robert Hooke, a recent graduate of the university, as his assistant. Some of the Oxford group moved to London and, Boyle among them, participated in the founding in 1660 of what would become the Royal Society for the Advancement of Knowledge. Boyle held to the Baconian concept that the development of science led to the improvement of the human condition. He was an important exponent and practitioner of experimentation and of new concepts about the nature of matter, but he remained undecided between the existence of atoms and vacua and Descartes' imperceptible "subtle" matter. He also wrote extensively on theology and on the relationship between science and religion, holding that each lent support to the other.

Much of Boyle's experimental activity was devoted to work with the vacuum pump built for him by Hooke. In a series of experiments in a glass chamber from which air had been partially or almost entirely evacuated, Boyle replicated earlier experiments by Pascal and others with a mercury-filled tube. Others were performed with animals while the chamber was being emptied of air. He demonstrated that in a space devoid of air, a feather and a piece of metal fell at the same rate. Boyle also investigated "the spring of the air," or air pressure; although the inverse relationship between the volume of air and its pressure was also noted by another, this relationship became known as Boyle's Law.

Boyle questioned the standard conceptions of chemical change in his day, notably in his *The Sceptical Chymist* (1661), in which he challenged Aristotelian and Paracelsian ideas and called for greater sophistication in ideas about the nature of matter and on causality. Boyle devoted a great deal of effort to alchemical pursuits, convinced that appropriate procedures could result in the transmutation of base metals into gold.

Boyle's religious activities were an important part of his life. He supported translations of the Bible into languages other than English as well as missionary work in the New World; he also provided in his will for an endowed annual lectureship in support of Christianity. Throughout his varied activities Boyle represented the new natural philosophy in its relationship to religion, in the important role of experimentation in it, and in fostering new ideas about the nature of matter and the changes it undergoes.

Tycho Brahe (1546–1601)

Tycho Brahe was born into a family of Danish nobles and was destined for a career in diplomacy, but he developed a passion for astronomy as a teenager and became the greatest observational astronomer since Antiquity. He also created an influential, geocentric, but non-Ptolemaic astronomical system. The Copernican system was unacceptable to him, as it was to almost all his contemporaries, since it appeared to violate the established principles of physics and of religious belief and could not be verified by observation.

Brahe became convinced as a young man that traditional astronomy needed to be reformed, and that the key to that was the determination of much more precise positions of the stars and planets. His wealth allowed him to begin to acquire the most precise observational instruments capable of being produced at that time. In 1572 he observed a new star, visible for many months, where none had been seen before. The following year he published *De stella nova* (On the New Star), concluding, contrary to the Aristotelian tradition of the unchanging nature of heavens, that it was beyond the sphere of the Moon.

Recognizing that Copernicus' *De revolutionibus* had a number of features that were superior to the Ptolemaic system, Brahe was determined to create an alternative geocentric system embodying some of the advantages of Copernicanism. His goal received substantial support when the King of Denmark donated the island of Hven, not far from Copenhagen, to Tycho. There the astronomer built his observatory, named Uraniborg, where he had assistants, a laboratory, and a printing press.

At Uraniborg, Brahe made a number of important discoveries, notably concerning the Moon. He found that contrary to traditional belief, the Moon does not move uniformly in its orbit, and he developed a better lunar theory than his predecessors. His observation of the comets of 1577 and 1585 also led him to conclude that like the supernova of 1572, they were beyond the sphere of the Moon. He eventually reached the conclusion that the traditional rotating solid spheres moving the planets did not exist. The elimination of the celestial spheres was a necessary requisite for the creation of his own planetary system.

Tycho never worked out the details of his system in a manner comparable to the geometrical models of Ptolemy or Copernicus. In some respects, however, although geocentric, his system accounted in a general way for observations of the planets. About the time Brahe proposed his model, in the 1580s, others were coming up with similar ones. It was geoheliocentric; that is, the Sun revolved about the motionless Earth, while the planets revolved about the Sun in the same order as in the Copernican theory. In general, heliocentric systems accounted in the pre-telescopic age for the observed motions of the planets as had the Ptolemaic or Copernican systems.

When Tycho's patron died, the new King of Denmark revoked his predecessor's gift of the island of Hven, and Tycho had to leave Uraniborg. The Holy Roman Emperor became his new patron and gave him a castle near Prague to pursue his astronomical work. It was there toward the end of the century that Johannes Kepler joined him as his assistant for the remaining year and a half of Tycho's life. Kepler arranged to acquire Tycho's observations and succeeded him in the emperor's patronage, allowing him to achieve his radical transformation of Copernican astronomy. Tycho's astronomy nevertheless gained a substantial following for several years, particularly after another of his assistants, Christian Severin Longomontanus, provided the geometrical details necessary for the Tychonic system.

Nicolaus Copernicus (1473–1543)

Nicolaus Copernicus is chiefly known for his highly significant astronomical achievement, the creation of his heliocentric theory. He was born in Thorn (Torun) in West Prussia, a province of the king of Poland, to a well-to-do merchant family. As a boy, upon the death of his father, he was cared for and aided by an uncle, who subsequently became a bishop and intended his nephew to pursue a career in the Church. From 1491 to 1495 Copernicus attended the University of Krakow, where he took courses in mathematics, astronomy, and astrology. He left without taking a degree. It is not known whether it was his attendance there that awakened his interest in astronomy, but he actively pursued that interest for the rest of his life. After leaving Krakow, Copernicus attended the Universities of Bologna, where he studied canon and civil law from 1496 to 1501. While there he assisted the professor of astronomy and made his first known astronomical observations. During the celebrations by the Church of the new century, Copernicus gave a lecture on astronomy in Rome. Copernicus' uncle arranged an appointment for him as a canon, or member of the administrative body of a cathedral, as well as an additional benefice, providing his nephew with a comfortable lifetime income, but Copernicus continued to pursue his interest in astronomy. From 1501 to 1503 Copernicus studied medicine at the University of Padua, and in 1503 he received a degree in canon law from the University of Ferrara.

He served for a time as an administrative assistant to his uncle, who appears to have intended his nephew for an important ecclesias-

An imaginative portrait from Pierre Gassendi's *N.*
Copernici vita (1654).

tical and political career. Copernicus turned his back on that opportunity to pursue his developing astronomical ideas. In 1509, however, he published a Latin translation of some not very interesting Byzantine Greek verses, which he dedicated to his uncle. By this time he was gaining some reputation as an astronomer.

In 1510 Copernicus, after living with his uncle, moved to Frauenburg (Frombork), where he erected an observation tower, carried out his canonical duties, proposed solutions to the debasement of the currency, and practiced medicine. He also began to develop his heliocentric system, and some time before 1514 circulated an anonymous manuscript describing an early stage of his heliocentric system. It was later named *Commentariolus* (Brief Commentary). He made a number of observations from about 1512 to 1529 and constructed tables necessary for the writing of his masterwork.

In Copernicus' time the foundation of the science of astronomy was based on Aristotelian and Ptolemaic hypotheses, as was much else in the world of learning. The term *hypothesis* was then used to apply to the geometric models used as means of calculating the positions of the celestial bodies as they moved around the sky. Copernicus had mastered the techniques employed by Ptolemy, but he was dissatisfied with several aspects of Ptolemaic astronomy. Each of the planetary models was independent of the others in the sense that a change in the parameters of one did not necessarily affect any of the others. Copernicus seemed to feel that a unified system was required to explain how various aspects of the planetary geometrical models could be seen as flowing from such a unitary system. He then began to work over the next few decades on the manuscript of what would become his epoch-making *De revolutionibus* (On the Revolutions).

Copernicus became increasingly reluctant to publish, since evidence in support of his theory required much more time and attention than he could give to it. He feared being thought foolish for having failed to provide adequate support for this theory. The appearance of Georg Joachim Rheticus to study with him, and the response to Rheticus' *First Account*, convinced Copernicus to have his work printed, which it was in 1547.

René Descartes (1596–1650)

René Descartes was an influential figure in the history of philosophy and in shaping the mechanical philosophy of the seventeenth century. He wrote on the nature and acquisition of knowledge and on mathematics, the nature of matter, mechanics, cosmology, optics, and physiology. Born in southern France to a financially comfortable middle-class family, he attended the Jesuit college of La Flèche, where he obtained an excellent education in mathematics and natural philosophy, among other subjects taught there. As a young man he spent some time studying law at the University of Poitiers. Although he traveled to and briefly lived in various parts of Europe, Descartes spent a good deal of his adult life in the Netherlands, which he entered having volunteered for the army of the Prince of Nassau.

Courtesy Oklahoma University Library.

Shortly after arriving there, he met Isaac Beeckman (1588–1637), who was an important influence on the development of Descartes' thought. Both were interested in mathematical relationships in mechanical processes. Beeckman, however, introduced Descartes to the idea of micro-mechanical processes handled mathematically to explain various aspects of the physical sciences. Over the next few years Descartes devoted a good deal of thought to the most effective means of thinking about philosophical issues. He spent much time writing, experimenting, and corresponding with other natural philosophers.

Descartes concluded early that the goal of natural philosophy should be the determination of clearly and unambiguously known fundamental principles from which the phenomena of nature could be deduced. In his *Discourse on Method and Rules for the Direction of the Mind*, he proposed that a series of linkages between the principles thus deduced would enlarge our knowledge of the natural world. These insights could be obtained by proper means of thinking. He rejected this approach later in his career, when the limitations of this method became apparent to him, since he was not led to his hypotheses and explanations about various aspects of natural philosophy by their derivation from first principles. Descartes was an avid experimenter who spent countless hours dissecting a variety of animals and experiments in a number of physical sciences. He prepared several works on the nature of the universe, light, and physiology, but he decided against publishing them when he learned of Galileo's condemnation in 1633. The works were published posthumously.

Descartes published his first work, *Discourse on Method*, in 1637, along with essays entitled *Geometry*, *Dioptrics*, and *Meteorology*. His major work, *Principles of Philosophy*, was published in 1644 in Latin and translated into French three years later. In that work he explained his notion of a plenary universe, that is, one completely full of matter, in which vacuums did not exist. Along with material substance, equivalent to extension, the universe contained soul, an immortal and immaterial thinking substance. The absence of void spaces meant that the space left by a moving object was immediately filled with matter moving into the space it had left. There were three types of matter for Descartes. The Cartesian universe of indefinite extent is composed of vortices, or whirlpools, with stars at their centers, each surrounded by planets. Vortices are constituted of three kinds of matter particles.

In the development of his dynamics Descartes was very concerned with developing mathematically based laws of nature. In the constant motion that is a feature of the Cartesian universe, he was concerned to develop laws of collision, in which each particle of matter possessed a force dependent on its magnitude, speed, and direction. A particle, or body, tended to persist in its motion and direction unless impeded or altered by collision with another body.

Descartes applied his principles of mechanics to light. Light consisted of a tendency to motion, or a force transmitted by the elementary kind of matter composing the vortices. Reflection was analogous to the bounce of a tennis ball on meeting an unyielding surface. Refraction was explained by the passage of the light force through a surface, thereby altering the extent of the force and its direction. Color was explained by Descartes on the analogy of a rotating tennis ball, whose speed of rotation determined the color. Descartes seems to have independently discovered the sine law of refraction and made an effort to show how it could be derived from his theory of optics.

In his explanation of magnetism Descartes began with William Gilbert's theory of the Earth and the planets as magnets. For Descartes, under certain conditions the particles of the elementary matter filling the spaces between the spherical particles become right- and left-hand screws as they move into a vortex above or below the axes of rotation of the planets. The particles then enter and pass through threaded channels in the planets. The same principle applied to the activities of magnets and electrified bodies.

Descartes' ideas on anatomy, physiology, and medicine were also based on mechanistic principles. Humans were unique beings, combining both mechanistically operating matter and immortal, reasoning souls. He modified William Harvey's theory of the circulation of the blood and Kepler's theory of vision. Involuntary muscle action, Descartes held, was independent of intervention by the soul or brain, unlike the ability of the mind to direct bodily actions.

Descartes was quite influential in promoting the belief that the secrets of nature could best be learned on principles analogous to those governing mechanics. He was widely read and discussed during his lifetime and after. Newton began as a Cartesian, but his *Principia* of 1687 showed Cartesianism to be quite inadequate in the areas of mechanics. In addition, work in optics, physiology, and medicine showed Cartesian ideas to be inadequate in those areas as well. Cartesianism had a longer life in France than in England, however, and continued to be actively studied and written about until well into the eighteenth century. A number of important natural philosophers were influenced by Cartesianism, including Christiaan Huygens and Wilhelm Leibniz.

Galileo Galilei (1564–1642)

Galileo played one of the most important roles in challenging traditional Aristotelian ideas in mechanics and astronomy, in establishing the importance of mathematics and precise measurement for natural philosophy, and in the creation of the Scientific Revolution. He was born in Pisa, and as a boy he studied music with his father, an important musical theorist; Galileo likely helped him with experiments on tones emitted by strings of different lengths and under varying tensions. Galileo studied at the University of Pisa, to which he subse-

From Galileo's *Dialogue Concerning the Two Chief World Systems.*

quently returned as an instructor in mathematics in 1589. He had by then discovered the isochronism of the pendulum and become convinced of the importance of experimentation in the development of natural philosophy.

During his three years on the faculty of the University of Pisa, Galileo had begun to question certain traditional Aristotelian notions regarding motion. Among them were the distinction between bodies moving to or from the center of the Earth and in free fall. He began to question the proposition that the speed of fall was uniform and proportional to the weight of the falling body, and he hypothesized that the speed of descent, although uniform, was proportional, instead, to the specific gravity of the falling body. Dropping bodies of widely differing specific gravities from heights and noting that they landed at approximately the same times necessitated the abandonment of that idea. Additional experiments led him to conclude that the speed with which bodies fell might be accelerating.

In 1592 Galileo was named to the faculty of the University of Padua in the Republic of Venice. He supplemented his salary by teaching students privately and selling his geometric military compass, a device he invented to be used by engineers for precise measurement. During his early years at Padua, Galileo became persuaded of the plausibility of the Copernican system, and he continued his researches on motion. He came to the conclusion that the distances fallen were in accordance with the odd numbers beginning with one; that is, after the second interval of time the total distance traversed equaled four equal units of distance, and after three equal time intervals, the distance traversed equaled nine equal units of distance. He also concluded that a ball given a push on the surface of the Earth would, in the absence of friction or collision, continue indefinitely.

In 1609 Galileo, having heard of the invention of an instrument in the Netherlands that could make distant objects appear nearer, constructed his own, nine-power version, later to be named a telescope. Realizing its advantages for maritime purposes, he donated it to the Republic of Venice, which thereupon tripled his salary and named him to a lifetime position to the university. A few months later he built a twenty-power instrument and turned it to the heavens. He observed that the Moon had mountains, that Jupiter had four moons circling it, and that the Milky Way was composed of innumerable, hitherto unseen, stars, as was the entire sky. In 1610 Galileo published his *Sidereus nuncius* (Sidereal Messenger) describing his observations. The little book created a sensation and made Galileo famous throughout Europe. He had dedicated it to the Duke of Tuscany and named Jupiter's satellites the Medicean Stars. Cosimo II de' Medici then became Galileo's patron, and Galileo moved to Florence, where he resided the rest of his life.

In 1611 Galileo discovered that the planet Venus had phases and therefore revolved about the Sun. He also observed sunspots, further challenging Aristotelian assumptions about the perfect nature of the heavens. The validity of the telescopic observations did not go unchallenged, but the observations were shortly thereafter verified by a number of Jesuits. Aristotelians continued to differ with Galileo's opinions, and some Jesuits became concerned with what were seen as his Copernican inclinations, which seemed to contradict biblical truths.

Denounced to the Inquisition in 1615, Galileo responded by writing a number of letters on the relationship of natural philosophy to theology, which were not published in his lifetime, though they were circulated. He took the position that there was one truth, that certain biblical passages were open to interpretation, and that natural philosophy and religion should be kept separate—and positions in each to be determined by experts in those fields. Theologians should not undertake to criticize positions satisfactorily established in natural philosophy. The Inquisition's theologians, however, decided that heliocentrism was untrue and heretical, and a moving Earth theologically erroneous. In 1616 Galileo was called before Cardinal Bellarmine, the leading theologian of the Holy Office, who presented him with its position. Galileo was told not to teach the Copernican theory on the threat of being accused of heresy, to which he agreed. Copernicus' *On the Revolutions* was placed on the Index of Prohibited Books "until it should be corrected."

In the wake of a debate over three comets that appeared in 1616, Galileo published his *Il saggiatore* (The Assayer), which he dedicated to the recently elected pope, Urban VIII, who, as Cardinal Barberini, had befriended Galileo. The book was a brilliant polemic on appropriate methods in the study of natural philosophy, in which traditional Scholastic methods were attacked and experimental mathematical ones defended. It made clear distinctions between characteristics of bodies such as weight, shapes, sizes, and motions that could be mathematically determined and those properties that were interpreted as qualities such as color, smell, and taste by those who perceived them. The work was very well received, including by the pope, and Galileo was encouraged to complete his manuscript comparing the Ptolemaic and Copernican systems in light of his earlier discoveries. His book, entitled *Dialogue Concerning the Two Chief World Systems—Ptolemaic and Copernican*, was published in 1632. It was written in Italian as conversations over four days among a learned natural philosopher, employing Galileo's discoveries and arguments, an open-minded individual, and one who employed traditional Aristotelian arguments in response to the Galileian ones. On the fourth "day" of the conversations, arguments were presented in favor of the tides as caused by the motions of the Earth. These were counterbalanced by the argument of the Aristotelians in the form given by Cardinal Bellarmine in 1616 that if proof of the Earth's motion were indeed demonstrated, interpretations of biblical passages would have to be altered.

A few months after its publication the pope became angered and, for reasons that are not entirely clear, ordered Galileo to be brought before the Inquisition for violating the order of 1616. After several weeks Galileo was found guilty in 1633 of strong suspicion of heresy, forced to abjure belief in the Copernican theory, and confined to house arrest near Florence for the remainder of his life. His *Dialogue* was banned.

Galileo's fame throughout Europe persisted, and he frequently received visitors, two of whom remained to work with him on scientific matters. He decided to publish the results of his work on mechanics, and he did so in the Netherlands in 1638. His *Dialogues on Two New Sciences* was devoted to his experiments and discoveries on falling bodies and projectiles, the strength of materials, harmonics, and speculations on the nature of matter and other unresolved problems. After his death in 1642 a number of Galileo's followers kept his mathematical experimental tradition alive and made new discoveries based on experimentation.

Pierre Gassendi (1592–1655)

Gassendi was born in a small town in southern France, and he prepared for the priesthood by studying theology and Aristotelian natural philosophy. He was a professor of philosophy at one institution and subsequently professor of mathematics at another. He was a member of that small group in the early seventeenth century determined to find alternatives to traditional Aristotelian approaches to the study of nature, and he kept fully abreast of the novel ideas of his contemporaries. He was instrumental in bringing the ancient atomistic theory of Epicurus (341–270 B.C.E.) as a component of European natural philosophy, where it had significant influence. Elements of Epicurean philosophy, however, contradicted certain aspects of Christian theology, and Gassendi modified some of its components to make it more palatable to his contemporaries.

Epicurus had assumed multiple material, divine entities, a plurality of worlds, creation of our eternal, infinite universe by chance out of nothing, a random motion of atoms, a lack of divine intervention, and the mortality of the human soul. These were replaced by traditional Christian components: creation of the universe by an omniscient and omnipotent God, who exercised providential care over its functions, and the immateriality and immortality of souls. The world, according to Gassendi, is composed of a finite number of atoms moving within void space, and it provides evidence of design.

The atomic theory, along with Descartes' theory of matter, which denied the existence of void spaces, became essential ingredients of the mechanical philosophy. The particulate nature of matter in both cases was used to account for the great variety of qualities in the objects of our world. The *atom*, a term taken from the Greek, meaning indivisible, in Gassendi's version also could not be divided, but possessed weight, size, shape, and solidity. The qualities we perceive in matter could be explained by the arrangements and motions of the the atoms composing them.

Gassendi investigated and wrote on all aspects of natural philosophy, including the most effective methodology, astronomy, physics, geology, meteorology, physiology, and botany. He adopted Copernicanism at first, but after the condemnation of Galileo in 1633, he proposed the Tychonian geoheliocentric system, but without a great deal of conviction. His posthumously published *Syntagma philosophicum* (The System of Philosophy) in 1658, which contained some works unpublished during his lifetime, continued to be of interest to natural philosophers during the century.

William Gilbert (1544–1603)

Gilbert was a well-known physician in England who at the height of his career was physician to Queen Elizabeth. He published one work in his lifetime—*On the Magnet, Magnetic Bodies, and on the Great Terrestrial Magnet* (1600)—that had significant influence in subsequent decades. Its importance lay in its use of observation and experimentation to gain new knowledge about nature, its new information about magnetism, and its partial support of the Copernican theory. Additional writings, published a half century after his death, revealed his acceptance of a full Copernicanism.

Gilbert's starting-point was his rejection of Aristotelian methods and the conception of the Earth as inert and imperfect in contrast to the perfection of the heavens. He made spherical lodestones, which he called "little Earths" and, in a series of experiments, concluded that they naturally rotated. Utilizing the observations of seamen made with the compass, he concluded that the Earth was a magnet and rotated just as his lodestones did. Gilbert was also interested in the comparison of lodestones with amber, which under friction exhibited what he termed electricity. He thought that electrical and magnetic effects were different in nature, although electrified bodies and magnets both attracted particular objects to themselves.

Gilbert's book was divided into sections dealing with various aspects of magnetic phenomena. Among them was the behavior of the compass needle in pointing approximately to the North Pole. Another dealt with vertical dip and its variation on different parts of the Earth. He claimed to have duplicated variations from the North Pole with terrellae modeled on the Earth, and he ascribed those variations to different configurations of the surface of the Earth in different regions. This hypothesis was useful in navigation and for confirmation of the Earth as a magnet. Gilbert's experimental philosophy may have been the result of his collaboration with navigators and mathematicians, which led him to emphasize the importance of empiricism and practical applications.

William Harvey (1578–1657)

Harvey's work on the circulation of the blood was recognized in his lifetime as a turning-point in physiology and medicine. He also worked and wrote on the fertilization and development of egg-laying animals and mammals. After obtaining his B.A. at Cambridge, Harvey enrolled in 1600 in the medical school at the University of Padua, the leading medical school in Europe and a center for anatomical research. Upon his return to England he joined and then held a number of offices in the London College of Physicians, which was both a learned society and a trade organization, where he lectured from time to time on anatomical subjects. He went on to serve as a royal physician and then as chief physician to King Charles I.

While Galen's long-accepted teachings on anatomy were being questioned and partially overturned in the sixteenth century, his views

From Fielding H. Garrison, *An Introduction to the History of Medicine* (1921).

on physiological processes were still accepted. Among them was the process by which ingested food is converted into blood by passing from the stomach to the liver, from which it passes to the vena cava and its branches to be absorbed by various parts of the body. Blood was considered the essential component in the functioning of living organisms, but there was among Harvey's contemporaries a variety of opinions on what the heart is actually doing in the course of a heartbeat. Familiar with the discovery of the movement of venous blood from the heart to the lungs, where it became brighter and was returned to the heart, Harvey began to investigate in detail how the heart functions in moving blood to the lungs and back to the heart and arteries.

The common view was that in a heartbeat the heart dilates, sucking blood from the vena cava into the left ventricle and absorbing air from the lungs, ventilating the heart. By 1616, however, after experiments with cold-blooded animals and dying mammals and following demonstrations that the valves in the veins allow blood to flow only to the heart, Harvey concluded that the heart contracts with a heartbeat, sending blood from both its ventricles and dilating the arteries. The heart then relaxes and is refilled with blood from the vena cava and pulmonary veins. It was only after a few years that Harvey began to turn his attention to the continuous sequence of heartbeats and determined that it was the same blood issuing from and returning to the heart, since there is not enough blood in the body for the process to continue with fresh blood each time. He thus came to the conclusion that the blood leaves the heart through the arteries, passes around the body in the course of about half an hour, returning to the heart through the veins. The passage of blood from successively smaller arteries to the veins could not yet be seen; nonetheless Harvey assumed that it did so through invisible passages.

In his work *Exercises on the Movement of the Heart and Blood in Animals* (1628) Harvey noted that in cases of severe hemorrhage, all the blood leaves the body in half an hour. Using ligatures, he demonstrated that the blood flows from the heart in the arteries, and that the valves in the veins permit the blood to flow only toward the heart.

In his later work Harvey devoted his attention to problems of generation in animals. His *Exercises on the Generation of Animals* (1651) challenged notions on the nature of fertilization that held it to be the result in viviparous animals of a combination of semen and blood. Harvey held otherwise, citing his own observations that there is no evidence of blood as a factor in fertilization, and an egg is the source of generation in both viviparous and oviparous animals. He concluded with the expression *ex ovo omnia* (all things come from an egg).

Robert Hooke (1635–1703)

One of the leading experimenters of his age, Hooke worked in a number of areas. Shortly after his graduation from Oxford University he was hired by Robert Boyle as an assistant in his experiments. Upon the founding of the Royal Society in London, he was hired as its curator of experiments, charged with performing experiments for its members at their weekly meetings. In the 1660s he built a vacuum pump for Boyle, and with it they performed a variety of experiments in a glass chamber from which the air had been evacuated. Among the discoveries made with the pump was the inverse proportion between the volume and pressure of the air. He also gave lectures in mechanics and geometry to the Royal Society. In 1677 Hooke was appointed secretary of the society, becoming responsible for a short time for the publication of its journal.

He was a strong believer in and forceful promoter of the mechanical philosophy, holding that all effects could be explained by the motion and configuration of the particles of which matter was composed. Because of his interest in springs, increasingly used in watches, he discovered was what is known as Hooke's Law, that the power of a spring is proportional to its tension. Among Hooke's inventions was the universal joint, the clock-driven telescope, and an iris diaphragm for telescopes.

Hooke theorized about a number of phenomena, including optics and gravity. He came into conflict with Isaac Newton over matters in those two areas. Hooke's theory about the nature of light and colors was advanced in 1665. He held that red and blue are primary colors, and that the other colors are dilutions of them. When refracted, light, a series of pulses, comes in contact with another medium; colors arise from a difference between the "orbicular" pulses of the light striking the new medium and the pulses of the matter of the medium entered. This theory would be challenged by Newton in his experiments with a prism.

Hooke built microscopes and increased their ability to represent invisible objects accurately by adding additional light through use of an attached mirror to focus more light on them. He made numerous microscopic observations, publishing his results in his *Micrographia* (1665).

In the 1670s Hooke proposed to the Royal Society that the planets were kept in their orbits by an inertial tendency to fly off in the direction of their orbital motion, counteracted by an inverse-square centripetal movement toward the Sun. This notion subsequently came to the attention of Newton, who was the only one at the time with the mathematical ability to prove that assumption and to derive Kepler's planetary laws from them.

After the London Fire of 1666, Hooke helped design several buildings, some designed entirely by himself.

He also did important work in geology, postulating that there were changes in the relationship of land to water on the Earth. Land masses might successively be eroding and emerging from the sea, and these changes would account for the appearance of fossils some distance from the sea.

Christiaan Huygens (1629–1695)

Huygens was influential in seventeenth-century natural philosophy for his work on mathematics, mechanics, optics, astronomy, and pneumatics and his invention of the pendulum clock. Educated at the University of Leiden, he became a devotee of the mechanical philosophy and was influenced by the work of Galileo and Descartes. He was elected as the first foreign fellow of the Royal Society of London, and he was invited by King Louis XIV of France to lead the Royal Academy of Sciences in Paris.

In mathematics Huygens addressed questions concerning more effective ways of approximating pi; the nature of a catenary curve, which is formed by a hanging chain, each end suspended at equal heights; and probability. In his work on motion he held that there was no absolute frame of reference, and that all motion was relative. He showed that bodies falling along a cycloidal path fell equal distances in equal times, and that the centrifugal force of a body in circular motion, as in a whirling sling, is proportional to the square of its velocity and inversely proportional to its radius. His work on the cycloid and its isochronism led to his invention of an improved pendulum clock in 1656; its details were published the following year and in 1673. The clock was accurate to within a few seconds in the course of a day. He made improvements on and observations with a number of inventions: the pendulum clock, the vacuum pump, the microscope, and a machine for grinding lenses.

Among Huygens' telescopic discoveries were Saturn's largest moon, Titan, and the recognition that what had been thought to be two other moons of Saturn were its rings. In optics Huygens proposed that the phenomenon of double refraction seen in some substances was caused by light traveling in waves, with each point on a wave front the source of successive weaker waves. The newer wave front was tangent to all the secondary waves. He also held that the speed of light is finite. This hypothesis was published in his *Treatise on Light* (1690).

Johannes Kepler (1571–1630)

Kepler attended the University of Tübingen, preparing himself to become a Lutheran minister. Michael Maestlin (1550–1631), a professor at the university, persuaded him to accept the Copernican theory. Because of some differences with Lutheran doctrine, Kepler was denied a pulpit. He taught instead at a secondary school and pursued his interest in astronomy and in the true structure of the universe. In an effort to unite his interests in religion, harmonics, and mathematical astronomy, he proposed, contrary to Copernicus, that planetary orbits should be calculated from the center of the Sun, rather than the cen-

Courtesy University of Oklahoma Library.

ter of the Earth's orbit. Convinced on religious grounds that the universe must be spherical, he held that the Trinity was represented by the circumference, center, and intervening space. He further proposed that the reason for the relative distances from the Sun of the planets, as determined by Copernicus, and why there were six of them, was that they were separated by the five regular solids that were known from Antiquity. Moreover, Kepler was convinced that the Sun has a physical role in moving the planets. A force from the Sun diminishes with distance, thus accounting for slower planetary motion at greater distance from the Sun. This also explained the usefulness of Ptolemy's equant—a point not at the center of an orbit—around which the planets appear from the Earth to move with varying speeds. Kepler published his ideas in 1596 in his *Mysterium cosmographicum* (Cosmographic Mystery). This publication initiated a correspondence with Galileo and led to the offer of a position in Prague as assistant to Tycho Brahe, the most noted astronomer of his time.

Although opposed to Kepler's Copernicanism, Brahe assigned Kepler to work at determining the orbit of Mars. Upon Brahe's death in 1601 Kepler acquired the most accurate and extensive set of astronomical observations made up to that time, and he succeeded Brahe as the official astronomer of the Holy Roman Emperor.

Kepler now discovered that the planes of all the planetary orbits passed through the Sun, confirming his belief in the physical function of the Sun in moving the planets. Calculating from Tycho's data for various circular orbits and employing uniform motions, Kepler was able to improve predictions of planetary positions beyond what had been achieved by others, but he found that there was still an error of 8' in parts of the orbit of Mars. After successive efforts involving extensive calculations, Kepler arrived at an elliptical orbit for Mars, with the Sun in one of its two foci. Moreover, a line drawn from the planet to the Sun sweeps out equal areas in equal times, representing the motion of the planet as more rapid when near the Sun and slower when distant from it. He then applied his discoveries about the Martian orbit to the motions of all the planets. These conclusions, now called Kepler's First and Second Laws of planetary motion, were published in his *Astronomia nova* (New Astronomy) of 1609. They represented a radical transformation of astronomy in their abandonment of uniform circular motion as characteristic of the heavens and in their union of the traditional object of astronomy to predict planetary position with the physics of the heavens.

How the Sun made the planets move was a continuing concern for Kepler throughout his career. At first he proposed souls in the planets as responding to the Sun, but later said that there was a force in the Sun, diminishing in proportion to distance, that moved the planets. He hypothesized that the Sun rotated, was magnetic, with only one of it poles active, and that the planets as magnets were alternately attracted and repelled, accounting for their varying distances from the Sun.

The relationship of the distances of the planets from the Sun to their orbital periods continued to preoccupy Kepler after writing his *Mysterium cosmographicum*. In 1618 he found that the cubes of the mean distances of all the planets were proportional to the squares of their periods. This is now referred to as Kepler's Third Law. This was published in his *Harmonice mundi* (Harmonics of the Universe, 1619), in which he put forward his theories about the relationship of the planetary motions to musical tones. In 1627 Kepler published his *Rudolphine Tables*, named in honor of his patron. They were soon accepted as the most accurate planetary tables published up to that time.

Kepler was also concerned with the science of optics. In 1604 he published a work in which he pointed to the retina as the place where an inverted image, refracted through the lens of the eye, was formed and transmitted to the nerves. He also indicated that the intensity of light diminishes as the square of its distance from the light source. After the publication of Galileo's discoveries with the telescope, Kepler proposed a theory of lenses that explained how telescopes worked. Substituting a convex lens for Galileo's concave eyepiece made possible improvements in the telescope. This suggestion was published in Kepler's *Dioptrice* (1611).

Very few astronomers accepted Kepler's astronomical ideas during his lifetime. Among the objections to it were his Copernicanism, resistance to his elimination of the traditional circles, the difficulty of applying his Second Law, which required complex approximations, and his insistence that physical explanations were part of the astronomer's tasks. The successes of his tables in predicting celestial events, however, along with a growing belief in the need to account for physical causes, persuaded most astronomers by the middle years of the seventeenth century of the validity of his approach. His description of planetary motions came to be accepted and was one of the foundations of Newton's laws of motion. Although Kepler's quasi-magnetic forces were rejected as the cause of planetary motion, his goal of determining the causes of planetary motion became important in the further development of astronomy, and other forces were proposed to account for them.

Marcello Malpighi (1628–1694)

Malpighi was an outstanding anatomist whose use of the microscope and improvements in techniques of observation led to a number of important discoveries in microscopic plant and animal structures. He was educated and received his medical degree at the University of Bologna. His achievements led to his election as a Fellow of the Royal Society and to his appointment as chief physician to Pope Innocent XII. He taught at the universities of Pisa and Bologna, and while at the latter published the results of his detailed microscopic investigations of the lungs in 1661.

He collected autopsy reports and the anatomical investigations of others, upon which he built his own observations. Among them were observations of certain of the sense organs and of the eye, concluding that Descartes' theory of vision was wrong. His detailed observations of the cerebral cortex, kidney, and spleen, combined with the influence of mechanical philosophy, led him to conclude that the glands filtered blood and produced fluids. He saw that each of the glands contained a follicle, with blood vessels, nerves, and a duct for emission of fluids. He found the capillaries connecting the microscopic venous and arterial blood vessels, and he was thereby convinced of the validity of Harvey's work. His investigations of lower animals and plants stemmed from his belief that they would increase knowledge of the anatomy and function of higher animals. He wrote on the anatomy of plants and on the microscopic development of the chick in the egg. His work was important in substantiating the importance of anatomy for the development of physiology and the practice of medicine.

Isaac Newton (1642–1727)

Isaac Newton was one of the greatest scientists who ever lived. His achievements in mathematics, mechanics, both terrestrial and celestial, and in optics brought together the achievements in the physical sciences of the previous several decades and were the capstone of

Courtesy Whipple Museum of Science, Wh.5588,
University of Cambridge.

the Scientific Revolution. His work had a lasting impact on the progress
of scientific knowledge and played a significant role in the nature and
practice of subsequent science.

Newton was born in a small town in England into a prosper-
ous farming family. He had a difficult childhood, was raised by his
grandparents, and left home for school at the age of twelve. In 1661 he
entered the University of Cambridge, where he encountered the traditional scholastic curriculum. He became enamored of mathematics,
however, and began to study on his own, mastering a great deal during his student years.

By the time he had completed his undergraduate studies, Newton, investigating tangents to a curve, thought of them as produced by
moving points and of areas under curves as produced by moving lines.

He saw patterns for finding tangents and inverse ones for finding areas, which he called the method of fluxions, a version of the calculus. By 1665 he had developed the binomial expansion, a major step toward finding areas under curves, which we call integration. By 1666 he had defined his method in systematic fashion, but he showed it to no one. This delay in publication later led to bitter arguments over priority with Leibniz, who had independently developed a somewhat more effective method for calculus.

During his undergraduate years Newton also familiarized himself with the works of Descartes, Gassendi, Boyle, and others, and he absorbed the ideas behind the mechanical philosophy. These ideas stimulated his interest in the study of impact, gravity, circular motion, and optics. He discovered that the center of mass of two bodies in impact either does not move or moves uniformly in a straight line. In circular motion he found the formula for the centrifugal force generated. His experiments with pendulums led him to determine the acceleration of gravity. Applying this discovery to the centrifugal tendency of bodies on the surface of the Earth, he found it to be minuscule compared to the force of gravity, thus answering one of the physical objections to a rotating Earth. He likewise compared the centrifugal force of the Moon in its orbit with the force of gravity and found the gravitational acceleration as approximately an inverse-square ratio.

Newton's investigations into light and colors likewise revealed hitherto unknown results, which challenged received opinions. The views of his contemporaries were that light is white by nature and modified into colors in the course of reflection and refraction. As a mechanical philosopher Newton held that light was corpuscular in nature, and its particles, depending on circumstances, of different colors. He therefore thought that light was a mixture of colors, making it appear white. He experimented in a dark room with a narrow beam of white light refracted through a prism and projected onto a distant wall. The round beam was dispersed into an elongated spectrum of colors from red to violet, each refracted at different angles. A second prism inserted in the paths of the various colored rays showed no further dispersion in color. A lens held in the path of the spectrum bringing it to a focus returned the original refracted beam to white light.

In an effort to perfect telescopes, Newton addressed the problem of chromatic aberration in telescopic images produced by telescopic lenses. He built a reflecting telescope with a parabolic mirror, which was hailed by the Royal Society, which elected him as a member. In 1672 he published the results of his experiments with the prism in the *Philosophical Transactions of the Royal Society*. This publication engendered a number of disputes with Robert Hooke and some clerics in Belgium that upset Newton considerably. He had little to do with the society for several years until publication of his masterwork, the *Principia*. He continued to pursue his work in optics, however, directing his attention to the colors in thin transparent films. He measured the alternating light and dark rings in the space between certain lenses and a sheet of glass. This experiment showed that colors could emerge from reflection as well as refraction and that light had periodic characteristics.

Beginning about 1670 Newton devoted about a quarter of a century to reading, writing, and experimenting in alchemy. He believed that true knowledge of the nature of matter, its components and transformations, had been known in antiquity and had since been lost. His object was to learn not only about matter and its transformations but also about its spiritual components. He was concerned, as were others, with an aspect of mechanical philosophy that seemed to eliminate any role for spirit in the functioning of the natural world and thus encouraged atheism. He thought he saw in alchemy a role for what he and others similarly concerned called "active principles." These would be transformed in Newton's later work into forces of attraction and repulsion in the particles of which matter was composed.

Newton also began to pay a great deal of attention, beginning in the 1670s, to theology and the roles of prophecy. Here too he read widely, in Scripture and especially in the writings of the Church Fathers, and became obsessed with the fourth-century controversy over the Trinity. He became convinced of the position of Arius, that Jesus was created as an intermediary between God and humanity, a position somewhat like that of modern Unitarianism. Newton did not dare make his unorthodox views known. Later in his life he had a circle of similar-minded friends, all of whom maintained the secrecy of their beliefs throughout their lives. Newton's views on religion did not become publicly known until the twentieth century.

In 1680, after a short correspondence with Robert Hooke about the path of a falling body on a rotating Earth, Newton turned his attention to the nature of circular motion and addressed the question of the force exerted on a revolving body from its center to keep it in orbit. He coined the term *centripetal force* for it and concluded that the force toward a focus of an elliptical orbit varies inversely as the square of the distance. He then put this theory aside until a visit in 1685 by Edmond Halley raised the question for him once more. Newton became fascinated by the problem and sent a short manuscript on the problem to Halley. He then concentrated for the next two and a half years on elaborating issues he had raised in that manuscript. The result was the publication in 1687 of his *Philosophiae naturalis principia mathematica* (Mathematical Principles of Natural Philosophy). Addressing issues in dynamics, Newton put forward his First Law as the principle of inertia. His Second Law stated the proportionality between the change of motion produced by a force, which included the concept that a change of direction is the same as the acceleration of a moving body. In dealing with planetary motion Newton clarified his concept of centripetal motion, and in his Third Law he stated in dynamic terms that in impact the motions of two bodies are equal and opposite. Newton's three laws of motion demonstrated how the achievements of Galileo and Kepler in mechanics and astronomy flowed from them as necessary consequences.

Devoting attention to the attractions of two bodies upon one another, and then the attractions of three bodies upon one another, Newton showed how the force of attraction depended on the mass of the attracting body, varied inversely with distance, and could account for perturbations in planetary motion, an improved lunar theory, and the tides. He also showed that Descartes' theory of vortices in a material medium could not obey Kepler's laws of planetary motion, and that therefore the planets moved through empty space.

The publication of the *Principia* immediately raised Newton to the forefront of the English scientific community. On the Continent there was resistance to the notion of attraction as contrary to the principles of the mechanical philosophy, but Newton's laws of motion and principle of gravitation found almost universal acceptance during his lifetime. Its success led to his publication of slightly revised second and third editions. He left Cambridge in 1696 to take a position in London as Warden and then Master of the Mint, where he mercilessly prosecuted and punished counterfeiters and reformed the currency. His later life had him involved in controversies over the source of his achievements in celestial dynamics, the invention of the calculus, and theological issues.

Newton was nevertheless recognized as the leading scientist of his day. He was elected president of the Royal Society in 1703 and held the position until his death. His optical experiments, carried out much earlier, were published in his *Opticks* in 1704; this work also raised a number of important unresolved issues in natural philosophy. Newton's funeral was a state occasion attended by the queen and by notables who carried his casket to Westminster Abbey, where he was buried.

Paracelsus (c. 1493–1541)

Theophrastus Philippus Aureolus Bombastus von Hohenheim, later known as Paracelsus, was a verbose and rough-tongued physician who attacked prevailing medical theory and practice. He proposed new remedies and treatments based on his own physiological theories and concepts of disease. He challenged the Galenic theory that the body contained four humors—blood, black bile, yellow bile, and phlegm— each with its particular qualities; that when the humors were in balance, the body was healthy; that disease resulted from their imbalance. Instead, Paracelsus held that the substances composing the body functions had spiritual components that needed to be freed to do their work while the toxic natures of the substances in which they were embedded had to be overcome.

These spiritual forces were chiefly of three kinds, reducible to Salt, Sulfur, and Mercury, and expressed themselves as chemical properties. Physiological processes, Paracelsus held, were governed by alchemist-like *archei*, which, when they failed in their duties, resulted in disease. Paracelsus subscribed to the notion of macrocosm-microcosm relationships—that humans reflected the universe as a whole, so that human functions corresponded to operations in the natural world, including the heavens. Examples included relationships between the Sun, the Moon, and the five known planets and seven principal bodily organs as well as seven metals. The duty of the physician was to provide medicines that corresponded in their natures to the spiritual characteristics of the malfunctioning bodily organs and thereby overcome the debilitating effects of the disease. The role of chemistry was very important for Paracelsus, and he employed chemical medicines never before used. Some of the medicines were composed of minerals with powerful effects, some even poisonous.

Paracelsus' medical philosophy was closely integrated with his religious beliefs, which included the divine nature of the body's spiritual essences, an interpretation of the Creation in terms of chemistry. In the course of his lifetime and for decades after, Paracelsus' teachings came under severe criticism on religious and medical grounds. In the course of the seventeenth century, however, his influence grew. His approach to prescriptions became quite influential, and a number of chemical medicines were adopted, elaborated, and included in standard pharmacopoeias.

Andreas Vesalius (1514–1564)

Vesalius is chiefly known for his *De humani corporis fabrica* (On the Structure of the Human Body), published in 1543. He was born in Brussels, the son of an apothecary to the Holy Roman Emperor, and obtained his M.D. degree from the University of Padua in 1537. He was immediately signed on as a guest lecturer in anatomy at Padua. The following year, with the aid of an artist who was working at the studio of Titian, he published an anatomical text with six plates. The teaching of anatomy in medical schools, as it had evolved during the Middle Ages, had the professor reading from a classical text, usually Galen, while assistants did the dissection and pointed out the appropriate parts. Cadavers for such exercises were difficult to obtain, and medical students witnessed such dissections infrequently.

Vesalius was fortunate, however, in that a judge, impressed by his work, saw to it that the corpses of a number of executed criminals were made available to him. A number of anatomists, in accord with the temper of the time, had began to do their own dissecting. Vesalius, who, early on, had been reduced to stealing cadavers of freshly executed people from the gallows at night, or exhuming buried bodies, was able to go further than others. He began to learn that a number of anatomical details differed from those described in Galen. Among the errors he found were that the jawbone was not composed of two bones, but one. Further, the septum dividing the right and left parts of the heart was not open to the passage of blood from its right to left ventricles, nor did a network believed by Galen to lie beneath the brain exist. A consequence of these latter two discoveries was the raising of impor-

Frontispiece of Vesalius' *De fabrica.*

tant questions about Galenic physiology. Vesalius' position, however, was that he was merely correcting Galen's errors, which had arisen from Galen's extrapolations from animal anatomy rather than from dissections of humans.

Recognizing the importance of his discoveries, Vesalius decided to publish a new kind of anatomical textbook that covered the entire human body, based chiefly on his own discoveries. It was magnificently illustrated by artists from Titian's studio with woodblocks, the creation of which were closely supervised by Vesalius himself, as was its printing. This rather large volume was unusual for its time, as it showed various organs in series of plates, as though successive layers of the body had been peeled away. Every illustration was accompanied by detailed comments, and they represented about 400 changes from the descriptions provided in the works of Galen. The book was immediately recognized as a classic. Because its cost was prohibitive for most medical students, Vesalius published shortly afterward a condensed version, the *Epitome of the Fabrica*, which was widely used.

Among Vesalius' principles was that because of the variations in organ structure in different persons, a proper science of anatomy required examination of the same structures in several different bodies. He expressed the hope that others would, from their own dissections, correct his where necessary and continue where he had left off. Shortly after the publication of his masterpiece Vesalius left the university and became a physician to the Holy Roman Emperor. In 1555 he published a second edition of *de fabrica*, correcting some of the mistakes in the first. He intended to return to academic life upon his return from a visit in 1564 to the Holy Land, but he died after a stormy voyage on the way home. His work had a powerful influence on subsequent anatomical discoveries, notably at Padua, and helped lay the foundation for very significant developments in physiology.

PRIMARY DOCUMENTS

Traditional Natural Philosophy

Aristotelianism

Document 1
Aristotle on the Nature of the Universe, Matter, Motion, and Life

The teachings of Aristotle embraced a wide range of subjects in a systematic and detailed manner and provided the foundation for much of natural philosophy for two millennia. His ideas were important in later Antiquity in the work of Galen, the most influential writer on anatomy, physiology, and medicine, and Claudius Ptolemy, the leading astronomer of the ancient world. When discovered by Muslims in the eighth century, Aristotle's works were adopted as the basis for natural philosophy in the world of Islam and translated into Arabic. Shortly after the foundation of universities in Western Europe in the twelfth and thirteenth centuries, Aristotelian texts, as well as Arabic commentaries on them, were translated into Latin and modified in accord with Christian doctrine, chiefly by St. Thomas Aquinas in the thirteenth century. University curricula were to a great extent based on Aristotle's teachings, and most natural philosophers during the Scientific Revolution had been schooled in them. By the end of the seventeenth century, however, most of Aristotle's ideas expressed in Document 1 had been overthrown or considerably modified.

The following passages are from three of Aristotle's works: *On the Heavens, Physics,* and *On the Soul.* The first describes the universe as a whole and the principles governing it. *Physics* deals with changes occurring in the world around us and the meaning of causality. The nature of living things as distinguished from matter in general is described in *On the Soul.*

For Aristotle the universe is finite and spherical; it is completely filled with five kinds of matter: four in the region from the center of the universe to the Moon, and one from the Moon to the edge of the universe. The Moon, the Sun, and each of the planets revolve with uniform motions about the motionless earth. In the region of the earth, its four elements, each with their individual properties, are constantly in motion. Those properties, the nature of motion, and Aristotle's concept of the quadruple nature of causality are described in Document 1.

The "soul," as used by Aristotle, is the essence and characteristics of living things as distinguished from ordinary matter or substance in general. All living things exhibit the ability to grow; plants have only that ability. Animals have in addition the capability of movement, which is shared by humans. The latter, however, are the only living beings possessing the ability to think. Aristotle's ideas on the nature of living things began to be modified in the course of the Scientific Revolution, but not nearly as much as his concepts of the physical world.

All natural bodies and magnitudes we hold to be, as such, capable of locomotion; for nature, we say, is their principle of movement. But all movement that is in place, all locomotion, as we term it, is either straight or circular or a combination of these two, which are the only simple movements. And the reason of this is that these two, the straight and the circular line, are the only simple magnitudes. Now revolution about the center is circular motion, while the upward and downward movements are in a straight line, 'upward' meaning motion away from the center, and 'downward' motion towards it. All simple motion, then, must be motion either away from or towards or about the centre.

There is no infinite body beyond the heaven. Nor again is there anything of limited extent beyond it. And so beyond the heaven there is no body at all.

[T]he natural movement of the earth, part and whole alike, is to the centre of the whole—whence the fact that it is now actually situated at the centre—but it might be questioned, since both centres are the same, which centre is it that portions of the earth and other heavy things move to. Is this their goal because it is the centre of the earth or because it is the centre of the whole? For fire and other light things move to the extremity of the area which contains the centre. It happens, however, that the centre of the earth and of the whole is the same. Thus they do move to the centre of the earth, but accidentally, in virtue of the fact that the earth's centre lies at the centre of the whole. That the centre of the earth is the goal of their movement is indicated by the fact that heavy bodies moving toward the earth do not move parallel but so as to make equal angles, and thus to a single centre, that of the earth. It is clear, then, that the earth must be at the centre and immovable, not only for the reasons already given, but also because heavy bodies forcibly thrown quite straight upward return to the point from which they started, even if they are thrown to an infinite distance. From these considerations then it is clear that the earth does not move and does not lie elswhere than at the centre.

In accordance with general conviction we may distinguish the absolutely heavy, as that which sinks to the bottom of all things, from the absolutely light, which that which rises to the surface of all things. . . . It is apparent that fire, in whatever quantity, so long as there is no external obstacle, moves upward, and earth downward; and, if the quantity is increased, the movement is the same, though swifter. But the heaviness and lightness of bodies which combine these qualities is different from this, since while they rise to the surface of some bodies, they sink to the bottom of others. Such are air and water. Neither of them is absolutely light or heavy. Both are lighter than earth—for any portion of either rises to the surface of it—but heavier than fire, since a portion of either, whatever its quantity, sinks to the bottom of fire; compared together, however, the one has absolute weight, the other absolute lightness, since air in any quantity rises to the surface of water, while water in any quantity sinks to the bottom of air. Now other bodies are severally light and heavy, and evidently in them the attributes are due to the difference of their uncompounded parts; that is to say, according as the one or other happens to preponderate the bodies will be heavy and light respectively.

The body, then, which moves in a circle cannot possibly possess either heaviness or lightness. For neither naturally nor unnaturally can it move either towards or away from the centre.

Since everything that is in motion must be moved by something, let us take the case in which a thing is in locomotion and is moved by something that is itself in motion, and that again is moved by something else that is in motion, and that by something else, and so on continually: then the series cannot go on to infinity, but there must be some first movement.

If people say the void must exist, as being necessary if there is to be movement, what rather turns out to be the case, if one studies the matter, is the opposite, that not a single thing can be moved if there *is* a void; for as with those who for a like reason say the earth is at rest, so, too, in the void things must be at rest; for there is no place to which things can move more or less than to another; since the void in as far as it is void admits no difference.

We see the same weight or body moving faster than another for two reasons, either because there is a difference in what it moves through, as between water, air, and earth, or because, other things being equal, the moving body differs from the other owing to excess of weight or of lightness.

Now there is no ratio in which the void is exceeded by body, as there is no ration of 0 to a number. For if 4 exceeds 3 by 1, and 2 by more than 1, and 1 by still more than it exceeds 2, still there is no ratio by which it exceeds 0; for that which exceeds must be divisible into the excess + that which is exceeded, so that 4 will be what it exceeds 0 by + 0. For this reason, too, a line does not exceed a point—unless it is composed of points! Similarly the void can bear no ratio to the full, and therefore neither can movement through the one to movement through the other, but if a thing moves through the thickest medium such and such a distance in such and such a time, it moves through the void with a speed beyond any ratio.

To sum the matter up, the cause of this result is obvious, viz. that between any two movements there is a ratio (for they occupy time, and there is a ratio between any two times, so long as both are finite), but there is no ratio of void to full.

Knowledge is the object of our inquiry, and men do not think they know a thing till they have grasped the "why" of it (which is to grasp its primary cause). . . .

In one sense. then, (1) that out of which a thing comes to be and which persists, is called 'cause', e. g. the bronze of the statue, the silver of the bowl, and the genera of which the bronze and the silver are species.

In another sense (2) the form or the archetype, i. e. the statement of the essence, and its genera, are called 'causes' (e. g. of the octave the relation of 2:1, and generally number), and the parts in the definition.

Again (3) the primary source of the change or coming to rest; e. g. the man who gave advice is a cause, the father is cause of the child, and generally what makes of what is made and what causes change of what is changed.

Again (4) in the sense of end or 'that for the sake of which' a thing is done, e. g. health is the cause of walking about. ('Why is he walking about?' we say. 'to be healthy', and having said that, we think we have assigned the cause.)

[W]hat has soul in it differs from what has not in that the former displays life. . . .
[P]lants are observed to possess in themselves an originative power through which they increase or decrease in all spatial directions; they grow up *and* down, and everything that grows increases its bulk alike in both directions or indeed in all, and continues to live so long as it can absorb nutriment.

This power of self-nutrition can be isolated from the other powers mentioned, but not they from it—in mortal things at least. The fact is obvious in plants; for it is the only psychic power they possess.

This is the originative power the possession of which leads us to speak of things as *living* at all, but it is the possession of sensation that leads us for the first time to speak of living things as animals. . . .

The primary form of sense is touch, which belongs to all animals. . . . [S]oul is the source of these phenomena and is characterized by them, viz by the powers of self-nutrition, sensation, thinking and motivity. . . .

Of the psychic powers above enumerated some kinds of living things . . . possess all, some less than all, others one only. Those we have mentioned are the nutritive, the appetitive, the sensory, the locomotive, and the power of thinking.

Source: The Works of Aristotle Translated into English under the Editorship of J. A. Smith and W. D. Ross (Oxford: Clarendon Press, 1922); vol. 2, *On the Heavens*, translated by J. L. Stocks, 269–271, 274, 311–312; *Physics*, translated by R. P. Hardie and R. K. Gaye, 195, 214–216, 241–242; vol. 3, *On the Soul*, translated by J. A. Smith, 413–414.

The Transformation of Cosmology and Astronomy

The distinction, and to a degree contradictions, between the physical nature of the universe as described by Aristotle and the observed motions of the celestial bodies and the geometrical techniques employed to predict their positions had long been noted. It was only with the achievement of Copernicus that a few of the issues involved began to be addressed. In the early part of the seventeenth century Aristotelian and theological objections to Copernicanism began to be strongly challenged, chiefly by Kepler and Galileo; the former by his revision of the nature of planetary orbital paths, the latter by his discoveries with the telescope. Kepler's insistence that physical forces must be united with precise observations and Galileo's discoveries about moving bodies also played important roles in the removal of Aristotelian objections to the Copernican theory. Newton's mechanics most effectively incorporated these earlier efforts, and the nature of astronomy and conceptions of our universe were forever changed. The foundations had been laid for the successive and continuous development of our astronomical knowledge.

Copernicus on the Nature of and Reasons for His Astronomical Theory

Document 2
Preface to *On the Revolutions of the Celestial Spheres*

Copernicus began to develop his heliocentric theory some time early in the sixteenth century, and he continued to polish it over the next few decades. When his disciple Georg Joachim Rheticus, as well as others who had seen his manuscript, urged Copernicus to publish his work, he agreed despite his fears of ridicule. The work was initially seen through the press in Nuremberg by Rheticus, and subsequently by Andreas Osiander, a Lutheran minister, who deleted Copernicus' introduction and inserted one of his own, indicating that the work was for the calculation of planetary positions alone and should not be taken to represent reality. That this was contrary to Copernicus' own beliefs is clear from his address to the pope. This passage represents his reasons for adopting a theory that strongly contradicted not only the traditional and at the time widely accepted geocentric models of Ptolemy, but well-established principles of physics, celestial observations, and concepts of the nature of astronomy as well.

Copernicus justifies his bold step, as was common during the Renaissance, by referring to positions taken in Antiquity. Appealing to the advantages of his system, however, Copernicus noted that it was capable of answering questions that the Ptolemaic models could not, for it dispensed with an objectionable technique used by Ptolemy and, above all, represented a unified system, unlike the Ptolemaic geocentric models that considered as a whole (to use a modern analogy) appeared like a Frankenstein monster. Note as well the ways in which Copernicus, while rejecting certain aspects of Aristotelianism, retained others. Moreover, an improvement in the ability to predict accurately the positions of celestial bodies, the primary function of the science of astronomy, was not listed among the advantages of his system.

To His Holiness, Pope Paul III, Nicolaus Copernicus' Preface to His Books on the Revolutions I can readily imagine, Holy Father, that as soon as some people hear that in this volume, which I have written about the revolutions of the spheres of the universe, I ascribe certain motions to the terrestrial globe, they will shout that I must be immediately repudiated together with this belief. For I am not so enamored of my own opinions that I disregard what others may think of them. I am aware that a philosopher's ideas are not subject to the judgement of ordinary persons, because it is his endeavor to seek the truth in all things, to the extent permitted to human reason by God. . . . I was impelled to consider a different system of deducing the motions of the universe's spheres for no other reason than the realization that [mathematicians] do not agree among themselves in their investigations of this subject. . . . [T]hose who devised the eccentrics seem thereby in large measure to have solved the problem of the apparent motions with appropriate calculations. But meanwhile they introduced a good many ideas which apparently contradict the first principles of uniform motion. Nor could they elicit or deduce from the eccentrics the principal consideration, that is, the structure of the universe and the [sure] symmetry of its parts. On the contrary, [with them it is just as though someone were to join together hands, feet, a head, and other members from different places, each part well drawn, but not proportioned to one and the same body, and not in the least matching each other, so that from these (fragments) a monster rather than a man would be put together]. Hence in the process of demonstration or "method," as it is called, those who employed eccentrics are found either to have omitted something essential or to have admitted something extraneous and wholly irrelevant. . . . For this reason I undertook the task of rereading the works of all the philosophers which I could obtain to learn whether anyone had ever proposed other motions of the universe's spheres than those expounded by the teachers of [mathematical arts] in the schools. And in fact first I found in Cicero that Hicetas supposed the earth to move. Later I also discovered in Plutarch that certain others were of this opinion. . . .

Therefore, having obtained the opportunity from these sources, I too began to consider the mobility of the earth. And even though the idea seemed absurd, nevertheless I knew that others before me had been granted the freedom to imagine any circles whatever for the purpose of explaining the heavenly phenomena. Hence I thought that I too would be readily permitted to ascertain whether explanations sounder than those of my predecessors could be found for the revolution of the celestial spheres on the assumption of some motion of the earth.

Having thus assumed the motions which I ascribe to the earth later on in the volume, by long and intense study I finally found that if the motions of the other planets [are brought into a relation with the circular course of the earth, and are reckoned for the revolution of each planet, not only do their phenomena follow therefrom but also the order and size of all the planets and spheres, and heaven itself is so linked together that nothing can be moved from its place without causing confusion in the remaining parts and the universe as a whole.] . . . [T]he order of the spheres is the following, beginning with the highest.

The first and the highest of all is the sphere of the fixed stars, which contains itself and everything, and is therefore immovable. It is unquestionably the place of the universe, to which the motion and position of all the other heavenly bodies are compared. Some people think that it also shifts in some way. A different explanation of why this appears to be so will be adduced in my discussion of the earth's motion. . . .

[The sphere of the fixed stars] is followed by the first of the planets, Saturn, which completes its circuit in 30 years. After Saturn, Jupiter accomplishes its revolution in 12 years. Then Mars revolves in 2 years. The annual revolution takes the series' fourth place, which contains the earth, . . . together with the lunar sphere as an epicycle. In the fifth place Venus returns in 9 months. Lastly, the sixth place is held by Mercury, which revolves in a period of 80 days.

At rest, however, in the middle of everything is the sun. For in this most beautiful temple, who would place this lamp in another or better position than that from which it can light up the whole thing at the same time? For, the sun is not inappropriately called by some people the lantern of the universe, its mind by others, and its ruler by still others. [Hermes] the Thrice Greatest labels it a visible god, and Sophocles' Electra, the all-seeing. Thus, indeed as though seated on a royal throne, the sun governs the family of planets revolving around it. . . .

In this arrangement, therefore, we discover a marvelous symmetry of the universe, and an established harmonious linkage between the motion of the spheres and their size, such as can be found in no other way. For this permits a not inattentive student to perceive why the forward and backward arcs appear greater in Jupiter than in Saturn and smaller than in Mars, and on the other hand greater in Venus than in Mercury. This reversal in direction appears more frequently in Saturn than in Jupiter, and also more rarely in Mars and Venus than in Mercury. Moreover, when Saturn, Jupiter, and Mars rise at sunset, they are nearer to the earth than when they set in the evening or appear at a later hour.

Source: Nicolaus Copernicus, *On the Revolutions of the Heavenly Spheres,* edited by Jerzy Dobrzycki, translated by Edward Rosen (Baltimore: Johns Hopkins University Press, 1978), 3–6.

Kepler and the Creation of a New Astronomy

Document 3
The New Astronomy

Johannes Kepler, having become a Copernican during his university days, decided early in his career that astronomy, traditionally considered a branch of applied mathematics, must be firmly united with the physics of the heavens. Using the data he had acquired from Tycho Brahe's observations, the most precise ever determined, he calculated the motions of the planets about the Sun, allied to a physical theory of why the planets move as they do. Familiar with William Gilbert's work *On the Magnet*, Kepler speculated that the Sun, by its rotation, moves the planets by magnetic means. His work on the planet Mars led him to a revolutionary revision of traditional ideas about the nature of planetary motion. He discovered, contrary to what Copernicus had thought, that the planes of all the planetary orbits intersected the Sun, and that the orbits of the planets were not circular, but elliptical, with the Sun in one of the foci of each orbit. Nor, contrary to what the ancients and Copernicus had thought, did the planets move with uniform speed. He published his results in 1609 in a work entitled *Astronomia nova* (A New Astronomy). The following passages from the introduction to the work present the basic ideas of Kepler's discoveries.

My aim in the present work is chiefly to reform astronomical theory (especially of the motion of Mars) in all three forms of hypotheses, so that our computations from the tables correspond to the celestial phenomena. Hitherto, it has not been possible to do this with sufficient certainty. In fact, in August of 1608, Mars was a little less than four degrees beyond the position given by calculation from the Prutenic tables. In August and September of 1593 this error was a little less than five degrees, while in my new calculation the error is entirely suppressed.

Meanwhile, although I place this goal first and pursue it cheerfully, I also make an excursion into Aristotle's *Metaphysics*, or rather, I inquire into celestial physics and the natural causes of the motions. The eventual result of this consideration is the formulation of very clear arguments showing that only Copernicus's opinion concerning the world (with a few small changes) is true, that the other two are false, and so on. . . .

Now my first step in investigating the physical causes of the motions was to demonstrate that [the planes of] all the eccentrics intersect in no other place than the very centre of the solar body (not some nearby point), contrary to what Copernicus and Brahe thought. . . . [I]n the fourth part of the work, . . . I demonstrate most soundly that Mars's eccentric is so situated that the centre of the solar body lies upon its line of apsides, and not any nearby point, and hence, that all the [planes of the] eccentrics intersect in the sun itself. . . . I have demonstrated that the circle in which the earth is moved around the sun does not have as its centre that point about which its motion is regular and uniform. . . .

For whether it is the earth or the sun that is moved, it has certainly been demonstrated that the body is moved in a nonuniform manner, that is, slowly when it is farther from the body at rest, and more swiftly when it has approached this body.

Thus the physical difference is now immediately apparent, by way of conjecture, it is true, but yielding nothing in certainty to conjectures of doctors on physiology or to any other natural science. . . . That Copernicus is better able than Brahe to deal with celestial physics is proven in many ways. Of whom, in all fairness, most honest and grateful mention is made, and recognition given, since I build this entire structure from the bottom up upon his work, all the materials being borrowed from him.

First, although Brahe did indeed take up those five solar theories from the theories of the planets, bringing them down to the centres of the eccentrics, hiding them there, and conflating them into one, he nevertheless left in the world the effects produced by those theories. For Brahe no less than for Ptolemy, besides that motion which is proper to it, each planet is still actually moved with the sun's motion, the two being mixed into one, the result being a spiral. That it results from this that there are no solid orbs, Brahe has demonstrated most firmly. Copernicus, on the other hand, entirely removed this extrinsic motion from the five planets, assigning its cause to a deception arising from the circumstances of observation. Thus the motions are still multiplied to no purpose by Brahe, as they were before by Ptolemy. . . .

For if the earth is moved, it has been demonstrated that the increases and decreases of its velocity are governed by its approaching towards and receding from the sun. And in fact the same happens with the rest of the planets: they are urged on or held back according to the approach toward or recession from the sun. So far, the demonstration is geometrical.

And now, from this very reliable demonstration, the conclusion is drawn, using a physical conjecture, that the source of the five planets' motion is in the sun itself. It is therefore very likely that the source of the earth's motion is in the same place as the source of the other five planets' motion, namely, in the sun as well. It is therefore likely that the earth is moved, since a likely cause of its motion is apparent.

That, on the other hand, that the sun remains in place in the centre of the world, is most probably shown by (among other things) its being the source of motion for at least five planets. For whether you follow Copernicus or Brahe, the source of motion for five of the planets is in the sun, and in Copernicus, for a sixth as well, namely, the earth. And it is more likely that the source of all motion should remain in place rather than move. . . . Many are prevented by the motion of heavy bodies from believing that the earth is moved by an animate motion, or better, by a magnetic one. They should ponder the following propositions.

A mathematical point, whether or not it is in the centre of the world, can neither effect the motion of heavy bodies not act as an object towards which they tend. Let the physicists prove that this force is in a point which neither is a body nor is grasped otherwise than through mere relation. . . .

Nor are heavy bodies driven in towards the middle by the rapid whirling of the *primum mobile*, as objects in whirlpools are. That motion (if we suppose it to exist) does not carry all the way down to these lower regions. If it did, we would feel it, and would be caught up by it along with the very earth itself. Indeed, we would be carried ahead, and the earth would follow. All these absurdities are consequences of our opponents' view, and it therefore appears that the common theory of gravity is in error.

Source: Johannes Kepler, *New Astronomy*, translated by William H. Donahue (Cambridge: Cambridge University Press, 1992), 48–52, 54.

The Role of the Telescope in Challenging the Aristotelian Cosmos

Document 4
Galileo on the Revelations of the Telescope

After hearing about a newly invented instrument that magnified distant objects, Galileo made one for himself. His use of it in examining the celestial bodies had a profound effect on traditional Aristotelian conceptions of the nature of the universe. The rapid publication of his observations in 1610 in his *Sidereus nuncius* (Starry Messenger) gave Galileo an international reputation overnight. His naming of Jupiter's moons after the ruling family of Tuscany, the Medici, resulted in its Grand Duke becoming his patron. The telescope immediately transformed the nature of astronomy and rapidly led to significant new discoveries. Observations made with it challenged the concepts of the perfect circularity of the heavenly bodies and therefore of the perfection of the heavens themselves, the size of the universe, and the notion that there was a single center of revolution. Shortly after the publication of Galileo's treatise, the observed phases of Venus contradicted the Ptolemaic theory. The subsequent discovery of sunspots led to the idea that the Sun rotated and to the possiblility of that rotation as the cause of planetary motion. Improvements in the design of telescopes came rapidly, leading to wider fields of view, improvements in magnification, and the insertion of micrometers, allowing an increasingly substantial improvement in precision and detailed measurement of celestial angles.

By oft-repeated observations . . . we have been led to the conclusion that we certainly see the surface of the Moon to be not smooth, even, and perfectly spherical, as the great crowd of philosophers have believed about this and other heavenly bodies, but, on the contrary, to be uneven, rough, and crowded with depressions and bulges. And it is like the face of the Earth itself, which is marked here and there with chains of mountains and depths of valleys. . . . [W]hen the Moon displays herself to us with brilliant horns, the boundary dividing the bright from the dark part does not form a uniformly oval line, as would happen in a perfectly spherical solid, but is marked by an uneven, rough, and very sinuous line. . . . For several, as it were, bright excrescences extend beyond the border between light and darkness into the dark part, and on the other hand little dark parts enter into the light. Indeed, a great number of small darkish spots, entirely separated from the dark part, are distributed everywhere over almost the entire region already bathed by the light of the Sun, except, at any rate, for that part affected by the large and ancient spots. We noticed, moreover, that all these small spots just mentioned always agree in this, that they have a dark part on the side toward the Sun while on the side opposite the Sun they are crowned with brighter borders like shining ridges. And we have an almost entirely similar sight on Earth, around sunrise, when the valleys are not yet bathed in light but the surrounding mountains facing the Sun are already seen shining with light. And just as the shadows of the earthly valleys are diminished as the Sun climbs higher, so those lunar spots lose their darkness as the luminous part grows. . . .

We will now report briefly on what has been observed by us thus far concerning the fixed stars. And first, it is worthy of notice that when they are observed by means of the spyglass, stars, fixed as well as wandering, are seen not to be magnified in size in the same proportion in which the other objects, and also the Moon herself, are increased. . . . The reason for this is that when the stars are observed wih the naked eye, they do not show themselves according to their simple, and, so to speak, naked size, but rather surrounded by a certain brightness and crowned by twinkling rays especially as the night advances. Because of this they appear much larger than if they were stripped of these extraneous rays. . . .

What was observed by us in the third place is the nature and matter of the Milky Way itself, which, with the aid of the spyglass, may be observed so well that all the disputes that for so many generations have vexed philosophers are destroyed by visible certainty, and we are liberated from wordy arguments. For the galaxy is nothing else than a congeries of innumerable stars distributed in clusters. To whatever region of it you direct your spyglass, and immense number of stars immediately offer themselves to view, of which very many appear rather large and very conspicuous, but the multitude of small ones is truly unfathomable. . . .

Moreover—and what is even more remarkable—the stars that have been called "nebulous" by every single astronomer up to this day are swarms of small stars placed exceedingly closely together. . . .

We have briefly explained our observations thus far about the Moon, the fixed stars, and the Milky Way. It remains for us to reveal and make known what appears to be most important in the present matter: four planets never seen from the beginning of the world right up to our day. . . .

[O]n the seventh day of January of the present year 1610, at the first hour of the night, when I inspected the celestial constellations through a spyglass, Jupiter presented himself. . . .

On the first of March, at 40 minutes, four stars were perceived, all to the east. . . .

These are the observations of the four Medicean planets recently, and for the first time, discovered by me. From them, although it is not yet possible to calculate their periods, something worthy of notice may at least be said. And first, since they sometimes follow and at other times precede Jupiter by similar intervals, and are removed from him toward the east as well as the west by only very narrow limits, and accompany him equally in retrograde and direct motion, no one can doubt that they complete their revolutions about him while, in the meantime, all together they complete a 12-year period about the center of the world.

Source: Galileo Galilei, *Sidereus Nuncius or the Sidereal Messenger*, translated by Albert van Helden (Chicago: University of Chicago Press, 1989), 40–41, 57, 62, 64, 82–84.

The Reform of the Medical Sciences

The study of anatomy and physiology, as well as the practice of medicine up to the sixteenth century, were, with some modifications, heavily based on the work of the great physician of Antiquity, Galen. Paracelsus, an alchemist and physician, strongly attacked contemporaneous medical practice and use of medicines, as well as medical education. His extensive publications put forward his own theories of disease and were linked to his alchemical notions. At about the same time Andreas Vesalius, dissatisfied with the teaching of anatomy in medical schools, wanted to learn about the organs of the body through his own dissections. The result of his investigations was the publication of his beautifully illustrated classic text *On the Structure of the Human Body*. It initiated a sequence of anatomical discoveries by others and led as well to new knowledge about physiological processes. Chief among them were the discoveries by William Harvey about the functions of the beating heart and the circulation of the blood.

Alchemy, the Nature of Matter, and Medical Practice

Document 5
Paracelsus on Alchemy and the Nature of Illness

Paracelsus wrote a considerable number of tracts, most of which were published only after his death by his followers, who were impressed by his reputed ability to cure diseases that had been considered incurable. In Document 5, Paracelsus unites religious themes with alchemical ones to explain both the nature of the universe and proper medical practice. He not only departs from traditional Aristotelian modes of explanation but also distinguishes his alchemical theories from the goal of converting base metals into gold, and he leans on the ideas expounded in the tracts attributed to the mythical Hermes Trismegistus. Note that whereas some Aristotelian ideas are condemned, some on the nature of matter are retained. Note, too, that illnesses are linked to chemical foundations.

He who learns nothing from [God and Nature] is like the heathen teachers and philosophers, who follow the subtleties and crafts of their own inventions and opinions. Such teachers are Aristotle, Hippocrates, Avicenna, Galen, and the rest, who based all their arts simply upon their own opinions. . . .

This it is which has moved and incited us to write a special book concerning Alchemy, basing it not on men, but on Nature herself, and upon those virtues and powers which God, with his own finger, has impressed upon metals. The initiator of this impression was Mercurius Trismegistus. He is not without due cause called the father of all wise men, and of all who followed this Art with love and earnest desire.

Know then that all the seven metals are born from a threefold matter, namely, Mercury, Sulphur, and Salt, but with distinct and peculiar colourings. In this way Hermes truly said that all the seven metals were made and compounded of three substances, and in like manner also tinctures and the Philosophers' Stone. These three substances he names Spirit, Soul, and Body. . . . Now, in order that these three distinct substances, may be rightly understood, . . . it should be known that they signify nothing else than the three principles, Mercury, Sulphur, [and Salt] from which all the seven metals are generated. For Mercury is the spirit, Sulpur is the soul, and Salt is the body. The metal between the spirit and the body, concerning which Hermes speaks, is the soul, which indeed is Sulphur. It unites those two contraries, the body and the spirit, and changes them into one essence.

In the creation of the world, the first separation began with the four elements, when the first matter of the world was one chaos. From that chaos God built the Greater World, separated into four distince elements, Fire, Air, Water, Earth. Fire was the warm part, Air only the cold, Water the moist, and, lastly, Earth was but the dry part of the Greater World.

Every thing which is generated and produced of its elements is divided into three, namely, into metal between the spirit and the body, concerning which Salt, Sulphur, Mercury. Out of these a conjunction takes place, which constitutes one body and an united essence. This does not concern the body in its outward aspect, but only the internal nature of the body.

Its operation is threefold. One of these is the operation of Salt. This works by purging, cleansing, balsaming, and by other ways, and rules over that which goes off in putrefaction. The second is the operation of Sulphur. Now, sulphur either governs the excess which arises from the two others, or it is dissolved. The third is of Mercury, and it removes that which changes into consumption. Learn the form which is peculiar to these three. One is liquor, and this is the form of mercury; one is oiliness, which is the form of sulphur; one is alkali, and this is from salt. Mercury is without sulphur and salt; sulphur is devoid of salt and mercury; salt is without mercury or sulphur. In this manner each persists in its own potency.

With regard to the generation of Gold, the true opinion is that it is Suphur sublimated to the highest degree by Nature, and purged from all dregs, blackness, and filth whatever, so transparent and lustrous . . . as no other of the metals can be, with a higher and more exalted body. Sulphur, one of the three primals, is the first matter of gold. If Alchemists could find and obtain this Sulphur, . . . it would certainly be the cause of effusive joy on their part. This is the Sulphur of the Philosophers, from which gold is produced, not from that other Sulphur from which come iron, copper, etc. . . . Moreover, Mercury, separated to the highest degree, according to metallic nature, and free from all earthly and accidental admixture, is changed into a mercurial body with consummate clearness. This is the Mercury of the Philosophers which generates gold, and is the second part of the primal matter. The third part of the primal matter of gold, . . . is salt, crystallized to the highest degree, and . . . highly separated and purified. . . . The physician should understand the three genera of all diseases as follows. One genus is of salt, one of sulphur, and one of mercury. Every relaxing disease is generated from salt, as dysentery, diarrhoea, lienteria, etc. Every expulsion is caused by salt, which remains in its place, whether in a healthy or suffering subject. The salt in the one case is, however, that of Nature, while in the other it is corrupted and dissolved. Cure must be accomplished by means of the same salts from which the disease had origin, even as fresh salt will rectify and purify dissolved salt. The sulphureous cure follows as a certain confirmation of the operation in salt.

All diseases of the arteries, ligaments, bones, nerves, etc., arise from mercury. In the rest of the body the substance of corporeal mercury does not dominate. It prevails only in the external members. Sulphur softens and nourishes the internal organs, as the heart, brain, and veins, and their diseases also may be termed sulphureous, for a sulphureous substance is present in them. Let us take colic as an example. Salt is the cause of this, because this predominates in the intestines. In its dissolved state it produces one kind of colic, and when it is excessively hard it produces another kind; for when it passes from its own temperature it becomes excessively humid or excessively dry. In the cure of colic by elemented salts the human salt must be rectified. But if a salt other than from sulphur be applied, you must regard it as a submersion of salt and not a cure of colic. Similarly, in the case of mercurial and sulphureous diseases, each must be administered to its counterpart, not a contrary to a contrary. The cold does not subdue the hot, nor vice versa, in congenital diseases. The cure proceeds from the same source as the disease, and has generated the place thereof.

Source: The Hermetic and Alchemical Writings of Paracelsus. 2 vols., translated by Edward E. Waite (London: Elliott and Co., 1894), I, 72–73, 125, 160, 349–350; II, 317–319.

Vesalius on the Reform of Medicine

Document 6
Introduction to the *De Fabrica*

Vesalius' epic work *De humani corporis fabrica* (On the Structure of the Human Body) was designed to reform the study of anatomy, based on his own dissections of human cadavers. In the course of those dissections he came to realize that there were a significant number of errors in the anatomical texts of Galen that were used in the curricula of medical schools. He felt that their correction was an essential step in the reform of medicine. He therefore decided to create an anatomical text with his own descriptions of the body's parts and illustrated beautifully and carefully by a trained artist. Another thing that was unusual about the text was that the sequence of text and illustrations followed a pattern that had begun to emerge in the Renaissance of the disassembly of complex structures, such as machines, to show the relationships of their components. This was the pattern followed by Vesalius. He, as had Copernicus about the same time, referred to certain ancient authorities for validation of his concept of the need for a reform of medicine. His work also challenged received opinion based on the greatest authority in his field in Antiquity. Vesalius saw his work as only a part of the need to reform the practice of his profession. That reform must begin in the medical schools.

The practice in classes on anatomy from the late Middle Ages to the Renaissance was, as described by Vesalius, to have the professor, seated above the cadaver, read from Galen as someone, very likely a butcher, cut open the body and its parts while an assistant pointed to the body parts described. The involvement of Vesalius in performing his own dissections to see what he could learn represented an emerging attitude about acquiring knowledge through the activities and interventions of the natural philosopher.

In ancient times there were three medical sects, to wit, the Dogmatic, the Empirical, and the Methodical, but the exponents of each of these embraced the whole of the art as the means to preserve health and to war against disease. To this end they referred all that they individually thought necessary in their particular sects, and employed the service of a threefold aid to health: first, a theory of diet; secondly, the whole use of drugs; and thirdly, manual operation. This last, above the rest, nicely proves the saying that medicine is the addition of that which is

defective and the removal of that which is in excess; as often as we re-
sort to the art of medicine for the treatment of disease we have occasion to employ it; and time and experience have taught, by the benefits
it has conferred, that it is the greatest aid to human health. . . .

But it was not at all my purpose to set one instrument of medicine above the rest, since the triple art of health, as it is called, cannot
at all be disunited and wrenched asunder, but belongs in its entirety to
the same practitioner; and for the due attainment of this triple art, all
the parts of medicine have been established and prepared on an equal
footing, so that the individual parts are brought into use with a success proportioned to the degree in which one combines the cumulative
force of all. How rarely indeed a disease occurs which does not at once
require the triple manner of treatment; that is to say, a proper diet must
be prescribed, some service must be rendered by medicine, and some
by the hand. . . .

For when, in the first place, the whole compounding of drugs was
handed over to the apothecaries, then the doctors promptly lost the
knowledge of simple medicines which is absolutely essential to them;
and they became responsible for the fact that the druggists' shops were
filled with barbarous terms and false remedies, and also that so many
elegant compositions of the ancients were lost to us, several of which
have not yet come to light; and, finally, they prepared an endless task
for the learned men, not only of our own age, but for those who pre-
ceded it by some years, who devoted themselves with indefatigable zeal
to research in simple medicines; so much so that they may be regarded
as having gone far to restore the knowledge of them to its former bril-
liance.

But this perverse distribution of the instruments of healing among
a variety of craftsmen inflicted a much more odious shipwreck and a
far more cruel blow upon the chief branch of natural philosophy [anat-
omy], to which, since it comprises the natural history of man and
should rightly be regarded as the firm foundation of the whole art of
medicine. . . .

And equally inevitably this deplorable dismemberment of the art
of healing has introduced into our schools the detestable procedure
now in vogue, that one man should carry out the dissection of the
human body, and another give the description of the parts. These latter are perched up aloft in a pulpit like jackdaws, and with a notable

air of disdain they drone out information about facts they have never approached at first hand, but which they merely commit to memory from the books of others, or of which they have descriptions before their eyes; the former are so ignorant of languages that they are unable to explain their dissections to the onlookers and botch what ought to be exhibited in accordance with the instruction of the physician, who never applies his hand to the dissection, and contemptuously steers the ship out of the manual, as the saying goes. . . .

[A]t Louvain, where I had to return on account of the disturbance of war, because during eighteen years the doctors there had not even dreamed of anatomy, and in order that I might help the students of that academy, and that I myself might acquire greater skill in a matter both obscure and in my judgment of prime importance for the whole of medicine, I did somewhat more accurately than at Paris expound the whole structure of the human body in the course of dissecting, with the result that the younger teachers of that academy now appear to spend great and very serious study in acquiring a knowledge of the parts of man, clearly understanding what invaluable material for philosophizing is presented to them from this knowledge.

Source: Proceedings of the Royal Society of Medicine, translated by B. Farrington (25 July 1932), 1357–1366.

Harvey and the Circulation of the Blood

Document 7
Harvey on the Motions of the Heart and Blood

William Harvey's studies at the University of Padua, the most influential medical school of his day, were important for his seminal work on the movement of the blood. It was at that university that its leading anatomist, Girolamo Fabrici (c. 1533–1619) had discovered the valves in the veins. Their function, as described by Fabrici, was to slow the movement of the blood toward the body's extremities. Although the work of Vesalius half a century earlier, as well as the discoveries of subsequent anatomists, had begun to question certain aspects of Galenism, traditional notions about the movements of the blood through the body were still based on Galenic ideas. Harvey began his investigations of the motions of the blood shortly after his return to England. In the emerging attitude with respect to observation and experiment, he felt it necessary to slow down the motions of the heart and movement of the blood better to observe the sequence of events in the course of a beating heart. He also thought it important to use a quantitative measure to support his conclusions. His observations and discoveries were published in 1628 in his *Exercitatio anatomica de motu cordis et sanguinis in animalibus* (Anatomical Exercises on the Movement of the Heart and Blood in Animals). Harvey's conclusions became relatively rapidly known, with the subsequent discovery of the capillaries provided the clinching argument for the circulation. They stimulated advances in physiology.

In the first place, then, when the chest of a living animal is laid open and the capsule that immediately surrounds the heart is slit up or removed, the organ is seen now to move, now to be at rest; there is a time when it moves, and a time when it is motionless.

These things are more obvious in the colder animals, such as toads, frogs, serpents, small fishes, crabs, shrimps, snails, and shell-fish. They also become more distinct in warm-blooded animals, such as the dog and hog, if they be attentively noted when the heart begins to flag, to move more slowly, and, as it were, to die: the movements then become slower and rarer, the pauses longer, by which it is made much more easy to perceive and unravel what the motions really are, and how they are performed.

We are therefore authorized to conclude that the heart, at the moment of its action, is at once constricted on all sides, rendered thicker in its parietes and smaller in its ventricles, and so made apt to project or expel its charge of blood.

Hence the very opposite of the opinions commonly received appears to be true; inasmuch as it is generally believed that when the heart strikes the breast and the pulse is felt without, the heart is dilated in its ventricles and is filled with blood; but the contrary of this is the fact, and the heart, when it contracts (and the impulse of the apex is conveyed through the chest wall), is emptied. Whence the motion which is generally regarded as the diastole of the heart, is in truth its systole. And in like manner the intrinsic motion of the heart is not the diastole but the systole; neither is it in the diastole that the heart grows firm and tense, but in the systole, for then only, when tense, is it moved and made vigorous.

From these and other observations of a similar nature, I am persuaded it will be found that the motion of the heart is as follows:

First of all, the auricle contracts, and in the course of its contraction forces the blood (which it contains in ample quantity as the head of the veins, the store-house and cistern of the blood) into the ventricle, which, being filled, the heart raises itself straightway, makes all its fibres tense, contracts the ventricles, and performs a beat, by which it immediately sends the blood supplied to it by the auricle into the arteries. The right ventricle sends its charge into the lungs by the vessel which is called vena arteriosa, but which in structure and function, and all other respects, is an artery. The left ventricle sends its charge into the aorta, and through this by the arteries to the body at large.

These two motions, one of the ventricles, the other of the auricles, take place consecutively, but in such a manner that there is a kind of harmony or rhythm preserved between them, the two concurring in such wise that but one motion is apparent, especially in the warmer blooded animals, in which the movements in question are rapid. Nor is this for any other reason than it is in a piece of machinery, in which, though one wheel gives motion to another, yet all the wheels seem to move simultaneously; or in that mechanical contrivance which is adapted to firearms, where, the trigger being touched, down comes the flint, strikes against the steel, elicits a spark, which falling among the powder, ignites it, when the flame extends, enters the barrel, causes the explosion, propels the ball, and the mark is attained—all of which incidents, by reason of the celerity with which they happen, seem to take place in the twinkling of an eye.

Lest anyone should say that we give them words only, and make more specious assertions without any foundation, and desire to innovate without sufficient cause, three points present themselves for confirmation. I conceive that the truth I contend for will follow necessarily, and appear as a thing obvious to all. First,—the blood is transmitted by the action of the heart from the vena cava to the arteries in such quantity that it cannot be supplied from the ingesta, by the food consumed, and in such wise that the whole mass must very quickly pass through the organ. Second,—the blood under the influence of the arterial pulse and is impelled in a continuous, equable, and incessant stream through every part and member of the body in much larger quantity than were sufficient for nutrition or than the whole mass of fluids could supply. Third,—the veins in like manner return this blood incessantly to the heart from all parts and members of the body.

These points proved, I conceive it will be manifest that the blood circulates, revolves, propelled and returning, from the heart to the extremities, from the extremities to the heart, and thus that it performs a kind of circular motion.

Source: The Works of William Harvey, translated by Robert Willis (Oxford: Sydenham Society, 1847), 21, 22, 31, 32, 48.

New Methods for the Development of Natural Philosophy

With the growth of knowledge about the natural world unknown to ancient thinkers, some natural philosophers began to deem Aristotelian methods inadequate for continuing to learn more about the nature of our world. In the early seventeenth century Kepler and Galileo were among them, and their new approaches were carried out in the practice of their sciences. Emphasis on the roles of observation, experiment, and mathematics became increasingly important. Among the most influential thinkers addressing the issues of scientific method in the course of the seventeenth century were Francis Bacon and René Descartes. Each approached the problem of the best ways to gain new knowledge with different emphases.

The founding of scientific discussion groups and formal societies with the goal of promoting the development of scientific knowledge saw the necessity of setting rules for their activities. England having emerged from a period of civil unrest and war, the Royal Society of London was keenly aware of the need to keep divisive religious and political issues from interfering with their goals and activities. Robert Hooke, as its only paid professional, expressed some of the society's rules to prevent disruptive controversies in those areas. At the end of the century William Wotton, a member of the Royal Society, summed up the distance traveled with respect to scientific method from concepts and practices of scientific method that had reigned for centuries before the modern era.

Francis Bacon

Document 8
On False Notions and the Importance of Experiments

Among Bacon's voluminous works, his two-part *Novum organum* (A New Instrument, 1620) was influential in urging a reconsideration of the most appropriate methods in the pursuit of natural philosophy. Book I offered a critique of traditional approaches to methods in the study of nature. Book II proposed an important role for observation and experiment linked to the proper use of reason in learning new things about the natural world and thereby providing means for the betterment of human life. A detailed analysis, along with examples, is provided about the best means for carrying out experiments and analyzing their results. The points he made were influential in the establishment of the goals of the Royal Society and other scientific societies later in the seventeenth century.

XXXVII

The doctrine of those who have denied that certainty could be attained at all has some agreement with my way of proceeding at the first setting out; but they end in being infinitely separated and opposed. For the holders of that doctrine assert simply that nothing can be known. I also assert that not much can be known in nature by the way which is now in use. But then they go on to destroy the authority of the senses and understanding; whereas I proceed to devise and supply helps for the same.

XXXVIII

The idols and false notions which are now in possession of the human understanding, and have taken deep root therein, not only so beset men's minds that truth can hardly find entrance, but even after entrance is obtained, they will again in the very instauration of the sciences meet and trouble us, unless men being forewarned of the danger fortify themselves as far as may be against their assaults.

XXXIX

There are four classes of Idols which beset men's minds. To these for distinction's sake I have assigned names, calling the first class *Idols of the Tribe*; the second, *Idols of the Cave*; the third, *Idols of the Market Place*; the fourth, *Idols of the Theater*.

XL

The formation of ideas and axioms by true induction is no doubt the proper remedy to be applied for the keeping off and clearing away of idols. To point them out, however, is of great use; for the doctrine of Idols is to the interpretation of nature what the doctrine of the refutation of sophisms is to common logic.

XLI

The Idols of the Tribe have their foundation in human nature itself, and in the tribe or race of men. For it is a false assertion that the sense of man is the measure of things. On the contrary, all perceptions as well as of the sense as of the mind are according to the measure of the individual and not according to the measure of the universe. And the human understanding is like a false mirror, which, receiving rays irregularly, distorts and discolors the nature of things by mingling its own nature with it.

XLII

The Idols of the Cave are the idols of the individual man. For everyone (besides the errors common to human nature in general) has a cave or den of his own, which refracts and discolors the light of nature, owing either to his own proper and peculiar nature; or to his education and conversation with others; or to the reading of books, and the authority of those whom he esteems and admires; or to the differences of impressions, accordingly as they take place in a mind preoccupied and predisposed or in a mind indifferent and settled; or the like. So that the spirit of man (according as it is meted out to different individuals) is in fact a thing variable and full of perturbation, and governed as it were by chance. Whence it was well observed by Heraclitus that men look for sciences in their own lesser worlds, and not in the greater or common world.

XLIII

There are also Idols formed by the intercourse and association of men with each other, which I call Idols of the Market Place, on account of the commerce and consort of men there. For it is by discourse that men associate, and words are imposed according to the apprehension of the vulgar. And therefore the ill and unfit choice of words wonderfully obstructs the understanding. Nor do the definitions or explanations wherewith in some things learned men are wont to guard and defend themselves, by any means set the matter right. But words plainly force and overrule the understanding, and throw all into confusion, and lead men away into numberless empty controversies and idle fancies.

XLIV

Lastly, there are Idols which have immigrated into men's minds from the various dogmas of philosophies, and also from wrong laws of demonstration. These I call Idols of the Theater, because in my judgment all the received systems are but so many stage plays, representing worlds of their own creation after an unreal and scenic fashion. Nor is it only of the systems now in vogue, or only of the ancient sects and philosophies, that I speak; for many more plays of the same kind may yet be composed and in like artificial manner set forth; seeing that errors the most widely different have nevertheless causes for the most part alike. Neither again do I mean this only of entire systems, but also of many principles and axioms in science, which by tradition, credulity, and negligence have come to be received.

But of these several kinds of Idols I must speak more largely and exactly, that the understanding may be duly cautioned.

XLVI

The human understanding when it has once adopted an opinion (either as being the received opinion or as being agreeable to itself) draws all things else to support and agree with it. And though there be a greater number and weight of instances to be found on the other side, yet these it either neglects and despises, or else by some distinction sets aside and rejects; in order that by this great and pernicious predetermination the authority of its former conclusions may remain inviolate. . . . Indeed in the establishment of any true axiom, the negative instance is the more forcible of the two.

XCV

Those who have handled sciences have been either men of experiment or men of dogmas. The men of experiment are like the ant, they only collect and use; the reasoners resemble spiders, who make cobwebs out of their own substance. But the bee takes a middle course: it gathers its material from the flowers of the garden and of the field, but transforms and digests it by a power of its own. Not unlike this is the true business of philosophy; for it neither relies solely or chiefly on the powers of the mind, nor does it take the matter which it gathers from natural history and mechanical experiments and lay it up in the memory whole, as it finds it, but lays it up in the understanding altered and digested. Therefore from a closer and purer league between these two faculties, the experimental and the rational (such as has never yet been made), much may be hoped.

Source: Francis Bacon, *Works*, VIII, translated by James Spedding, Robert L. Ellis, and Douglas D. Heath (Boston: Taggard and Thompson, 1863), 33–37, Aphorisms, Book One, with some changes in spelling.

René Descartes

Document 9
On Right Reasoning and the Mechanical Philosophy

It was during his military service in the Netherlands that René Descartes began to think about the best ways to acquire certain knowledge in natural philosophy. He saw the certainty of mathematical demonstration as a worthy model to replace the logical certainty associated with the use of the Aristotelian syllogism. The manner in which mechanical devices functioned provided a useful model for explanation in natural philosophy. Spiritual components of the universe, souls, angels, and aspects of divinity were in a separate compartment, not subject to mechanical causes.

Descartes' *Discourse on Method*, published in 1637, was very influential in promoting the mechanical philosophy.

I was delighted with Mathematics because of the certainty of its demonstrations and the evidence of its reasoning; but I did not yet understand its true use, and, believing that it was of service only in the mechanical arts, I was astonished that, seeing how firm and solid it was, no loftier edifice had been reared thereupon.

I shall not say anything about Philosophy, but that, seeing that it has been cultivated for many centuries by the best minds that have ever lived, and that nevertheless no single thing is to be found within it which is not subject of dispute, and in consequence which is not dubious, I had not enough presumption to hope to fare better there than other men had done. And also, considering how many conflicting opinions there may be regarding the self-same matter, all supported by learned people, while there can never be more than one which is true, I esteemed as well-nigh false all that only went as far as being probable.

Then as to the other sciences, inasmuch as they derive their principles from Philosophy, I judged that one could have built nothing solid on foundations so far from firm.

I had in my younger days to a certain extent studied Logic; and . . . observed . . . that the syllogisms and the greater part of the other teaching served better in explaining to others those things that one knows . . . than in learning what is new. . . . [I]nstead of the great number of precepts of which Logic is composed, I believed that I should find the four which I should state quite sufficient, provided that I adhered to a firm and constant resolve never on any single occasion to fail in their observance.

The first of those was to accept nothing as true which I did not clearly recognise to be so: that is to say, carefully to avoid precipitation and prejudice in judgments, and to accept in them nothing more than what was presented to my mind so clearly and distinctly that I could have no occasion to doubt it.

The second was to divide up each of the difficulties which I examined into as many parts as possible, and as seemed requisite in order that it might be resolved in the best manner possible.

The third was to carry on my reflections in due order, commencing with objects that were the most simple and easy to understand, in order to rise little and little, or by degrees, to knowledge of the most complex, assuming an order, even if a fictitious one, among those which do not follow a natural sequence relatively to one another.

The was in all cases to make enumerations so complete and reviews so general that I should be certain of having omitted nothing.

[W]hat . . . is most remarkable of all, is the generation of the animal spirits, which resemble a very subtle wind, or rather a flame, which is very pure and very vivid, and which, continually rising up in great abundance from the heart to the brain, thence proceeds through the nerves to the muscles, thereby giving the power of motion to all the members. And it is not necessary to suppose any other cause to explain how the particles of blood, which, being most agitated and most penetrating, are the most proper to constitute these spirits, proceed towards the brain, rather than elsewhere, than that the arteries which carry them thither are those which proceed from the heart in the most direct lines.

[W]hat should be regarded as the 'common sense' by which these ideas are received, and what is meant by the memory which retains them, by the fancy which can change them in diverse ways and out of them constitute new ideas, and which, by the same means, distributing the animal spirits through the muscles, can cause the members of such a body to move in as many diverse ways and in a manner as suitable to the objects which present themselves to its senses and to its internal passions, as can happen in our own case apart from the direction of our free will. And this will not seem strange to those, who, knowing how many different *automata* or moving machines can be made by the industry of man, without employing in so doing more than a very few parts in comparison with the great multitude of bones, muscles, nerves, arteries, veins, or other parts that are found in the body of each animal. From this aspect the body is regarded as a machine which, having been made by the hands of God, is incomparably better arranged, and possesses in itself movements which are much more admirable, than any of those which can be invented by man. . . . [W]hile Reason is a universal instrument which can serve for all contingencies, these organs have need of some special adaptation for every particular action. From this it follows that it is morally impossible that there should be sufficient diversity in any machine to allow it to act in all the events of life in the same way as our reason causes us to act.

Source: René Descartes, *Discourse on Method*, translated by Elizabeth S. Haldane and G.R.T. Ross (Cambridge: Cambridge University Press, 1911), I, 85–86, 91–92, 115–116.

The Nature, Outlook, and Methods of the Royal Society

Document 10
Robert Hooke

Robert Hooke, upon his graduation from Oxford University, became Robert Boyle's assistant in carrying out experiments and went on to become the Royal Society's official "Curator of Experiments" upon its founding in 1662. He was required to perform experiments at the regular meetings of the society and to provide occasional presentations of new scientific ideas. The passage in Document 10 represents the approach and philosophical outlook of the society. Note the justification of its undertakings and the desire to avoid conflict with political and religious opinions.

Memorandum on the Royal Society (1663)
The business and design of the Royal Society is—

To improve the knowledge of naturall things, and all useful Arts, Manufactures, Mechanick practices, Engynes and Inventions by Experiments—(not meddling with Divinity, Metaphysics, Moralls, Politicks, Grammar, Rhetorick, or Logick).

To attempt the recovering of such allowable arts and inventions as are lost.

To examine all systems, theories, principles, hypotheses, elements, histories, and experiments of things naturall, mathematicall, and mechanicall, invented, recorded, or practised, by any considerable author ancient or modern. In order to the compiling of a complete system of solid philosophy for explicating all phenomena produced by nature or art, and recording a rationall account of the causes of things.

All to advance the glory of God, the honour of the King, the Royall founder of the Society, the benefit of his Kingdom, and the generall good of mankind.

In the mean time this Society will not own any hypothesis, system, or doctrine of the principles of naturall philosophy, proposed or mentioned by any philosopher ancient or modern, nor the explication of any phenomena whose recourse must be mad [sic] to originall causes (as not being explicable by heat, cold, weight, figure, and the like, as effects produced thereby); nor dogmatically define nor fix axioms of scientificall things, but will question and canvass all opinions adopting nor adhering to none, till by mature debate and clear arguments, chiefly such as are deduced from legitimate experiments, the truth of such experiments be demonstrated invincibly.

And till there be a sufficient collection made of experiments, histories, and observations, there are no debates to be held at the weekly meetings of the Society, concerning any hypothesis or principal of philosophy, nor any discourses made for explicating any phenomena, except by speciall appointment of the Society or allowance of the President. But the time of the assembly is to be employed in proposing and making experiments, discoursing of the truth, manner, grounds and use thereof, reading and discoursing upon letters, reports and other papers concerning philosophicall and mechanicall matters, viewing and discoursing of curiosities of nature and art, and doing such other things as the Council or the President shall appoint.

Source: Charles Richard Weld, *A History of the Royal Society*, I (London, 1848), 146–148.

Appropriate Methods in Natural Philosophy as Seen at the End of the Seventeenth Century

Document 11
Wotton on Appropriate Methods in the Pursuit of Natural Philosophy

William Wotton (1666–1726), a Fellow of the Royal Society and a divine, in the passage in Document 11 sums up the transformation of appropriate methods to be employed in the pursuit of natural philosophy. Note the emphasis on the roles of experiment, mathematics, and the mechanical philosophy.

I am now to enquire into the Comparative Excellency of Ancient and Modern *Books of Philosophy*, thereby to see in which of them Nature, and its Operations, are explained best. Here I shall first enquire into the several *Methods of Philosophizing*; and afterwards, into the Intrinsick Worth of the Doctrines themselves.

As for *Modern Methods of Philosophizing*, as compared with the *Ancient*, I shall only observe the following particulars. (1.) No Arguments are perceived as cogent, no Principles are allowed as current, among the celebrated Philosophers of the present Age, but what are themselves intelligible. . . . Matter and Motion, with their several Qualities, are only considered in Modern Solutions of Physical Problems. *Substantial Forms, Occult Qualities (b), Intentional Species, Idiosyncrasies, Sympathies and Antipathies of Things*, are exploded; not because they are Terms used by Ancient Philosophers, but because they are only empty Sounds. Words whereof no Man can form a certain and determinate Idea, forming of Sects and Parties in Philosophy, that shall take their Denominations from, and think themselves obliged to stand by the Opinions of any particular Philosophers, is, in a manner, wholly laid aside. *Des Cartes* is not more believed upon his own Word, than *Aristotle:* Matter of Fact is the only Thing appealed to; and Systems are little further regarded. . . . Mathematicks are joyned along with Physiology, not only as Helps to Men's understandings, and Quickners of their Parts; but as absolutely necessary to the comprehending of the Oeconomy of Nature, in all her works. . . . The new Philosophers, as they are commonly called, avoid making general Conclusions, till they have collected a great Number of Experiments or Observations upon the Thing in hand; and, as new Light comes in the old Hypotheses, fall without any Noise or Stir. So that the Inferences that are made from any Enquiries into Natural Things, though perhaps set down in general Terms, yet are (as it were by Consent) received with this Tacit Reserve, *As far as the Experiments or Observations already made, will warrant.* How much these. . . . Things will enlarge Natural Philosophy is easie to guess. . . . The old Philosophers seemed still to be afraid that the common People should despise their Arts if commonly understood;

this made them keep for the most Part to those Studies which required few Hands and Mechanical Tools to compleat them: Which to any Man that has a right Notion of the Extent of a natural Philosopher's Work, will appear absolutely necessary. Above all, the Ancients did not seem sufficiently to understand the Connection between Mathematical Proportions of Lines and Solids, in an abstracted Proposition, and in every Part of the Creation; at least in their reasonings about the Causes of Natural Things, they did not take any great pains to shew it. . . . [T]here was little Correspondence between Mathematical and Physical Sciences, and that Mankind did not believe that there was so intimate a Relation between them as it is now generally known there is. . . .

Now as this Method of Philosophizing laid down above, is right, so it is easie to prove that it has been carefully followed by Modern Philosophers. My Lord *Bacon* was the first great Man who took much pains to convince the World that they had hitherto been in a wrong Path, and that Nature her self, rather than her Secretaries, was to be addressed to by those who were desirous to know very much of her Mind. Monsieur *Des Cartes*, who came soon after, did not perfectly tread in his Steps, since he was for doing most of his Work in his Closet, concluding too soon, before he had made Experiments enough; but then to a vast Genius he joined exquisite Skill in Geometry, and working upon intelligible Principles in an intelligent Manner; though he very often failed of one Part of his End, namely a right Explication of the Phaenomena of Nature, yet by marrying Geometry and Physicks together, he put the World in hopes of a Masculine Offspring in process of Time, though the first Productions should prove abortive. This was the State of Natural Philosophy, when those great Men who after King Charles II's Restoration joined in a Body, called by that Prince himself, the ROYAL SOCIETY, went on with the Design; they made it their Business to let their Members awork to collect a perfect History of Nature, in order to establish thereupon a Body of Physicks. . . .

Had experimental Philosophy been anciently brought upon the Stage, had Geometry been solemnly and generally applied to the Mechanism of Nature, and not solely made use of to instruct Men in the Art of Reasoning, and even that too, not very generally neither, the Moderns would not have had so great Reason to boast as now they have: For these are things which come under ocular Demonstration, which do not depend upon the Fancies of Men for their Approbation, as Oratory and Poetry very often do. So that one may not only in general say that the Ancients are out-done by the Moderns in these Matters, but also assign most of the particulars, and determine the Proportion wherein and how far they have been exceeded, and shew the several Steps whereby this sort of Learning has from Age to Age received Improvement; which ends Disputes and falsifies the Understanding at once.

Source: William Wotton, *Reflections upon Ancient and Modern Learning* (London: Peter Buck, 1694), 229–310.

Experiment and Measurement in Natural Philosophy

Although experiments had been performed occasionally in Antiquity and the Middle Ages, experimentation was hardly a significant part of Aristotelian methodology. The growth of scepticism during the Renaissance, the growing interest in doing as as well as thinking exhibited in the crafts, and the desire to see for oneself, as evidenced, for example, in the work of Vesalius, was complemented by varying and controlling the conditions of the phenomena under study. The urgings of Francis Bacon and the examples set by Gilbert and Galileo early in the seventeenth century were increasingly followed after them. The use of mathematics and measurement expanded beyond the traditional mathematical sciences and slowly began to be applied to other branches of science.

Magnetic Experiments and Celestial Motion

Document 12
William Gilbert on the Magnet and Magnetism

William Gilbert's *On the Magnet* (1600) was the first work since the thirteenth century to deal extensively with magnetic phenomena. Until Gilbert's work it had been held that the poles of a magnet pointed to the celestial poles. The growing interest in geography and navigation during the explorations of the sixteenth century led to greater attention to the compass, as well as to magnetic bodies and their properties. Mariners had noted that the compass needle varies from due north in different ways in different parts of the earth, and also that the manner in which a needle mounted perpendicularly varies in different areas. It was thought that these phenomena, along with celestial observation, might prove useful in locating position at sea. Gilbert was familiar with the discoveries and ideas of navigators concerning the movements of the compass. The link between studies of magnetic behavior and celestial phenomena was very much on Gilbert's mind as he pursued his studies. He came to the conclusion that magnetism was a terrestrial phenomenon, and that the earth was a lodestone. The first part of his book was devoted to the various movements associated with a compass or lodestone. After a number of experiments Gilbert came to the conclusion that a globular lodestone, which he called a terrella, was like a little earth, that it had poles and naturally rotated. The idea was an old one, based on ancient ideas about the nature of spheres, but Gilbert's attribution of rotation to the earth was his own idea and one of the earliest published expressions of that component of the Copernican theory.

The fact is trite and familiar, that the loadstone attracts iron; in the same way, too, one loadstone attracts another. Take the stone on which you have designated the poles, N. and S., and put it in its vessel so that it may float; let the poles lie just in the plane of the horizon, or at least in a plane not very oblique to it; take in your hand another stone the poles of which are also known, and hold it so that its south pole shall lie toward the north pole of the floating stone, and near it alongside; the floating loadstone will straightway follow the other (provided it be within the range and dominion of its powers), nor does it cease to move nor does it quit the other till it clings to it, unless, by moving your hand away, you manage skillfully to prevent the conjunction. In like manner, if you oppose the north pole of the stone in your hand to the south pole of the floating one, they come together and follow each other. For opposite poles attract opposite poles. But, now, if in the same way you present N. to N. or S. to S., one stone repels the other; and as though a helmsman were bearing on the rudder it is off like a vessel making all sail, nor stands nor stays as long as the other stone pursues. One stone also will range the other, turn the other around, bring it to right about and make it come to agreement with itself. But when the two come together and are conjoined in nature's order, they cohere firmly. For example, if you present the north pole of the stone in your hand to the Tropic of Capricorn (for so we may distinguish with mathematical circles the round stone or terrella, just as we do the globe itself) or to any point between the equator and the south pole: immediately the floating stone turns round and so places itself that its south pole touches the north pole of the other and is most closely joined to it. In the same way you will get like effect at the other side of the equator by presenting pole to pole; and thus by art and contrivance we exhibit attraction and repulsion, and motion in a circle toward the concordant position, and the same movements to avoid hostile meetings. Furthermore, in one same stone we are thus able to demonstrate all and are interfered with in their movements. If the loadstone be oblong, with vertices at the extremities and not at the sides, it attracts best at the vertex; for the parts convey to the poles a greater force in right lines than in oblique. Thus do the loadstone and the earth conform magnetic movements.

The magnetic force is given out in all directions around the body; around the terrella it is given out spherically; around loadstones of other shapes unevenly and less regularly. But the sphere of influence does not persist, nor is the force that is diffused through the air permanent or essential; the loadstone simply excites magnetic bodies situate at convenient distance. And as light—so opticians tell us—arrives instantly in the same way, with far greater instantaneousness, the magnetic energy is present within the limits of its forces; and because its act is far more subtile than light, and it does not accord with non-magnetic bodies, it has no relations with air, water, or other non-magnetic body; neither does it act on magnetic bodies by means of forces that rush upon them with any motion whatever, but being present solicits bodies that are in amicable relations to itself. And as a light impinges on whatever confronts it, so does the loadstone impinge upon a magnetic body and excites it. And as light does not remain in the atmosphere above the vapors and effluvia nor is reflected back by those spaces, so that magnetic ray is caught neither in air nor in water. The forms of things are in an instant taken in by the eye or by glasses; so does the magnetic force seize magnetic bodies.

[T]he earth revolves, not fortuitously nor by chance, nor with a headlong motion, but evenly, with a certain high intelligence and with a wonderful steadiness, even like the rest of the movable stars which have fixed periods for their movements.

Thus, inasmuch as the sun itself is the mover and inciter of the universe, the other planets that are situate within the sphere of his forces, being impelled and set in motion, do also with their own forces determine their own courses and revolve in their own periods, according to the amplitude of their greater rotation and the differences of the forces effused and the perception of a greater good. . . . We have asserted that the earth turns on its centre, making one day in its revolution sunward. . . . [T]he sun is the cause of both the earth's and the moon's motions. . . . So, then, the earth rotates in the space of 24 hours, even as the moon does in her monthly course, by a magnetical compact of both, the globes being impelled forward according to the ratio of their orbits. . . . But as between the moon and the earth, it is more reasonable to believe that they are in agreement, because, being neighbor bodies, they are very like in nature and substance, and because the moon has a more manifest effect on the earth than have any of the other stars, except the sun; also the moon alone of all planets directs its movements as a whole toward the earth's centre, and is near of kin to earth, and as it were held by ties to earth.

Source: William Gilbert, *De Magnete*, translated by P. Fleury Mottelay (New York: Wiley, 1893), 28–30, 123, 344–345.

The Reformation of Mechanics

Document 13
Galileo on Falling Bodies

The traditional view of the motion of bodies, although slightly modified during the Middle Ages, was still essentially Aristotelian in character by 1600. The view that all objects on the earth or between the earth and the Moon were either heavy or light was the standard one. Heavy objects tended to move toward their natural place, the center of the universe, which coincided with the center of the earth; light objects tended away from the center of the earth. These were natural motions. Thrown objects, or objects moving other than toward or away from the center, had to be moved by something, in accordance with the principle that everything moved must be moved by something. Freely falling bodies moved with a speed proportional to their weight.

Galileo had begun to challenge these ideas early in his career, but he published little on the subject until the latter part of his life. After his condemnation by the Inquisition for his Copernican beliefs, he was confined to his house near Florence. There his reputation led to visits by notables foreign and domestic. Persuaded by some of his followers to publish his novel ideas on mechanics, he did so in a style he had used earlier in the form of a conversation between three men, two of whom are represented in the passage in Document 13, Salviati expressing Galileo's opinions, and Simplicio, an Aristotelian. Galileo thought it best that his book on mechanics and strength of materials be published abroad, and the volume was published in the Spanish Netherlands in 1638. It had a very considerable influence.

[SALVIATI] My purpose is to set forth a very new science dealing with a very ancient subject. There is, in nature, perhaps nothing older than motion, concerning which the books written by philosophers are neither few nor small; nevertheless I have discovered by experiment some properties of it which are worth knowing and which have not hitherto been either observed or demonstrated. Some superficial observations have been made, as, for instance, that the free motion . . . of a heavy falling body is continuously accelerated; but to just what extent this acceleration occurs has not yet been announced; for so far as I know, no one has yet pointed out that the distances traversed, during equal intervals of time, by a body falling from rest, stand to one another in the same ratio as the odd numbers beginning with unity.

It has been observed that missiles and projectiles describe a curved path of some sort; however no one has pointed out the fact that this path is a parabola. But this and other facts, not few in number or less worth knowing, I have succeeded in proving; and what I consider more important, there have been opened up to this vast and most excellent science, of which my work is merely the beginning, ways and means by which other minds more acute than mine will explore its remote corners.

Theorem II, Proposition II

The spaces described by a body falling from rest with a uniformly accelerated motion are to each other as the squares of the time-intervals employed in traversing these distances. . . .

SIMPLICIO. . . . I am convinced that matters are as described, once having accepted the definition of uniformly accelerated motion. But as to whether this acceleration is that which one meets in nature in the case of falling bodies, I am still doubtful; and it seems to me, not only for my own sake but also for all those who think as I do, that this would be the proper moment to introduce one of those experiments—and there are many of them, I understand—which illustrate in several ways the conclusions reached.

SALVIATI. The request which you, as a man of science, make, is a very reasonable one; for this is the custom—and properly so—in those sciences where mathematical demonstrations are applied to natural phenomena, as is seen in the case of perspective, astronomy, mechanics, music, and others where the principles, once established by well-chosen experiments, become the foundations of the entire superstructure. . . . I have attempted in the following manner to assure myself that the acceleration actually experienced by falling bodies is that above described.

A piece of wooden moulding or scantling, about 12 cubits long, half a cubit wide, and three finger-breadths thick, was taken; on its edge was cut a channel a little more than one finger in breadth; having made this groove very straight, smooth, and polished, and having lined it with parchment, also as smooth and polished as possible, we rolled along it a hard, smooth, and very round bronze ball. Having placed this board in a sloping position, by lifting one end some one or two cubits above the other, we rolled the ball, as I was just saying, along the channel, noting, in a manner presently to be described, the time required to make the descent. We repeated this experiment more than once in order to measure the time with an accuracy such that the deviation between two observations never exceeded one-tenth of a pulse-beat. Having performed this operation and having assured ourselves of its reliability, we now rolled the ball only one-quarter the length of the channel; and having measured the time of its descent, we found it precisely one-half of the former. Next we tried other distances, comparing the time for the whole length with that for the half, or with that for two-thirds, or three-fourths, or indeed for any fraction; in such experiments, repeated a full hundred times, we always found that the spaces traversed were to each other as the squares of the times, and this was true for all inclinations of the plane, i.e., of the channel, along which we rolled the ball. We also observed that the times of descent for various inclinations of the plane bore to one another precisely that ratio which, as we shall see later, the Author had predicted and demonstrated for them.

For the measurement of time, we employed a large vessel of water placed in an elevated position; to the bottom of this vessel was soldered a pipe of small diameter giving a thin jet of water, which we collected in a small glass during the time of each descent, whether for the whole length of the channel or for a part of its length; the water thus collected was weighed, after each descent, on a very accurate balance; the differences and ratios of these weights gave us the differences and ratios of the times, and this with such accuracy that although the operation was repeated many, many times, there was no appreciable discrepancy in the results.

Source: Galileo Galilei, *Dialogues Concerning Two New Sciences*, translated by H. Crew and A. De Salvio (New York: Macmillan, 1914), 153–154, 174, 178–179.

Experiment, Measurement, and the Vacuum

Document 14
Pascal's Suggested Experiments with the Torricelli Tube

A number of important experiments were conducted in the second half of the seventeenth century after the discovery of the space above the mercury in a vertical tube at least three feet long, sealed at one end, with its open end placed in a dish of mercury; the concept of the vacuum had been rejected by Aristotle, as well as by Descartes. For the followers of both Aristotle and Descartes the universe was a plenum, that is, completely filled with matter, some of which was imperceptible to the senses.

Blaise Pascal (1623–1662), a brilliant mathematician and experimenter, had been interested in the science of fluids and made important discoveries in hydrodynamics. He also devised a number of experiments with what had come to be called the Torricelli tube, after Evangelista Torricelli's (1608–1647) insightful suggestion, as described in Document 14, that the weight of the mercury, or quicksilver as it was then also called, in the tube was equal to the weight of the atmosphere pressing on the mercury in the dish in which its open end rested. Pascal made a number of experiments clearly demonstrating that the size of the space above the mercury had no effect on the height of the mercury. He also thought that he had a definitive experiment that would test Torricelli's hypothesis about the weight of the atmosphere. Pascal wrote to his brother-in-law, Florin Perier, with his suggestions, and Perier then carried them out, as reported by him in the letter reproduced in Document 14. The experiments carried out on a mountain in France were influential in convincing some natural philosophers of the existence of vacua and led to the creation of vacuum pumps with which a number of new experiments were capable of being performed. Pascal's results were not published until 1663.

My dear reader, since certain considerations prevent my publishing at this time in its entirety a treatise in which I have reported many new experiments I have made concerning the vacuum together with the conclusions I have drawn from them, I decided to give an account of the chief of them in this summary, where you will see in advance the plan of the whole work.

The occasion of these experiments was as follows: *About four years ago in Italy it was found that a glass tube four feet in height, with one end open and the other hermetically sealed, having been filled with quicksilver and the open end then stopped by a finger or in some other way and the tube placed vertically with the stopped end down and plunged two or three fingers' breadths into some more quicksilver contained in a vessel half full of quicksilver and half full of water; if the stopper is removed, the tube remaining plunged into the quicksilver of the vessel, the quicksilver of the tube descends part way, leaving at the top of the tube an apparently empty space, the bottom of the tube remaining full of quicksilver up to a certain height. And if the tube is lifted a little until its open end, which had been dipped in the quicksilver of the vessel, leaving this quicksilver, reaches the region of water, the quicksilver of the tube rises to the top with the water and these two liquids are mingled in the tube, but finally all the quicksilver falls, and the tube is found to be entirely filled with water.*

Source: Blaise Pascal, *New Experiments Concerning the Vacuum* (1647), translated by Richard Scofield in *Great Books of the Western World,* edited by Robert M. Hutchins (Chicago and London: Encyclopedia Britannica, 1952), vol. 33, 359.

Copy of the letter of Monsieur Pascal the Younger to Monsieur Perier,
November 15, 1647

You know the views of the Philosophers on this subject. They have all endorsed the principle that nature abhors a vacuum, and most of them have gone further and maintained that nature cannot admit of it, and would perish sooner than suffer it. Thus opinions have been divided: some have been content to say only that nature abhors a vacuum, others have maintained that she could not tolerate it. I have tried in my pamphlet on the vacuum to refute the latter opinion, and I believe that the experiments recorded there suffice to show indubitably that nature can, and does, tolerate any amount of space empty of any of the substances that we are acquainted with, and that are perceptible to our senses. I am now engaged in testing the truth of the former statement, namely, that nature abhors a vacuum, and am trying to find experimental ways to show whether the effects ascribed to the abhorrence of a vacuum are really attributable to that abhorrence, or to the weight and pressure of the air. . . .

To this end I have devised [an experiment] that is in itself sufficient to give us the light we seek if it can be carried out with accuracy. This is to perform the usual experiment with a vacuum several times over in one day, with the same tube and with the same quicksilver, sometimes at the base and sometimes at the summit of a mountain at least five or six hundred fathoms high, in order to ascertain whether the height of the quicksilver suspended in the tube will be the same or different in the two situations. You see at once, doubtless, that such an experiment is decisive. If it happens that the height of the quicksilver is less at the top than at the base of the mountain (as I have many reasons to believe it is, although all who have studied the matter are of the opposite opinion), it follows of necessity that the weight and pressure of the air is the sole cause of this suspension of the quicksilver, and not the abhorrence of a vacuum: for it is quite certain that there is much more air that presses on the foot of the mountain than there is on its summit, and one cannot well say that nature abhors a vacuum more at the foot of the mountain than at its summit.

Copy of the Account of the Experiment submitted by
Monsieur Perier

I notified several people of standing in this town of Clermont, who had asked me to let them know when I would make the ascent. . . .

On that day, therefore, at eight o'clock in the morning, we started off all together for the garden of the Minim Fathers, which is almost the lowest spot in the town, and there began the experiment in this manner.

First, I poured into a vessel six pounds of quicksilver which I had rectified during the three days preceding; and having taken glass tubes of the same size, each four feet long and hermetically sealed at one end but upon at the other, I placed them in the same vessel and carried out with each of them the usual vacuum experiment. Then, having set them up side by side without lifting them out of the vessel, I found that the quicksilver left in each of them stood at the same level, which was twenty-six inches and three and a half lines above the surface of the quicksilver in the vessel. . . .

With the other tube and a portion of the same quicksilver, I then proceeded with all these gentlemen to the top of the Puy de Dôme, some 500 fathoms above the Convent. There, after I had made the same experiments in the same way that I have made them at the Minims, we found that there remained in the tube a height of only twenty-three inches and two lines of quicksilver; whereas in the same tube, at the Minims we had found a height of twenty-six inches and three and a half lines. Thus between the heights of the quicksilver in the two experiments there proved to be a difference of three inches one line and a half. . . .

Later, on the way down at a spot called Lafon de l'Arbre, far above the Minims but much farther below the top of the mountain, I repeated the same experiment, still with the same tube, the same quicksilver, and the same vessel, and there found that the height of the quicksilver left in the tube was twenty-five inches. I repeated it a second time at the same spot. . . . All these experiments yielded the same height of twenty-five inches, which is one inch, three lines and a half less than we had just found at the top of the Puy de Dôme. It increased our satisfaction not a little to observe in this way that the height of the quicksilver diminished with the altitude of the site.

On my return to the Minims I found that the [quicksilver in the] vessel I had left there in continuous operation was at the same height at which I had left it, that is, at twenty-six inches, three lines and a half. . . .

I repeated it again a last time, not only in the same tube I had used on the Puy de Dôme, but also with the same quicksilver and in the same vessel that I had carried up the mountain; and again I found the quicksilver at the same height of twenty-six inches, three lines and a half which I had observed in the morning, and thus finally verified the certainty of our results.

The next day. . . . I carried out the ordinary experiment of the vacuum in a private residence which stands on the highest ground of the city, some six or seven fathoms above the garden of the Minims, and on a level with the base of the tower. There we found the quicksilver at the height of about twenty-six inches and three lines, which is less than that which was found at the Minims by about half a line. I next made the experiment on the top of the same tower, which was twenty fathoms higher than its base and about twenty-six or twenty-seven fathoms above the garden of the Minims. There I found the quicksilver at the height of about twenty-six inches and one line, that is, about two lines less than its height at the base of the tower, and about two and a half lines lower than it stood in the garden of the Minims.

Source: The Physical Treatises of Pascal, translated by I.H.S. Spiers and A.G.H. Spiers (New York: Columbia University Press, 1937), 98–107.

Newton on the Laws of Motion and the Principle of Universal Gravitation

Document 15
Newton's Laws of Motion

What had begun as a debate within the Royal Society on the cause of planetary motion, when brought to Newton's attention in 1684, led him to develop the principles of mechanics and the principle of gravitation that have been influential in the science of mechanics to the present day. The publication in 1687 of Newton's *Mathematical Principles of Natural Philosophy* marked a culmination in the transformation of natural philosophy that had begun more than a century earlier. His laws of motion, although slightly modified since they were first published, remain the foundation for beginning the study of physics in university curricula today. From them and the law of universal gravitation, the discoveries of Kepler and Galileo could be derived mathematically. Newton's laws of motion subsequently led to many further discoveries in both astronomy and mechanics.

AXIOMS, OR THE LAWS OF MOTION

Law 1   *Every body perseveres in its state of being at rest or of moving uniformly straight forward except insofar as it is compelled to change its state by forces impressed.*

Projectiles persevere in their motions, except insofar as they are retarded by the resistance of the air and are impelled downward by the force of gravity. A spinning hoop, which has parts that by their cohesion continually draw one another back from rectilinear motions, does not cease to rotate, except insofar as it is retarded by the air. And larger bodies—planets and comets—preserve for a longer time both their progressive and their circular motions, which take place in spaces having less resistance.

Law 2   *A change in motion is proportional to the motive force impressed and takes place along the straight line in which that force is impressed.*

If some force generates any motion, twice the force will generate twice the motion, and three times the force will generate three times the motion, whether the force is impressed all at once or successively by degrees. And if the body was previously moving, the new motion (since motion is always in the same direction as the generative force) is added to the original motion if that motion was in the same direction or is subtracted from the original motion if it was in the opposite direction or, if it was in an oblique direction, is combined obliquely and compounded with it according to the directions of both motions.

Law 3   To any action there is always an opposite and equal reaction; in other words, *the actions of two bodies upon each other are always equal and always opposite in direction.*

Whatever presses or draws something else is pressed or drawn just as much by it. If anyone presses a stone with a finger, the finger is also pressed by the stone. If a horse draws a stone tied to a rope, the horse will (so to speak) also be drawn back equally toward the stone, for the rope, stretched out at both ends, will urge the horse toward the stone and the stone toward the horse by one and the same endeavor to go slack and will impede the forward motion of one as much as it promotes the forward motion of the other. If some body impinging upon another body changes the motion of that body in any way by its own force, then, by the force of the other body (because of the equality of their mutual pressure), it also will in turn undergo the same change in its own motion in the opposite direction. By means of these actions, equal changes occur in the motions, not in the velocities—that is, of course, if the bodies are not impeded by anything else. For the changes in velocities that likewise occur in opposite directions are inversely proportional to the bodies because the motions are changed equally. This law is valid also for attractions.

Proposition 75   Theorem 35 *If toward each of the points of a given sphere there tend equal centripetal forces decreasing in the squared ratio of the distances from the points, I say that this sphere will attract any other homogeneous sphere with a force inversely proportional to the square of the distance between the centers.*

For the attraction of any particle is inversely as the square of its distance from the center of the attracting sphere . . . , and therefore is the same as if the total attracting force emanated from one single corpuscle situated in the center of this sphere. Moreover, this attraction is as great as the attraction of the same corpuscle would be if, in turn, it were attracted by each of the individual particles of the attracted sphere with the same force by which it attracts them. And that attraction of the corpuscle . . . would be inversely proportional to the square of its distance from the center of the sphere; and therefore the sphere's attraction, which is equal to the attraction of the corpuscle, is in the same ratio. Q.E.D.

Thus far I have explained the phenomena of the heavens and of our sea by the force of gravity, but I have not yet assigned a cause to gravity. Indeed, this force arises from some cause that penetrates as far as the centers of the sun and planets without any diminution of its power to act, and that acts not in proportion to the quantity of the *surfaces* of the particles on which it acts (as mechanical causes are wont to do) but in proportion to the quantity of *solid* matter, and whose action is extended everywhere to immense distances, always decreasing as the squares of the distances. Gravity toward the sun is compounded of the gravities toward the individual particles of the sun, and at increasing distances from the sun decreases exactly as the squares of the distances as far out as the orbit of Saturn, as is manifest from the fact that the aphelia of the planets are at rest, and even as far as the farthest aphelia of the comets, provided that those aphelia are at rest. I have not as yet been able to deduce from phenomena the reason for these properties of gravity, and I do not feign hypotheses. For whatever is not deduced from the phenomena must be called a hypothesis; and hypotheses, whether metaphysical or physical, or based on occult qualities, or mechanical, have no place in experimental philosophy. In this experimental philosophy, propositions are deduced from the phenomena and are made general by induction. The impenetrability, mobility, and impetus of bodies, and the laws of motion and the law of gravity have been found by this method. And it is enough that gravity really exists and acts according to the laws that we have set forth and is sufficient to explain all the motions of the heavenly bodies and of our sea.

Source: Isaac Newton, *The Principia: Mathematical Principles of Natural Philosophy*, translated by I. B. Cohen and Anne Whitman (Berkeley and Los Angeles: University of California Press, 1999), 416, 594, 943.

The Nature of the Universe and Its Laws as Arguments for Design by a Creator

Document 16
Newton's Letter to Richard Bentley

By the terms of Robert Boyle's will an endowment was created for a series of lectures to show how the growth of scientific knowledge provided evidence for the existence, omniscience, and omnipotence of God. Richard Bentley (1662–1742) was the first one chosen to give a lecture. He decided that the best way to prepare for it was to consult Newton, whose *Mathematical Principles of Natural Philosophy* had given him the reputation of being the greatest scientist of the day. Newton's responses to Bentley's queries were based on a long-existing tradition of ascribing certain patterns evident in the world as examples of divine intention. Newton's use of the consequences of his recent discoveries as such evidence was a pattern since applied to a whole range of scientific discoveries up to the present day.

When I wrote my treatise upon our System, I had an Eye upon such Principles as might work with considering Men, for the belief of a Deity, and nothing can rejoice me more than to find it useful for that Purpose. But if I have done the Public any service this way, it is due to nothing but Industry and patient Thought.

As to your first Query, it seems to me that if the Matter of our Sun and Planets, and all the Matter of the Universe, were evenly scattered throughout all the Heavens, and every Particle had an innate Gravity towards all the rest, and the whole Space, throughout which this Matter was scattered, was but finite; the Matter on the outside of this Space would by its Gravity tend towards all the Matter on the inside, and by consequence fall down into the middle of the whole Space, and there compose one great spherical Mass. But if the Matter was evenly disposed throughout an infinite Space, it could never convene into one Mass, but some of it would convene into one Mass and some into another, so as to make an infinite Number of great Masses, scattered at great Distances from one to another throughout all that infinite Space. And thus might the Sun and fixt Stars be formed, supposing the Matter were of a lucid Nature. But how the Matter should divide itself into two sorts, and that Part of it, which is fit to compose a shining Body, should fall down into one Mass and make a Sun, and the rest, which is fit to compose an opaque Body, should coalesce, not into one great Body, like the shining Matter, but into many little ones; or if the Sun at first were an opaque Body like the Planets, or the Planets lucid Bodies like the Sun, how he alone should be changed into a shining Body, whilst all they continue opaque, or all they be changed into opaque ones, whilst he remains unchanged, I do not think explicable by meer natural Causes, but am forced to ascribe it to the Counsel and Contrivance of a voluntary Agent.

The same Power, whether natural or supernatural, which placed the Sun in the Center of the six primary Planets, placed *Saturn* in the Center of the Orbs of his five secondary Planets, and *Jupiter* in the Center of his four secondary Planets, and the Earth in the Center of the Moon's Orb; and therefore had this Cause been a blind one, without Contrivance or Design, the Sun would have been a Body of the same kind with *Saturn, Jupiter*, and the Earth, that is, without Light and Heat. Why there is one Body in our System qualified to give Light and Heat to all the rest, I know no Reason, but because the Author of the System thought it convenient; and why there is but one Body of this kind I know no Reason, but because one was sufficient to warm and enlighten all the rest. For the *Cartesian* Hypothesis of Suns losing their Light, and then turning into Comets, and Comets into Planets, can have no Place in my System, and is plainly erroneous; because it is certain that as often as they appear to us, they descend into the System of our Planets, lower than the Orb of *Jupiter*, and sometimes lower that the Orbs of *Venus* and *Mercury*, and yet never stay here, but always return from the Sun with the same Degrees of Motion by which they approached him.

To your second Query, I answer, that the Motions which the Planets now have could not spring from any natural Cause alone, but were impressed by an intelligent Agent. For since Comets ascend into the Region of our Planets, and here move all manner of ways, going sometimes the same way with the Planets, sometimes the contrary way, and sometimes in cross ways, in Planets inclined to the Plane of the Ecliptick, and at all kinds of Angles, 'tis plain that there is no natural Cause which could determine all the Planets, both primary and secondary, to move the same way and in the same Plane, without any considerable Variation: This must have been the Effect of Counsel. Nor is there any natural Cause which could give the Planets those just Degrees of Velocity, in Proportion to their Distances from the Sun, and other central Bodies, which were requisite to make them move in such concentrick Orbs about those Bodies. Had the Planets been as swift as Comets, in Proportion to their Distances from the Sun (as they would have been, had their Motion been caused by their Gravity, whereby the Matter, at the first Formation of the Planets, might fall from the remotest Regions towards the Sun) they would not move in concentrick Orbs, but in such eccentrick ones as the Comets move in. . . . To make this System therefore, with all its Motions, required a Cause which understood, and compared together, the Quantities of Matter in the several Bodies of the Sun and Planets, and the gravitating Powers resulting from thence; the several distances of the primary Planets from the Sun, and of the secondary ones from *Saturn*, *Jupiter*, and the Earth; and the Velocities with which these Planets could revolve about those Quantities of Matter in the central Bodies; and to compare and adjust all these Things together, in so great a Variety of bodies, argues that Cause to be not blind and fortuitous, but very well skilled in Mechanicks and Geometry.

Source: Four Letters from Sir Isaac Newton to Doctor Bentley. Containing Some Arguments in Proof of a Deity (London: R. and J. Dodsley, 1756), 1–6.

GLOSSARY

Active Principles: Internal principles that account for the behavior of bodies that cannot be explained solely on the grounds of mechanical actions, as for example with gravitation or in alchemical reactions. Active principles also allowed a role for divine providence in the operations of the universe.

Aerial Nitre: A hypothetical substance in the air that, when ingested by the lungs and then passing into the blood, nourishes the body.

Aether: A rarefied substance constituting the matter of the heavens.

Alchemy: The science involving the search for material and spiritual perfection through the treatment and interactions of various substances. Among its objectives were the transfer of other metals into gold and the growth of metals.

Aphelia: In the course of their orbits, the farthest distances of the planets from the Sun.

Archaeus: In the theory of Paracelsus, an entity like a spiritual alchemist within the human body that governs metabolic processes.

Book of Nature: The interpretation of the natural world conceived as a companion to the Bible, both revealing the nature of God.

Diastole: The relaxation of the heart muscle after its contraction in the heartbeat.

Eccentric: A circle used by astronomers to describe a planetary orbit whose center is slightly distant from the Earth or Sun.

Empiricism: The acquisition of knowledge based on the collection of facts by use of the senses in observation or experimentation.

Epicycle: In the plotting of planetary motion, a circle on which a planet revolves, while the center of the epicycle revolves on a larger circle about the Earth or Sun.

Epigenesis: The theory that the offspring of living things gradually develop from undifferentiated material.

Equant: In Ptolemaic astronomy, a point not at the center of an orbit, around which a planet moves with uniform motion.

Generation: The process by which plants or animals are reproduced.

Geoheliocentrism: The theory that all the planets revolve around the Sun, which revolves around the Earth in the course of a year.

Herbals: Books with illustrations and descriptions of plants and their properties.

Homocentric Spheres: In the Aristotelian system, spheres carrying the planets, all revolving about a common center, the Earth.

Humors: In Galenic physiology and medicine, the four bodily fluids, whose balance or imbalance determines the effectiveness of the body's functions and and an individual's health.

Impetus: A medieval theory based on the Aristotelian principle that everything moved must have a mover. It holds that an immaterial force is imparted to all hurled or propelled objects, keeping them in flight and gradually diminishing until they fall to Earth.

Intelligencers: Individuals acting as centers of correspondence and the transmission of scientific ideas to natural philosophers throughout Europe.

Isochronism of the Pendulum: The motions of a pendulum, regardless of the length of its swing, take equal lengths of time.

Kepler's Area Rule: Now called Kepler's Second Law, holds that a line from the Sun to a planet sweeps out equal areas in equal times, resulting in a more rapid motion of the planet when it is closer to the Sun than when farther from it.

Lodestone: An iron ore with magnetic properties.

Mechanical Philosophy: A system of explanation developed during the Scientific Revolution employing the size, shape, organization, and motions of invisible particles as the causes of natural events through contact, on analogy with the operations of mechanical devices.

Macrocosm/Microcosm: The idea that the small world embodies the large one—specifically, that man mirrors the entire universe—and that there are correspondences between them; underlies principles behind magic, astrology, and alchemy.

Micrometer: A device inserted in telescopes allowing for much greater precision in measurement between celestial objects than is possible by estimation.

Mixed Sciences: A term developed in Antiquity for the sciences that used mathematics, such as astronomy, mechanics, optics, and music.

Natural Philosophy: The study of all aspects of the natural world and including the methods of learning about them; what we would call science today.

Occult Sciences: The sciences, such as astrology, alchemy, and magic, whose effects are conceived as occurring through the operation of imperceptible forces.

Parallax: The angle at a star, or at the Sun, subtending the radius of Earth's orbit.

Peripatetics: Another name for Aristotelians, derived from the alleged practice by Aristotle of leading discussions among his followers while walking about in ancient Athens.

Philosopher's Stone: The goal sought by alchemists enabling the creation of gold from other metals, as well as spiritual purification.

Planetary Parameters: The various components used for the prediction of planetary positions; among them were the closest and farthest distances of a planet from the Sun, the length of time taken to complete an orbit, and the distance of a planet's center of revolution from the center of its orbit.

***Pneuma*:** In Stoic philosophy, a world soul, the fundamental substance pervading all bodies, and a life-giving ingredient in the air.

Preformation: The theory that all living things exist fully formed, or with analogous structures, either in the egg or male seed, and that the process of generation involves a trigger initiating growth, development, and birth.

Retrograde Motions: The periodic apparent motions of the planets in the opposite direction from their normal paths.

Spontaneous Generation: The birth of lower forms of life, such as worms or insects, from inanimate matter.

Syllogism: A logical form of reasoning by deduction, involving a major premise, a minor premise, and a conclusion; for example: All men are mortal; Aristotle is a man; therefore Aristotle is mortal.

Sympathy and Antipathy: The means by which occult forces affected similar or dissimilar entities in the concept of the microcosm/ macrocosm relationship.

Systole: The contraction of the heart muscle in a heartbeat.

Taxonomy: The classification into a hierarchy of the components of various categories; chiefly used in classifying living things.

Vital Spirits: The philosophical position that all things have immaterial components, or, in the case of living things, "souls," as the governing principles of their activities.

Vortex Theory: The theory that the Sun is surrounded by a substance whirling around it like a whirlpool. For Kepler, the vortex is caused by the rotation of the Sun, which is the cause of planetary motion; for Descartes, the vortex, emerging just after the Creation, accounts for the motions of the planets.

ANNOTATED BIBLIOGRAPHY

General Works and Surveys

Applebaum, Wilbur, ed. *Encyclopedia of the Scientific Revolution: From Copernicus to Newton*. New York: Garland, 2000. Includes entries by leading scholars on concepts, methods, intellectual and social contexts, developments in various sciences, and individuals.

Cohen, H. Floris. *The Scientific Revolution: A Historiographical Inquiry*. Chicago: University of Chicago Press, 1994. Detailed survey of conceptions of the Scientific Revolution and the different ways historians have described it and its origins.

Dear, Peter. *Revolutionizing the Sciences: European Knowledge and Its Ambitions, 1500–1700*. Princeton, NJ: Princeton University Press, 2001. The development of the Scientific Revolution, its various aspects, and the forces shaping them.

Goodman, David and Colin A. Russell, eds. *The Rise of Scientific Europe, 1500–1800*. Sevenoaks, England: Hodder and Stoughton, 1991. An introductory survey dealing with issues concerning the unique context of Europe contrasted with China and the world of Islam in the rise of new scientific ideas.

Hall, A. R. *The Revolution in Science, 1500–1750*. New York and London: Longman, 1983. Detailed survey of changing scientific ideas, although with little regard for contextual issues.

Henry, John. *The Scientific Revolution and the Origin of Modern Science*. Houndmills, England and New York: Palgrave, 2002. Succinct account of the development of aspects of the new philosophy and their contextual frameworks.

Jardine, Lisa. *Ingenious Pursuits: Building the Scientific Revolution*. New York: Nan A. Talese, 1999. Well-written accounts with excellent illustrations of various aspects of natural philosophy in the seventeenth century, mostly, but not entirely, in England.

Rossi, Paolo. *The Birth of Modern Science*. Translated by Cynthia De Nardi Ipsen. Oxford: Blackwell Publishers, 2001. How the growth of new scientific concepts encompassed various aspects of the social, cultural, and intellectual life of the time.

Shapin, Steven. *The Scientific Revolution*. Chicago: University of Chicago Press, 1996. An attempt to challenge the notion of the Scientific Revolution while addressing the emergence of new ideas in their cultural contexts.

Taton, René, ed. *The Beginnings of Modern Science: From 1450 to 1800*. Translated by A. J. Pomerans. London: Thames and Hudson, 1964. Essays covering the entire Scientific Revolution and its various components.

Wolf, Abraham. *A History of Science, Technology, and Philosophy in the 16th and 17th Centuries*. London: Allen and Unwin, 1935, reprinted. Well-illustrated articles on the growth of ideas in the various branches of science and their relations to technology and philosophy.

Contextual Issues in the Scientific Revolution

Atherton, Margaret, ed. *Women Philosophers of the Early Modern Period*. Indianapolis: Hackett, 1994. Selections on philosophical issues written by seven women during the Scientific Revolution.

Bono, James J. *The Word of God and the Languages of Man: Interpreting Nature in Early Modern Science and Medicine*. Vol. 1: *Ficino to Descartes*. Madison: University of Wisconsin Press, 1995. Describes different theories of language and how they reflected opposing attitudes about humankind's capacity to learn the nature of the created world.

Eamon, William. *Science and the Secrets of Nature: Books of Secrets in Medieval and Early Modern Culture*. Princeton, NJ: Princeton University Press, 1994. On the roles of the crafts and magic in the origins of modern science.

Feingold, Mordechai. *The Mathematicians' Apprenticeship: Science, Universities, and Society in England, 1560–1640*. Cambridge: Cambridge University Press, 1984. A very detailed examination of teaching practices, demonstrating that ideas of the new natural philosophy were beginning to find a place in the English universities.

Field, Judith V. and Frank A.J.L. James, eds. *Renaissance and Revolution: Humanists, Scholars, Craftsmen, and Natural Philosophers in Early Modern Europe*. Cambridge: Cambridge University Press, 1993. Examines issues connected with the nature of scientific disciplines and their interactions with other fields.

Findlen, Paula. *Possessing Nature: Museums, Collecting, and Scientific Culture in Early Modern Italy*. Berkeley and Los Angeles: University of California Press, 1994. Shows how the private collections of the Italian elites became centers of civic culture, scientific debate, and of learning.

Ford, Brian. *Images of Science: A History of Scientific Illustration*. London: The British Library, 1992. Magnificent reproductions from various sciences; most from the period of the Scientific Revolution.

Freudenthal, Gideon. *Atom and Individual in the Age of Newton*. Translated by Peter McLaughlin. Dordrecht and Boston: Reidel, 1986. A fairly sophisticated effort to link the development of Newton's concepts of matter and mechanics to philosophical positions emerging from social changes in seventeenth-century England.

Garin, Eugenio. *Science and Civic Life in the Italian Renaissance*. Translated by Peter Munz. Garden City, NY: Doubleday, 1969. Advances the thesis that the development of the culture of the Italian cities in the late Middle Ages and the Renaissance laid the foundation for the origins of modern scientific ideas.

Gouk, Penelope. *Music, Science, and Natural Magic in Seventeenth-Century England*. New Haven, CT: Yale University Press, 1999. A study of how changing musical theory and practice in the seventeenth century mediated between natural philosophy and magic.

Hadden, Richard W. *On the Shoulders of Merchants: Exchange and the Mathematical Conception of Nature in Early Modern Europe*. Albany: State University of New York Press, 1994. Argues that problems arising from increasing trade in commodities led to mathematical approaches differing from classical mathematics and important for the new natural philosophy.

Kline, Morris. *Mathematics in Western Culture*. Oxford: Oxford University Press, 1953. Chs. VIII–XV. Well-written account of the relation of mathematics to various aspects of natural philosophy, music, the arts, and the culture of Early Modern Europe.

Lindberg, David C. *The Beginnings of Western Science: The European Scientific Tradition in Philosophical, Religious, and Institutional Context, 600 B.C. to A.D. 1450*. Chicago: University of Chicago Press, 1992. Useful as an introduction to the importance of ancient ideas and their medieval modifications as the starting-point of the Scientific Revolution.

Mayr, Otto. *Authority, Liberty, and Automatic Machinery in Early Modern Europe*. Baltimore: Johns Hopkins University Press, 1986. The role of technology, particularly that of the clock, in understanding nature and aspects of social life.

McKnight, Stephen A., ed. *Science, Pseudo-Science, and Utopianism in Early Modern Thought*. Columbia: University of Missouri Press, 1992. Chapters on alchemy, utopianism, Hermeticism, and the context of the Scientific Revolution and its consequences.

Moran, Bruce T., ed. *Patronage and Institutions: Science, Technology, and Medicine at the European Court, 1500–1750*. Woodbridge, England: Boydell,

1991. How the interests of the various courts of Europe influenced the development of science.

Olson, Richard. *Science Deified and Science Defied: The Historical Significance of Science in Western Culture*. 2 vols. Berkeley and Los Angeles: University of California Press, 1982. I, chs. 7–9; II, chs. 1–3. Excellent accounts of changes in natural philosophy, based on changes in the social and intellectual milieus, and their effects on culture.

Porter, Roy and Mikulás Teich, eds. *The Scientific Revolution in National Context*. Cambridge and New York: Cambridge University Press, 1992. Discusses differences among the nations of Europe in their approaches to natural philosophy.

Righini Bonelli, Maria. L., and William R. Shea, eds. *Reason, Experiment, and Mysticism in the Scientific Revolution*. London: Macmillan, 1975. Several essays critically address the thesis that the ideas attributed to Hermes Trismegistus helped shape the Scientific Revolution.

Rossi, Paolo. *Philosophy, Technology, and the Arts in the Early Modern Era*. Translated by Salvatore Attanasio. New York: Harper and Row, 1970. On the role of new attitudes toward technology in the development of new approaches to nature.

Schiebinger, Londa. *The Mind Has No Sex? Women in the Origins of Modern Science*. Cambridge, MA: Harvard University Press, 1989. Women's contributions to the development of early modern science.

Shumaker, Wayne. *The Occult Sciences in the Renaissance: A Study in Intellectual Patterns*. Berkeley: University of Californa Press, 1972. Descriptions and analyses of the patterns of thought and debates about astrology, witchcraft, white magic, alchemy, and hermeticism.

Smith, Alan G. R. *Science and Society in the Sixteenth and Seventeenth Centuries*. New York: Harcourt Brace Jovanovich, 1972. A superbly illustrated brief acount of how social changes in the sixteenth and seventeenth centuries led to developments in the various branches of science and their effect on society.

Vickers, Brian, ed. *Occult and Scientific Mentalities in the Renaissance*. Cambridge: Cambridge University Press, 1984. Articles by experts on the occult sciences within various institutions, in different locations, and in the thinking of certain individuals.

Webster, Charles. *From Paracelsus to Newton: Magic and the Making of Modern Science*. Cambridge: Cambridge University Press, 1964. Addresses the relationship between magic and natural philosophy as an essential component of the Scientific Revolution.

Westman, Robert and J. E. McGuire. *Hermeticism and the Scientific Revolution*. Los Angeles: Clark Memorial Library, 1977. Analyses of theses about the importance of Hermetic ideas in the Scientific Revolution.

Astronomy and Cosmology

Aiton, Eric J. *The Vortex Theory of Planetary Motions*. London and New York: Science History Publications, 1972. Traces the development, history, influence, and demise of Descartes' vortex theory of planetary motion.

Crowe, Michael J. *Theories of the World from Antiquity to the Copernican Revolution*. New York: Dover, 1990. Excellent brief survey, well illustrated, up to and including Galileo's discoveries with the telescope.

Curry, Patrick. *Prophecy and Power: Astrology in the Early Modern Period*. Princeton, NJ: Princeton University Press, 1989. Analyzes the social context of the belief in astrology and its roles and uses among different social classes and areas of knowledge.

Garin, Eugenio. *Astrology in the Renaissance: The Zodiac of Life*. Translated by Carolyn Jackson, June Allen, and Clare Robertson. London: Routledge & Kegan Paul, 1983. Brief description of astrological ideas and practices and their relation to Platonism, Hermetism, and magic.

Gingerich, Owen. *The Book Nobody Read*. New York: Walker & Co., 2004. An interesting story with many fascinating and surprising details concerning the reception of Copernicus' *De Revolutionibus* and the fate of the individual volumes of the first two printings.

Grant, Edward. *Planets, Stars, and Orbs: The Medieval Cosmos, 1200–1687*. Cambridge: Cambridge University Press, 1994. Explores medieval versions of Aristotelo-Christian cosmologies, their modifications, and rejection in the seventeenth century.

Henry, John. *Moving Heaven and Earth: Copernicus and the Solar System*. Cambridge: Totem Books, 2001. Chapters on Copernicus' biography, astronomical details of his system, and reactions to and consequences of his heliocentrism.

King, Henry C. *The History of the Telescope*. New York: Dover, 1979. Chs. I–VI. Beginning with the early history of astronomical observation, traces the technical developments leading to improvements in capabilities of the telescope.

Kuhn, Thomas S. *The Copernican Revolution: Planetary Astronomy in the Development of Western Thought*. Cambridge: Harvard University Press, 1957. Well-written account, with excellent and useful diagrams, of the development of astronomy and cosmology from ancient times up to Newton.

Martens, Rhonda. *Kepler's Philosophy and the New Astronomy*. Princeton, NJ: Princeton University Press, 2000. An exposition of Kepler's philosophical outlook and how it paved the way for his revolutionary astronomical achievements.

Moss, Jean D. *Novelties in the Heavens: Rhetoric and Science in the Copernican Controversy*. Chicago: University of Chicago Press, 1993. Shows how rhetoric was employed to counter opposition to the new astronomy from traditional views in astronomy and religion.

Rosen, Edward, ed. and trans. *Three Copernican Treatises: The* Commentariolus *of Copernicus, the* Letter against Werner, *the* Narratio prima *of Rheticus*. New York: Octagon, 1971. Early versions of Copernicus' ideas with a useful introduction to the significant issues involved.

Taton, René and Curtis Wilson, eds. *Planetary Astronomy from the Renaissance to the Rise of Astrophysics*. Part A: *Tycho Brahe to Newton* (The General History of Astronomy), vol. 2. Cambridge: Cambridge University Press, 1989. Excellent coverage by a number of experts in a readable narrative of all significant aspects of the subject.

Van Helden, Albert. *Measuring the Universe: Cosmic Dimensions from Aristarchus to Halley*. Chicago: University of Chicago Press, 1985. The best account of efforts to measure the extent and components of the universe from Antiquity through the Scientific Revolution.

Westman, Robert S., ed. *The Copernican Achievement*. Berkeley and Los Angeles: University of California Press, 1975. Important essays on various aspects of Copernicus' astronomy.

The Advancement of Knowledge and the Methods of Science

Copenhaver, Brian P. and Charles B. Schmitt. *Renaissance Philosophy*. Oxford: Oxford University Press, 1992. Descriptions of Aristotelian, Platonic, and other ancient philosophies, as adapted and modified during the Renaissance.

Gaukroger, Stephen. *Francis Bacon and the Transformation of Early-Modern Philosophy*. Cambridge: Cambridge University Press, 2001. Analyses Bacon's thinking on proper scientific method. Includes a number of significant and detailed quotations.

Hacking, Ian. *The Emergence of Probability: A Philosophical Study of the Early Ideas about Probability, Induction, and Statistical Inference*. Cambridge: Cambridge University Press, 1975. Shows how the increasing prominence of the non-mathematical sciences in the seventeenth century led to the development of probability theory and statistical inference.

Henry, John. *Knowledge Is Power: How Magic, the Government and an Apocalyptic Vision Inspired Francis Bacon to Create Modern Science*. Duxton, Cambridge: Icon Books, 2003. Engagingly written brief analysis of how various aspects of Bacon's life and the intellectual life of his time led to the development of his influential philosophical outlook.

Martin, Julian. *Francis Bacon, the State, and the Reform of Natural Philosophy*. Cambridge: Cambridge University Press, 1992. Analyzes the relationship between Bacon's effort to increase the power of the state, the roles of legal practice and patronage, and the development of his philosophy of science.

Rossi, Paolo. *Francis Bacon: From Magic to Science*. London: Routledge & Kegan Paul, 1968. Deals with the role of magic in the development of Bacon's thoughts on natural philosophy.

Shapin, Steven and Simon Schaffer. *Leviathan and the Air-Pump: Hobbes, Boyle, and the Experimental Life*. Princeton, NJ: Princeton University Press, 1985. A study of the different approaches to the nature of knowledge and its relation to government and the social order in the works of Hobbes and Boyle.

Voss, Stephen, ed. *Essays on the Philosophy and Science of René Descartes*. Oxford: Oxford University Press, 1993. Articles on all aspects of Descartes' thought, including some novel interpretations.

Scientific Communication and Organizations

Brown, Harcourt. *Scientific Organizations in Seventeenth-Century France*. Baltimore: Johns Hopkins University Press, 1934. Examines the structures and functions of formal and informal organizations for the advancement and spread of new knowledge.

Hahn, Roger. *The Anatomy of a Scientific Institution: The Paris Academy of Sciences, 1666–1803*. Berkeley and Los Angeles: University of California Press, 1971. Chs. 1, 2. Describes the character of the organization in the context of the reign of Louis XIV.

Hall, Marie B. *Promoting Experimental Learning: Experiment and the Royal Society, 1660–1727*. Cambridge: Cambridge University Press, 1991. Emphasizes the role of experiments in the meetings of the Royal Society and their roles in the manner in which the society functioned.

Middleton, W.E.K. *The Experimenters: A Study of the Accademia del Cimento*. Baltimore: Johns Hopkins University Press, 1971. History of an early scientific society founded in 1657 by followers of Galileo and devoted to experimental science.

Ornstein, Martha. *The Rôle of Scientific Societies in the Seventeenth Century*. Hamden, CT, and London: Archon Books, 1963. Discusses the societies in several countries and their journals and relationships to universities.

Stroup, Alice. *A Company of Scientists: Botany, Patronage, and Community at the Seventeenth–Century Parisian Academy of Sciences*. Berkeley and Los Angeles: University of California Press, 1990. Although concentrating on the botanical and medical pursuits of the society's members, the work also deals with the structure of the organization and its royal patronage.

The Nature of Matter

Debus, Allen G. *The Chemical Philosophy: Paracelsian Science and Medicine in the Sixteenth and Seventeenth Centuries.* Mineola, NY: Dover Publications, 2002. Traces the history of alchemy, the ideas of Paracelsus, reactions to them, their modifications by others, and their influence on subsequent chemical ideas.

Hannaway, Owen. *The Chemists and the Word: The Didactic Origins of Chemistry.* Baltimore: Johns Hopkins University Press, 1975. Treats the emergence of chemistry as a distinct discipline from its roots in alchemy, metallurgy, distilling, pharmacy, and other crafts during the early modern period.

Jammer, Max. *Concepts of Mass.* Cambridge, MA: Harvard University Press, 1961. Chs. 1–7. History of ideas leading to the concept of mass up to and including Newton's.

Kargon, Robert. *Atomism in England from Hariot to Newton.* Oxford: Oxford University Press, 1966. Discusses stages in the evolution of theories about the atomic nature of matter in seventeenth-century England.

McMullin, Ernan. *Newton on Matter and Motion.* Notre Dame, IN: University of Notre Dame Press, 1978. An analysis of the history of Newton's efforts to cope with problems concerning the relationship between the nature of matter and his concepts of force and gravitation.

Pullman, Bernard. *The Atom in the History of Human Thought.* Translated by Axel Reisinger. Oxford: Oxford University Press, 1998. Chs. 12, 13. The modification of ancient ideas on atomism in the context of the new natural philosophy and culture of the Early Modern period.

Van Melsen, Andrew G. *From Atomos to Atom: The History of the Concept of Atom.* New York: Harper, 1960. Part I. Evolution of the concept from ancient times through the seventeenth century.

Physical and Mathematical Sciences

Boyer, Carl B. *A History of Mathematics.* Princeton, NJ: Princeton University Press, 1985. Chs. 16–19. Technical account of mathematicians and their achievements during the Scientific Revolution.

———. *The History of the Calculus and Its Conceptual Development.* New York: Dover, 1959. Chs. I–V. Traces the development of aspects of mathematics from ancient times leading to the development of calculus by Newton and Leibniz.

Clavelin, Maurice. *The Natural Philosophy of Galileo: Essays on the Origin and Formation of Classical Mechanics.* Translated by A.J. Pomerans. Cambridge, MA: MIT Press, 1974. Development of Galileo's ideas on mechanics, their relation to Aristotelian theories and Copernicanism and to subsequent ideas.

Cohen, I. Bernard. *The Birth of a New Physics*. New York: W. W. Norton, 1985. Describes the development of new ideas in mechanics in the course of the Scientific Revolution.

De Gandt, François. *Force and Geometry in Newton's* Principia. Translated by Curtis Wilson. Princeton, NJ: Princeton University Press, 1995. A historical analysis of the physical and mathematical concepts leading up to Newton's initial study of the problems analyzed in his *Principia*.

Densmore, Dana. *Newton's* Principia: *The Central Argument*. Translations by William H. Donahue. Santa Fe, NM: Green Lion Press, 1995. Excellent and detailed analyses, designed for students, of the physical principles of Newton's classic work.

Dijksterhuis, Eduard J. *The Mechanization of the World Picture*. Translated by C. Dikshoorn. Oxford: Clarendon Press, 1961. Parts III, IV. A history of the mathematized physical sciences seen as key to the mechanical conception of nature in the Scientific Revolution.

Hall, A. Rupert. *All Was Light: An Introduction to Newton's Opticks*. Oxford: Clarendon Press, 1993. Beginning with the optical ideas of Newton's predecessors in the seventeenth century, Hall goes on to describe Newton's work and theories, the creation of his book on optics, and its reception.

Lindberg, David C. *Theories of Vision from Al-Kindi to Kepler*. Chicago: University of Chicago Press, 1976. Surveys theories from Antiquity to Kepler of how the visual process works.

Mancosu, Paolo. *Philosophy of Mathematics and Mathematical Practice in the Seventeenth Century*. Oxford: Oxford University Press, 1996. Analyzes the philosophical and methodological concerns behind the transformation of the mathematics inherited from ancient Greece.

Rose, Paul L. *The Italian Renaissance of Mathematics*. Geneva: Librairie Droz, 1975. Shows how the recovery of classical Greek texts was instrumental in the subsequent growth and development of mathematics.

Sabra, A. I. *Theories of Light from Descartes to Newton*. London: Oldbourne, 1967. Examines seventeenth-century experiments and theories of the nature of light and its propagation.

Westfall, Richard S. *Force in Newton's Physics: The Science of Dynamics in the Seventeenth Century*. New York: Science History Publications, 1971. Traces the development of Newton's concept from earlier ideas, beginning with Galileo's on the nature of motion.

The Science of Living Things and the Practice of Medicine

Bylebyl, Jerome, ed. *William Harvey and His Age: The Professional and Social Context of the Discovery of the Circulation*. Baltimore: Johns Hopkins University Press, 1979. Three substantial articles placing Harvey in his social and philosophical context and discussing how he overcame the physiological conceptions of his time.

Cole, F.J.A. *A History of Comparative Anatomy from Aristotle to the Eighteenth Century*. New York: Dover, 1975. Detailed and extensively illustrated survey.

Ford, Brian J. *The Leeuwenhoek Legacy*. London: Farrand, 1991. Details of Leeuwenhoek's biography, his investigations, discoveries, and instruments.

Fournier, Marian. *The Fabric of Life: Microscopy in the Seventeenth-Century*. Baltimore: Johns Hopkins University Press, 1996. Descriptions and analyses of the work of the leading microscopists of the time.

Frank, Robert G., Jr. *Harvey and the Oxford Physiologists: A Study of Scientific Ideas*. Berkeley and Los Angeles: University of California Press, 1980. Shows how in the wake of Harvey's discovery of the circulation of the blood, new discoveries were made concerning respiration, the blood, metabolism, and other physiological functions.

French, Roger K. *William Harvey's Natural Philosophy*. Cambridge: Cambridge University Press, 1994. Discusses the contrast between Harvey's approach to physiology and Descartes' and how the idea of the circulation of the blood came to be accepted.

French, Roger K. and Andrew Wear, eds. *The Medical Revolution of the Seventeenth Century*. Cambridge: Cambridge University Press, 1992.

Hall, Thomas S. *History of General Physiology: 600 B.C. to A.D. 1900*. 2 vols. Chicago: University of Chicago Press, 1969. Vol. 1. Extended survey of theories about the nature of life and the functions of organs in living beings.

Pagel, Walter. *Paracelsus: An Introduction to Philosophical Medicine in the Era of the Renaissance*. Basel and New York: Karger, 1982. Examines the influence of the occult components in Paracelsus' medical doctrines and considers the nature of his personality.

Porter, Roy. *The Greatest Benefit of Mankind: A Medical History of Humanity*. New York and London: W. W. Norton, 1997. Chs. VIII, IX. Beautifully written account of medicine and its practice in the context of changing ideas in Early Modern Europe.

Siraisi, Nancy. *Medieval and Early Renaissance Medicine: An Introduction to Knowledge and Practice*. Chicago: University of Chicago Press, 1990. Discusses the various complex factors, drawn from ancient and medieval sources, religious, folk, and magical traditions, and the growth of medical education making up medical practice during the period.

Wilson, Catherine. *The Invisible World: Early Modern Philosophy and the Invention of the Microscope*. Princeton, NJ: Princeton University Press, 1995. Examines the interplay between philosophical ideas and microscopical practices and discoveries during the Scientific Revolution.

Religion and Natural Philosophy

Alexander, H. G., ed. *The Leibniz-Clarke Correspondence*. Manchester: Manchester University Press, 1956. A debate between Wilhelm G. Leibniz and Samuel Clarke, a spokesman for Isaac Newton, on the philosophical and theological implications of Newton's science and his religious opinions, with explanatory comments by the editor.

Brooke, John H. *Science and Religion: Some Historical Perspectives*. Cambridge: Cambridge University Press, 1991. Chs. 4–6. An examination of the great variety of issues surrounding aspects of the new natural philosophy from a number of religious and philosophical perspectives.

Cohen, I. Bernard, ed. *Puritanism and the Rise of Modern Science: The Merton Thesis*. New Brunswick, NJ: Rutgers University Press, 1990. Detailed analyses by a number of scholars of this influential thesis on the role of certain Protestant ideas in the development of the new natural philosophy in England and Europe.

Fantoli, Annibale. *For Copernicanism and for the Church*. Translated by George Coyne. Notre Dame, IN: University of Notre Dame Press, 1996. Most detailed and even-handed account of Galileo's encounters with the Inquisition.

Feingold, Mordechai, ed. *Jesuit Science and the Republic of Letters*. Cambridge: Cambridge University Press, 2003. Articles on the role of Jesuit teaching and its relationship to the changing nature of natural philosophy.

Funkenstein, Amos. *Theology and the Scientific Imagination from the Middle Ages to the Seventeenth Century*. Princeton, NJ: Princeton University Press, 1986. Shows how the interaction between ideas in natural philosophy and theology shaped and modified the nature of both.

Lindberg, David C. and Ronald L. Numbers, eds. *God and Nature: Historical Essays in the Encounter between Christianity and Science*. Berkeley and Los Angeles: University of California Press, 1986. Chs. 3–9. Essays on the relation of various aspects of the Scientific Revolution to religious beliefs and practices.

Osler, Margaret J. *Divine Will and the Mechanical Philosophy: Gassendi and Descartes on Contingency and Necessity in the Created World*. Cambridge: Cambridge University Press, 1994. Different approaches to the nature of God as Creator examined in the work of two of the leading proponents of mechanical philosophy.

Westfall, Richard S. *Science and Religion in Seventeenth-Century England*. New Haven, CT: Yale University Press, 1958. Tells of the religious opinions of scientists and how the new science of the seventeenth century modified traditional religious ideas.

Intellectual Biographies

Armitage, Angus. *Copernicus: The Founder of Modern Astronomy*. New York: Thomas Yoseloff, 1957. Presents biographical details, examines explanations of Copernicus' heliocentric theory, and describes its reception.

Bainton, R. H. *Hunted Heretic: Life and Death of Michael Servetus*. Boston: Beacon, 1953. Account of the life and important work in medicine and physiology in the early sixteenth century of the discoverer of the pulmonary circulation of the blood, his pursuit as a heretic by both Catholics and Calvinists, and his burning at the stake by the latter.

Bennett, Jim, Michael Cooper, Michael Hunter, and Lisa Jardine. *London's Leonardo: The Life and Works of Robert Hooke*. Oxford: Oxford University Press, 2003. Four essays on Hooke's life, career, and scientific achievements.

Bertoloni Meli, Domenico, ed. *Marcello Malpighi: Anatomist and Physician*. Florence: Olschki, 1997. Essays on theory and practice of medicine in the second half of the seventeenth century and on Malpighi's work with the microscope.

Caspar, Max. *Kepler*. Translated by C. Doris Hellman. New York: Dover, 1993. The standard biography by an editor of Kepler's collected works.

Cohen, I. Bernard and George E. Smith, eds. *The Cambridge Companion to Newton*. Cambridge: Cambridge University Press, 2002. Sixteen articles on all aspects of Newton's scientific, philosophical, and theological ideas.

Dobell, Clifford. *Antoni van Leeuwenhoek and His "Little Animals."* New York: Dover, 1960, Part I. Excellent account from diverse sources of Leeuwenhoek's life and his outstanding achievements with the microscope.

Drake, Ellen T. *Restless Genius: Robert Hooke and His Earthly Thoughts*. Oxford: Oxford University Press, 1996. A brief biography, followed by a detailed survey of his work in a great many areas of natural philosophy in the second half of the seventeenth century.

Drake, Stillman. *Galileo at Work: His Scientific Biography*. Chicago: University of Chicago Press, 1978. Presents accounts with considerable detail of both Galileo's personal life and his scientific work.

Gaukroger, Stephen. *Descartes: An Intellectual Biography*. Oxford: Oxford University Press, 1995. Describes the growth of Descartes' ideas and the forces shaping them.

Gillispie, Charles C., ed. *Dictionary of Scientific Biography*. 16 vols. New York: Scribner's, 1970–1980. Biographies of scientists and accounts of their scientific work throughout history, including several hundred in the sixteenth and seventeenth centuries. A useful index is provided.

Jardine, Lisa and Alan Stewart. *Hostage to Fortune: The Troubled Life of Francis Bacon*. London: Gollancz, 1998. Highly detailed and entertainingly written account of Bacon's life and ideas.

Jones, H. *Pierre Gassendi, 1592–1655: An Intellectual Biography*. Nieuwkoop, Netherlands: B. de Graaf, 1981. Provides details of Gassendi's life, his criticisms of Descartes and Aristotelians, and his promotion of Epicurean atomism.

Machamer, Peter, ed. *The Cambridge Companion to Galileo*. Cambridge: Cambridge University Press, 1999. Articles on all aspects of Galileo's scientific activities and their religious contexts.

Manuel, Frank. *A Portrait of Isaac Newton*. Cambridge, MA: Harvard University Press, 1968. Although containing little on his science, an interesting biography of Newton as a man, his personality, and his outlook on life.

McMullin, Ernan, ed. *Galileo: Man of Science*. New York: Basic Books, 1967. Very useful collection of essays on various aspects of Galileo's scientific work.

O'Malley, Charles D. *Andreas Vesalius of Brussels, 1514–1564*. Berkeley and Los Angeles: University of California Press, 1964. The detailed definitive biography, with extensive translations of Vesalius as an appendix.

Principe, Lawrence M. *The Aspiring Adept: Robert Boyle and His Alchemical Quest*. Princeton, NJ: Princeton University Press, 1997. Brings a wholly new approach to the work of Boyle, showing his intense involvement in alchemy and belief in transmutation. The work overturns a number of long-standing beliefs about Boyle's attitude toward chemistry.

Raven, Charles E. *John Ray, Naturalist: His Life and Works*. Cambridge: Cambridge University Press, 1950. Provides details of Ray's life and career and his work in the natural history and taxonomy of a variety of life forms.

Shapiro, Barbara. *John Wilkins, 1614–1672: An Intellectual Biography*. Berkeley and Los Angeles: University of California Press, 1968. A founding member of the Royal Society, Wilkins was closely involved with the major intellectual currents of his time and was an early popularizer of the ideas of Kepler and Galileo.

Shea, William. *The Magic of Numbers and Motion: The Scientific Career of René Descartes*. Canton, MA: Science History Publications, 1991. A masterful intellectual biography, presenting the various strands of Descartes' philosophy and science as a unified system.

Shirley, John W. *Thomas Harriot: A Biography*. Oxford: Clarendon Press, 1983. Points out Harriot's importance as an early-seventeenth-century innovator in mathematics, astronomy, optics, cartography, and many other areas.

Sobel, Dava. *Galileo's Daughter: A Historical Memoir of Science, Faith, and Love*. New York: Walker & Co., 1999. Galileo's correspondence with his daughter provides well-written details of his life and scientific activities.

Sturdy, David J. *Science and Social Status: The Members of the Académie des Sciences, 1666–1750.* Woodbridge: Boydell, 1995. Provides excellent biographies of the members up to 1750 and details about the structure and activities of the academy.

Thoren, Victor E. *The Lord of Uraniborg: A Biography of Tycho Brahe.* Cambridge: Cambridge University Press, 1990. History of all aspects of the life of one of the most important astronomers of the Early Modern period.

Voelkel, James R. *Johannes Kepler and the New Astronomy.* Oxford: Oxford University Press, 1999. Brief well-written account of Kepler's life and scientific achievements in astronomy, optics, and mathematics.

Westfall, Richard S. *The Life of Isaac Newton.* Cambridge: Cambridge University Press, 1993. A shorter version of Westfall's *Never at Rest.*

———. *Never at Rest: A Biography of Isaac Newton.* Cambridge: Cambridge University Press, 1980. The definitive full-scale biography, covering all aspects of Newton's life and achievements.

Wilson, Catherine. *Leibniz's Metaphysics: A Historical and Comparative Study.* Princeton, NJ: Princeton University Press, 1989. A detailed picture of Gottfried W. Leibniz, an influential philosopher of the later seventeenth century whose ideas reflected the thinking and context of his time.

Yoder, Joella G. *Unrolling Time: Christiaan Huygens and the Mathematization of Nature.* Cambridge: Cambridge University Press, 1988. Excellent survey of Huygens' achievements, particularly in mechanics.

Zagorin, Perez. *Francis Bacon.* Princeton, NJ: Princeton University Press, 1998. Covers biographical detail, Bacon's ideas on the practice of natural philosophy, and also his views on morals, literature, politics, law, and history.

Websites and Links to Topics on the Scientific Revolution

The following sites have links to other sites with topics on various scientific concepts, contextual and historiographical issues, and biographies.

www.bbk.ac.uk/Boyle. Has detailed and well-illustrated biographical and scientific material on Robert Boyle.

www.clas.ufl.edu/users/rhatch/pages. The most useful site for the variety of its offerings and links, including narratives of the Scientific Revolution, biographies, and bibliographies.

www.fordham.edu/halsall/. Check Internet Modern History Sourcebook/Transformation of the West/Scientific Revolution.

www.math.nus.edu/aslaksen/teaching/heavenly.shtml. Has many links to various astronomical topics.

www.newtonproject.ic.ac.uk/. Covers a variety of topics on Isaac Newton.

www.rice.edu/. Click The Galileo Project, which is devoted to all aspects of Galileo's life and career. It also has links to other sites and to biographical information on about 600 sixteenth- and seventeenth-century scientists.

www.vos.ucsb.edu/browse.asp?id=2731. Contains hyperlinks to a great many web pages devoted to a variety of topics on science, technology, and culture.

INDEX

About the Author

WILBUR APPLEBAUM is Professor Emeritus, Department of Humanities, Illinois Institute of Technology, where he taught history of science for many years. He has published on various aspects of the Scientific Revolution and on astronomy in the seventeenth century. He is the editor of the *Encyclopedia of the Scientific Revolution* (2000).